The Oldest We've Ever Been

The Oldest We've Ever Been

Seven True Stories of Midlife Transitions

edited by *Maud Lavin*

The University of Arizona Press

Tucson

To our families, extended and otherwise

The University of Arizona Press
© 2008 The Arizona Board of Regents

Library of Congress Cataloging-in-Publication Data appear on
the last printed page of this book.

Manufactured in the United States of America on acid-free,
archival-quality paper.

13 12 11 10 09 08   6 5 4 3 2 1

Contents

Editor's Introduction   vii

  Maud Lavin

Nothing Gained   1

  William Davies King

When the Middle Is the End   25

  Kim Larsen

My Mother, My Sight   54

  Allan deSouza

Through the Looking Glass   71

  Ellen McMahon

My Dead   103

  Calvin Forbes

Tax Time   132

  Peggy Shinner

Reuniting   141

  Maud Lavin and Locke Bowman

Acknowledgments   205

Contributors   207

Editor's Introduction

Maud Lavin

Middle age is a busy, thickly layered life stage. Its stories, though fascinating, are curiously underexplored in contemporary U.S. culture.

The personal essays in this book provide a montage of midlife; they were solicited and developed to convey, in different ways, the richness of midlife experience. They don't, though, attempt to cover every aspect of middle age. The writers were asked to choose stories that reveal confusing, emotional, sometimes humorous, sometimes sad, engaging transitions and to style them to offer readers literary pleasure as well as points of identification and connection. The authors explore common middle-age experiences such as celebrating remarriage and mourning family deaths and raising teenagers and weaving friendships. Yet they give these idiosyncratic spins, creating very individual anecdotes of collecting bacon boxes and beach boulders, visiting a sister's former church, and dating a college sweetheart decades later.

These writers are, in a way, a related group of people. Though born into quite different situations in terms of class, race, religion, and geography, each writer is now a member of the professional class. They are professors, lawyers, artists, and so on: their occupations each involve cultural or societal analysis, and for this book these analytical skills have been turned on themselves and their own midlife experiences, as well as used to connect to the experiences of others at this middle stage.

In turn, they are each members of the baby boom (those born between 1946 and 1964), and perhaps it's the overabundance of writing on this generation *as* a generation—its roots in the '60s and '70s, its size, its consumer trends, etc.—that has contributed to the upstaging of more intriguingly personal stories of what it feels like to be at midlife. Some generational and historical perspective is useful, though, and serves as a reminder that this is a time when the extension of the life span (for most, not all) has allowed a greater variation of experience and simply more time in the years between being young and being elderly. According to the U.S. Department of Health and Human Services, the average life expectancy for those citizens born in 1900 was 47.3 years, whereas the average life expectancy for those born in 1960 is 69.7 years—quite a leap.

We as a generation have been lucky concerning our place in medical history. As much as we boomers might like to think of ourselves as the individual authors of our opportunities for prolonged life span due to our lifestyle choices—our vegetarianism, say, or our Pilates, or our taking hormones or refusing to take them—it is much more so the strides since World War II in mainstream medicine that are primarily responsible for opening the door to more years for many of us. Taking for granted the unglamorous but widely used and decidedly life-extending statins, antibiotics, and blood pressure medicines now in common use allows us to imagine a long life—and therefore that we might have options and the time to realize them in the middle years. Many of these are quite recent developments, though. For instance, penicillin was made available to civilians only in 1945; Dr. Salk's polio vaccine was licensed in 1955; and cholesterol-reducing statins were released in the U.S. market as recently as 1987. However, access to these medicines and to health care in general is unfairly class-limited in the U.S., and, as Katherine Newman has reported in her book *A Different Shade of Gray: Midlife and Beyond in the Inner City*, premature aging and great physical hardship follow an absence of decent health care, a deprivation falling disproportionately on the middle-aged of color. There are other reasons, too, not to idealize our midlife status. In general, Margaret Morganroth Gullette has argued in her *Declining to Decline: Cultural Combat and the Politics of the Midlife*, people in their forties, fifties, and older can be targets of ageism in the workplace. We have to deal as well with negative stereotypes of aging in consumer culture. Accordingly, there is a great need to resist and recast these discouraging images instead of interiorizing their negativity or (another version of the same thing) desperately trying to act just the opposite. Stereotypes flatten. In contrast, complexity, engaging and engaged complexity represented in culture, is one countering strategy—we're trying for that here.

In selecting the book's contributors, I looked among friends, colleagues, and acquaintances for those whose publications showed them as talented ruminators as well as storytellers, and I especially sought those who would work to make the multifaceted nature of middle age come to life. Kim Larsen, a New York–based writer whose work deals with the intersection of conservation, culture, and economics, is a close friend (and she shows up as a character in the story "Reunited" I cowrote for this book with Locke Bowman). Her work to date addresses fraught situations of environmental change. Calvin Forbes is a well-known writer and the head of the writing program at the School of the Art Institute of Chicago, where we both teach. I'd heard him give a public reading and was enticed by his balance of everyday speech and incisive observation. Dave King, a theater professor at University of California, Santa Barbara, I met when I was ten, in our shared hometown of Canton, Ohio, and as an adult I've appreciated how Dave's cultural criticism brings together the eccentric and the mainstream—in his writing on caustic playwright and character actor Wallace Shawn, for instance. Ellen McMahon I first got to know at a conference: she is a designer, artist, and writer who teaches at the University of Arizona, Tucson, and whose series of artworks and writings on motherhood have been shown in galleries and published in books, such as *Mother Reader*, edited by Moyra Davey. Her pieces stand out as sophisticated blends of personal analysis and large cultural issues. Allan deSouza's work too—as a visual and performance artist and as a fiction and nonfiction writer—has been praised in reviews for its deft mix of personal and societal issues. Locke Bowman is a legal activist for justice-system reform; his writing includes newspaper op-ed pieces that combine analytical argument with personal emotion to advocate for pressing causes. Peggy Shinner is an activist as well, promoting nonviolence and women's self-defense through the Thousand Waves Martial Arts and Self-Defense Center in Chicago. She publishes her creative nonfiction in literary journals such as *Broom*, *The Gettysburg Review*, and *Fourth Genre*.

For this book, these writers tackled widespread midlife challenges and transitions. *The Oldest We've Ever Been* starts with Dave King's story about divorce and dating told, with self-irony and wit, through the lens of his eccentric collecting. King describes how our daily obsessions can mediate the larger transitions of our lives. He collects, as he likes to put it, nothing, a *lot* of nothing, that is, the detritus of everyday life—cereal boxes, roadside metallic debris, canned food labels. Somehow, around time devoted to work and family, and then work and divorce and its aftermath, he continued, and still continues, to grow these collections. Musing about value, he questions his own worth and his legacy to his two much-loved daughters. We see his children tolerate and enjoy his eccentricities, even as he holds some of his own oddities at arm's length.

Next, Kim Larsen writes about a deep relationship with a female friend with whom she shared politics, work interests, motherhood—and at times a difficult dynamic. Unexpectedly, her friend became seriously ill when she was in her forties. Larsen explores how her friend dealt with her disease, and how their friendship changed during its course.

Midlife can be a time when we realize the vulnerability of our own bodies, as well as others', in increasingly acute ways, ones that can raise anxieties and fears but also stir new perceptions about empathy and experience. Allan deSouza's story deals with recognizing himself—and his body's fragilities—in his mother. DeSouza also relates his physical vulnerabilities to his work life. His birth country, and his mother's, is Kenya; he was raised in England; and he teaches in the United States. DeSouza brings together scenes from these different locales to ask complex questions about sight and memory.

Ellen McMahon's story is about raising her teenage daughter while she was going through menopause; she explores the complex interfaces between biological aging and love. McMahon also brings in what happens when one sees one's younger self in one's child but even that knowledge can only be of limited help. She describes the mix of compassion, affection, anger, and worry involved in parenting an adolescent and the toll this can take on the body.

Calvin Forbes then addresses head-on challenges of maturing during middle age. He points out that among the many hurts connected to the deaths of parents and siblings is losing the comfort of feeling like there will always be some older family member to offer protection, someone who could, in a pinch, provide security and literally a second home. Gone is that childhood safety net. With these passings, too, come shifts in family dynamics and responsibilities. At the same time, Forbes writes about balancing his continued independence with his loving embeddedness within his now-diminished family.

Peggy Shinner's "Tax Time" involves the reader in the midlife emotions clustering around the deceptively simple April task of filing taxes, emotions that involve her father's legacy—financial and emotional, her own will concerning her partner, Ann, and her somewhat insecure middle-class status. This story is set in the context of the culture she was raised in, as are so many of the book's essays, and addresses how it rubs up against the context she's built for herself as an adult.

The book closes with the bittersweet piece Locke Bowman and I wrote about our efforts to rekindle our romance twenty-two years after we broke up in college, a story more common than we knew at the time, and one which throws the similarities and differences between youthful and middle-aged love into a bright light. In some ways, the feelings are exactly the same and as powerful, but perhaps they can thrive at midlife only if they mesh well with a more broadly realized context, one that includes a world outside the couple, and if they involve a mutual acceptance of each person's growth away from a youthful identity.

Together these stories seek to offer readers mirrors and windows for the pleasure and necessity of regarding one's own and others' middle years. Those of us in our forties and fifties need the intricacies of seeing ourselves and our differences when we read true tales of others in midlife transitions. So we aim here to share stories and to honor our readers' stories, too, by appreciating middle age not as the problem child of self-help books (those many manuals that try to tell us what to do about menopausal mood swings or abdominal fat or bone thinning), but as a wealth of events and perceptions and thoughts and feelings such as we've never experienced before. This book at its heart is an honoring of the simple fact that this is the oldest we've ever been—and we want to savor that.

The Oldest We've Ever Been

Nothing Gained

William Davies King

> You leave home one afternoon, you never return as yourself.
> —Joyce Carol Oates, *Middle Age: A Romance*

On a hot summer day in 1998, I arrived at the house I still jointly owned with the woman who was fast becoming my ex-wife to find that she had removed every item remotely connected with me and deposited them all in the garage. My surprise was not at the fact of displacement, though I would rather have done the work myself, but at the spectacle of what an immense and unattractive volume of me there was, and much of it retained only because I collect, as a cat collects fleas, and have collected since my childhood. There were the usual black plastic bags of shoes and canted piles of shirts on hangers, portable radios and razors and power tools, but also such stuff as I had scraped from the bottom of the pan, collected things of no clear value to anyone but me. Forty-three, wearing shorts and an old T-shirt not suitable for the faculty club and already thick with sweat in the dusty glare of desert suburbia, Ryder truck still clicking and ticking at my back as the garage door swung open with a shudder and shriek, I was beginning to have my doubts. I am a collector, which is something a lot of people can understand. And . . . well, I am a collector of nothing, which will require explanation.

I once thought about starting a collection of the lint pads that are formed by the dryer, circles of pseudo-felt. I thought it would be rich to have a binder filled with them, mounted on paper, all slightly different in color and texture, depending on which towels or blue jeans or cat-haired sweaters had been tumbled, but all basically the same—the fibers of wear. The great heap of my belongings seemed to amount to little more than that, a lot of not much, a little of everything else, somehow more than me and less, richness and vacuity.

I am on the small side as a person. A neighbor told my parents I was the only toddler he'd ever seen who could walk under a table, and I was typically one of the moon-eyed kids sitting on the floor to the side in class photographs, among the minis. Eventually I grew to a more normal height, but I sometimes think of myself as an overgrown boy. My weight has always hovered just above normal, which is typical, I think, among people who grew up in food competition with siblings. I have three—two younger brothers who could easily be cheated, though I chose not to, and an older sister, who always wanted it all and whom I could not cheat because she was disadvantaged, disabled, disastrous, and later insane. I have long experience measuring my fair and healthy share, then sneaking a little bit more. My one unrestrained indulgence has been in the cubic yards of my culling.

I've read accounts of those people who one day just give away everything, purging themselves of material association. They report feeling liberated. It's a Buddhist or Gnostic or Henry David Thoreau experience. I suppose the moment of my divorce might have been a good moment for me to do something like that. As I stared into the garage, I did not like what I saw. During the twenty years in which I had lived with my wife, two decades of steady accumulation, I had found ways of inserting my collections carefully into the assemblage of our life together, mostly concealed. Removed to the garage, however, arranged in heaps, not carelessly but also not artfully, the things could be seen as symptoms of hoarding, which is a diagnosis, not a hobby. On that hot summer day, I took a moment to ask myself if my collecting could be a disease. Or could it be an art? I could not say, so I laboriously conveyed the cumbersummation of me to a new residence. It seems I had to keep the array in order to catch myself somewhere in the web.

I left behind just one collection, naturally sculpted beach rocks with which I had decorated the lawn and gardens. I had gathered them, two or three at a time, on the countless long drives I took between the house in Claremont, California, where I lived with my college professor wife and two daughters, and my university professor job in Santa Barbara, two to three hours away. For a decade, I spent the mid-week at work, the weekends at home. I would often stop at a beach on the way home, hoping the night air might stave off freeway drowsiness. It was then I fell in love with these Brancusi boulders. They looked like naked bodies in the moonlight, wrapped warm and tight to each other. Soon I was rolling large rocks up a board into the trunk of my car. I imagine I collected a thousand or so, five or six at a time, and the next day I would place them in the yard or gardens, like a curator of antiquities, home from Rome.

This collection, now left behind, was the most beautiful of all my collections and the only one that was constantly on display. To set these boulders off, I practiced a sort of topiary mowing of our lawn, sculpting patches of alligator grass with my Murray 20 mower to accent the sea-worn contours. In the spring, lush green would arabesque over salty gray. By late summer, the grass would turn sharp and sallow amid the dusty rocks, and huge wolf spiders would finish the brutal composition with no-nonsense webs. Finally, I would mow everything down, hose the stones, and start a new configuration for the next year. Many people commented on them, and perhaps they still do, though the lawn now has the conventionally trimmed look of bimonthly mow-and-blow gardeners. The stones remain. So I have left some of my heaviness behind, the heaviest of all that I was, and they look good. When I glance inside the house now, it does not seem the same house, nor does my ex-wife seem like the same person. The house looks better.

My collecting continues to be oppressive to others and myself, and you'll soon know why. What I collect is not what anyone would want, you see; for example, the labels of virtually all the products I buy at the supermarket: 1,700 cereal boxes, 800 soup-can labels, 400 water-bottle wrappers, and on and on, numbers daily escalating. When the breakup finally came to the three-year relationship that followed the end of my marriage, the woman remarked how relieved she was not to have to save labels any more. I admit it was sweet how enthusiastic she was about helping me with the collections initially, and together we created one new collection, the "kitchen collection," which began as just a wall full of the little stickers you find on fruit—"price lookups," they are called. At a certain point, I put up two pieces of black paper in unglazed frames, and we affixed those little labels, as well as other bits of ephemera that might come in the junk mail, odds and ends really, which we arranged in haphazard compositions as they came along. Eventually, though, I was the one who was putting all the effort into this collection, and eventually she was the one with the Ryder truck.

Love. Romantic love. Not my area of expertise.

Divorce does not most often happen in middle age, as some people think, and has not become increasingly common at a faster pace then than at any other age. The great majority of divorces continue to happen in the early years, and the increase in the rate of divorce in the middle years just keeps pace with the increase across the board. However, middle-aged divorces have more . . . everything: headlines, repercussions, furniture, complicated photo albums, well-paid attorneys, heart-broken innocents. People tend to notice and remember such splits. These divorces divide the already riven world, such that few can escape the impact. Mine had more grocery by-products than most. With one daughter (5) wailing on my lap, and the other (9) drenching the kitchen table with tears, I knew, at least, at last, that I had awakened to something deep at the bottom of why I would happen to have an album of fifty-seven tuna-fish can labels:

Albertson's Solid White Tuna
Angelo Parodi Tonno a Filletti All'Olio di Oliva
Bela-Olhão Portugal Skipjack Tuna Fillets in Water with Salt
Budgens Skipjack Tuna Chunks
Bumble Bee Chunk Light Tuna—Touch of Lemon
Bumble Bee Solid White Albacore in Water (blue label)
Bumble Bee Solid White Albacore in Water (green label)
Bumble Bee Solid White Tuna in Vegetable Oil
Bumble Bee Prime Fillet Solid White Albacore in Water
Cento Solid Pack Light Tuna
Chicken of the Sea Albacore in Water
Chicken of the Sea Chunk Light Tuna
Chicken of the Sea Lite Chunk Light Tuna in Spring Water
Chicken of the Sea Chunk Light Tuna in Spring Water

Crown Prince Natural Chunk Light No Salt Added Tongol Tuna
Dolores Chunk Light Yellowfin Tuna
Geisha Albacore Solid White Tuna in Water
Geisha Light Tuna in Water
Genova Tonno Solid Light Tuna in Olive Oil
Genova Tonno Solid Light Tuna in Olive Oil Seasoned with Salt
Lady Lee Albacore Solid White Tuna in Water
Polar All Natural Tuna Chunk Light in Water
Polar All Natural Tuna Solid White Albacore in Water
Ralph's Private Selection Albacore Solid White Tuna Packed
    in Water
Royal Reef Albacore Solid White Tuna in Water
Sea Trader Chunk Light Tuna
Sea Trader Chunk Light Tuna in Water
Skagg's Alpha Beta Chunk Light Tuna
StarKist Chunk Light Tuna in Spring Water
StarKist Chunk Light Tuna in Spring Water (with measuring
    tape motif)
StarKist Chunk Light Tuna in Vegetable Oil
StarKist Chunk White Albacore Tuna in Water
StarKist Charlie's Chunk White
StarKist Solid White Tuna in Pure Vegetable Oil
Trader Joe's Albacore Solid White Tuna (red label)
Trader Joe's Albacore Solid White Tuna (red label with clipper
    ship print)
Trader Joe's Albacore Solid White Tuna (blue label)
Trader Joe's Albacore Solid White Tuna in Olive Oil
Trader Joe's Skipjack Tuna Packed in Water
Trader Joe's Tongol Chunk Light in Water Salt Added
Trader Joe's Wild Solid White Tuna in Water
Tuny Atun al Chipotle en Trozos Aleta Amarilla
Von's Chunk Light Tuna

I'll spare you the clams, crab meat, mussels, sardines, snails, herring, salmon, and kipper snacks. All that, and more, remained with me—the labels, that is ("Sorry, Charlie!"). The tuna had long ago been eaten, by the ones I love.

So, I am a collector, a divorced and loving collector. I collect nothing—with a passion.

That is to say, I collect hardly anything that is collectible, not a thing anyone would wish to collect, but at the end of the day, having myself wanted all these unwanted things, having procured them and organized them and understood them, I have a collection. By now, I have a big collection, since I started as a boy and now am of an age in the middle, fifty. So, I am a collector, but in a sense I am not, since I am not like any one of the millions of collectors out there, who collect collectibles. I am not the person who has beaten you out at the last minute in the eBay auction, nor am I the person whom you beat. In fact, I have never bought anything through eBay, haven't even made a bid. Of markets, I prefer super to flea. I've never been to Sotheby's or Christie's or a comic-books fair. I am not the price-guided, nose-to-the-wind, pocket-full-of-wheat-pennies kind of collector, yet I am most definitely a collector.

Of course, no collector is exactly like any other, since collectors are defined by their collections, and most collectors occupy some special corner of the world of collectibles. A collector of fountain pens is not clearly analogous to a coin collector or to a collector of Coleman Hawkins sides or Currier & Ives prints—or forty-nine brands of canned sardines.

The widely shared impulse to collect comes partly from a wound we feel deep inside this richest, most materialistic of all societies, and it also comes from a wound that many of us feel in our personal histories. Collecting is maybe not the most direct means of healing those wounds, but it serves well enough. It finds order in things, virtue in preservation, knowledge in obscurity, and above all it uncovers and even creates value.

I do not recall having a security blanket or a special teddy bear, but I surely must have found objects to give me infantile comfort. Before memory kicks in, we need mnemonic devices of that sort to remind us that parental love is continuous, even if it is not immediately at hand. Even when the capacity for memory has developed, an attachment to objects might help compensate for the troubling phases of existence. I remember a large and terrifying black cat. I remember the bald, breast-like dome of my baby brother's skull, as he was being nursed. I remember the fearful experience of trying to sleep at 7:00 or 7:30, with the night and darkness and sleep and dreams far off. But I don't remember having anything I could call my own, except this clamorous, always needy older sister, physically and mentally a wreck, hot on my neck, and two younger brothers, physically and mentally superb, hot on my heels. Middle-class suburban Ohio did not offer me much of plenty, but what I came upon, I kept—stones, bottle caps, odd bits of metal, squirrel skulls, travel brochures, political buttons, etc. My drawers and pockets filled with everything that was free for the taking.

When I was eleven and my sister eighteen, she had a complete mental breakdown, which left me with a vague sense of guilt and a new respect for the irrational. She spewed blame everywhere, and I absorbed as much as possible (free for the taking). Shortly after that, I was sent away to a boarding school, which was my release from the lockstep of Ohio, and my eyes opened amply to art and literature and such. I turned to the task of remaking myself, from such. However, I also became aware of a deep cavity in my life—loss of home, loss of love, loss of self-confidence—which was exacerbated by the fact that I was surrounded by wealthy, sophisticated boys, scions of the haves. I soon became aware that I was underprivileged, in the literal, not euphemistic sense. I was not poor, but I lacked the privileges by which the other boys defined themselves.

To compensate, I became a collector of undervalued, neglected, discarded things, tokens of my self-pity. At that time, the collection consisted of odd pieces of metal, found along the roadside, in the woods, or in basements, which I polished and then treated as the ultimate *objets d'art*. Remove the rust and grease from almost any twisted piece of steel, and there will be a touching story of form deformed. Railroad spikes, pliers, spigots, stopcocks, saws: I probably had half a ton of these gems. They were my Rossignol skis, my Bass Weejuns, my Pioneer amp, my Jack Kramer tennis racket, my subscription to *Esquire*. I could nail a frozen crescent wrench to the wall, mouth open to the ceiling, like a Russian icon.

Even a lead wheel balance arcs gracefully. One day, I "presented" all these things, in a gallery, and talked of them like a Dada connoisseur.

A few years later I channeled my collecting into lighter, less back-breaking objects, like labels, chain letters, chopsticks wrappers, "Inspected by . . . " tags, but lest you wonder, I still threw away all the dryer lint. I'd still have all the prep-school metal if I hadn't moved every two years or so (another cost of being young). The key factor was, then and now, that my collectibles should cost nothing. They should be overlooked by the world, and they should be glorified only by my having them. Out of that came my sense of fulfillment.

Fulfill, a transitive verb of Old English heritage, originally meant "to fill to the full." You could fulfill a material container, and later any void at all, however abstract, if only need or desire attended, and eventually the word stood for the filling full of need or desire. The longing-for makes possible the fulfillment, which is the aim of all collectors and a miraculous effect always pursued, bringing the magical potency of the desired object within one's grasp.

Fulfillment is never attained, because the effect of acquisition constantly drains away in ownership, and so the hunt goes on. Every collector is still waiting. Attain fulfillment, and the collection ends. Always there is one more possibly graspable thing, the object of still higher longing. Someone once called this effect "the kiss of possession." A kiss answers a desire, but it also stirs a desire, for another and another. For me, the kiss is of nothing. I collect nothing, or nearly so. For others, the hoarders (sick ones, of which category I'm a near miss), they kiss everything. For most, the kiss is selective, choice objects in between.

For all of us, the pursuit has its pleasures, and some sensation of fulfillment comes in the rhythm of acquisition. Seeing the album fill up—or the shelf, cabinet, or closet—feels good. The sensation is akin to the "belly full," and we all want that—the long day of skiing, followed by hundred-year-old brandy and Belgian chocolate, dinner at Silver Palate or Au Pied du Cochon, Puccini with Domingo, days of Bali Hai, wherever human beings have gone for transcendence of the beast. (Note: I have done *none* of those things, since I have had my own ways to belly up, like collecting 350 Altoids-type candy boxes, wintergreen, cinnamon . . . sugar-free, caffeinated, carbonated . . . echinacea . . . shaped like a football or Rugrat or . . .) Wilhelm Stekel called collecting one of the *Disguises of Love* in his 1922 book of the same title, emphasizing its erotic aspect: "No doubt the stamp-collector travels round the globe by means of his stamps; he lives in the history of the stamp; he dethrones kings and celebrates memorable historic events through the possession of a particular stamp. But, when all is said and done, it is but a harem that every collector establishes for himself. . . . All collectors draw their sustenance from spirits; they feed their love-hunger with shadowy phantoms. For this reason the collector never attains peace; he never ceases to collect."

It takes twenty or thirty years for some of us to recognize that we lead our lives through patterns of behavior as insistent and unconscious as that phrase "love-hunger" implies. Middle age is a time of review and revision. Some just accept the customs and practices that sustain them through the weeks and years. Others tweak the text or add a new layer of order. Others throw out the first draft and try desperately to find some blank paper to start anew. Collectors take stock; inventories and databases grow from this, also questions about how, or if, the collecting will continue. When I took stock, at midlife, I found I had my own peculiar problem in determining how it all adds up.

For most collectors, those who operate in the marketplace, the valued objects speak to many; hence, there is a market. Yet I respond to the mute, meager, practically valueless object, like a sea-washed spigot, its mouth stoppered by a green stone. My collecting is perverse and paradoxical in this sense. It is collecting still, but my habit answers to a different god within the object. In a sense, I'd call it the god Not-There, the absence of immanence. What I like is the potency of the impotent thing, the renewed and adorable life I find in a dead and despised object. I am held by this god, and I like to think there is warmth there, also forgiveness and love. Still, when I stand back, I see very little amid all the stuff.

When I meet someone I will often ask, "Are you a collector?"

And they will very often tell me they are and then show off a rack of floater pens, a closet of T-shirts, a wall of silhouette cutouts, or a barn full of buggies. What I share with them is a fascination with property and all the ghosts that inhabit an object (the maker, former owners, dealer, and the many others who might have wanted to be owners). I respond to the fact that a collected object connects me to the past, if only to the moment when I acquired it. It puts me in contact with a world out there, though of course that contact is through an object, not a person. Possessing a new object feels very much like learning something or meeting someone, and there is happiness in that. But in my case the knowledge gained is not very useful (I'm not a collector of Caravaggio or Cartier or cartoon cels), and the experience of meeting is one-sided. My objects are surprised to find me at the door.

A collector of collectors would find me rare.

Collecting wraps tightly around me, now with warmth, now with strangulation. As I entered the routine of adulthood, I allowed it to coil around me so that I might feel lovable and rich. I had this boa (constrictor) of feathers that weighed a ton, so much of so little. My collecting had the shape of desire, huge but pulled tight to the heart, as if to devour.

There were the great moments of transition in my life—first love, first job, first marriage, first house, first first child, and first second—and I went through them all as a collector, more and more wrapped up in things. A young man lays down a couple of dots, and from that beginning one may draw a straight line, to middle age and death, but there might still be a swoop or sudden discontinuation in the line. The line I traced was thick with excrescences, a giant crayon line, waxy and indistinct. By the time I was in graduate school, I was amassing labels, and all the rest followed, for example, the little squares you find on envelopes that say something like "Place Stamp Here." I have eight or nine hundred of them.

Let's get back to tuna fish. Would you marry me? Am I a catch?

I was, in my early twenties, a member of a visionary, progressive food co-op, the sort of place where you must begin your membership by listening to a lengthy Marxist lecture in the basement (rough draft of the manager's MA thesis in poli sci). This store was not friendly to labeling, which was, after all, a celebration of surplus value, so a lot of stuff came from bins, none too clean. Of course, the New Haven Food Co-op itself was a giant package, but inside were the scoops and ladles, towers of beans, vats of honey and peanut butter, wheels of cheese, the fields of amber grain. To stock Kellogg's or Nabisco in this place was a crime against society. Jif was capitulation. Nestlé was murder. Still, even in this store one could buy locally produced honey in a labeled jar or Dr. Bronner's Castille Soap, the stuff you could use to wash your hair *or* brush your teeth. Between the co-op and my sinful, counterrevolutionary purchases from the library vending machines (Hostess, Little Debbie, Payday), I intercepted a steady stream of labels. If you leave behind the world of progressive food retailing, as I did when I'd had my fill of the guilt trip and the bugs in the garbanzo beans, then it is hard to find any unlabeled consumer product. Nowadays, virtually every vegetable or piece of fruit is individually labeled. Trader Joe's even labels every single egg it sells. Soon it will be every gene.

At first, the assembling of the collection was just a matter of rounding up every label I had in my life at the time, but soon I found my life itself was changed. When I went to the store for supplies, I scouted for the new and interesting labels. Sometimes I made a conscious choice to pay more (or less) for a product simply because I wanted a different label. Instead of remaining loyal to a brand I had always used, I started exploring all the other brands, and the crunchy as well as the smooth; cinnamon as well as plain; small, medium, large, and jumbo. The effect was that a collection that was initially "about my consumption" at an unexamined moment became about my consumption as a collector of labels. A self-consciousness began to develop in the collecting. Of course, the notion of "having every label" was impossible, because I could not consume (or ingest) the world but only the portion of it for which I had appetite and cash.

Still, when I bought soup, I thought, I want *all* soup, and even if Progresso's Hearty Bean did not agree with me, or Campbell's Scotch Broth appeal, by golly I must have those labels. And I do have those labels, through several progressive generations of label, as labeling styles changed. I was nourished to the degree that those soup-can wrappers state their inner soups nourish, but as a collector I was incrementally enriched by the acquisition of each one of those labels I might not otherwise have had, now nearly nine hundred. I have had my teeth now whitened, now cavity-protected, now baking-sodaed, with gel and regular, mint, herbal mint, and "original," by Crest, Colgate, and a number of other dentifricatriciers. Would my teeth look better if I had stuck to the one best brand? Who knows? (I wish!) All I know is that I have a twenty-five-year array of toothpaste brands (ninety-five different boxes), but hardly a complete history. I buy toothpaste maybe three or four times a year, and I have not always been the one to make the purchase. Sometimes, when my motivation is low, I just buy the same old brand. But other times I'll think, why not Close-Up or Stripe or Tom's? A store around the corner from me now sells brands of toothpaste for five or six dollars a tube, mainly on the basis of their herbal enhancements or organic conciliations. I don't buy those, any more than I would buy an Eames chair or a Tiffany lamp. My collection fits me more exactly, ordinary but extreme.

Cereal is a category where I have adapted myself most radically to the product. I am at the mercy of the marketers when I stand before their showcase of overpriced grain. Any new flavor or shape or puzzle or movie tie-in or sports celebrity or free toy inside or CD-ROM-game-included will likely draw my eye and motivate purchase. Cereal manufacturers have always had to work hard to keep up the illusion that their puffing or flaking, sugaring and/or coloring had enormously inflated the value of a handful of rice or corn. I once heard that it would be just about as nutritious to eat the Wheaties *box* as to eat the cereal, but the psychological boost of eating anything bearing the image of a decathlete or a lady golfer could not be underestimated. Still, if ever I lack for fiber, I have a supply.

A recent Web search turned up collectors of candy wrappers, full sugar packets, and cereal boxes depicting NASCAR drivers, but I have not yet located another collector of Philadelphia Cream Cheese boxes or Doritos bags. Honeycombs does not figure prominently on the big board, ditto Rice Chex, or G.I. Joes (the cereal). I doubt that anyone has attended as closely as I have to the labeling of mushrooms (I have a whole book just for mushroom labels, more than fifty different varieties) or the tagging of onion bags. Immense notebooks labeled "Candy," "Candy 2," "Candy Bar," and "More Candy" attest to my sweet tooth. A relatively thin book with "Prepared Foods" shows that I prefer to cook my food fresh and from basic ingredients rather than buy frozen or takeout.

As an upper-middle-income, upper-middle-aged urbanite, I cut as wide a swath as I can through the field of consumer products. Since, after all, I am shopping at a supermarket, not a five-star restaurant, I can generally afford to exercise my market position freely, opting for the latest five-grain-*plus*-blueberry cereal rather than someone's generic flake or, worse, the cereal that shows up naked and undocumented in bags. (Shudder!) My freedom meets itself in the mirror when I face the limits of my imperial desire, and I tremble at yet another new bean soup, because I know I cannot bear the flatulence.

At this point, I estimate there are about 17,000–18,000 labels of all sorts in the collection, and it continues to grow daily. There are also about 500 crown bottle caps (only the kind with crinkly edges), also kept in binders, in the plastic pages meant to hold photographic slides. All of these caps were collected in my adult life, but I recall saving bottle caps as a kid since they seemed so obviously similar to coins. I recently discovered that there are a number of bottle-cap collectors out there, especially in Europe, where bottling still summons up the picture of a red-nosed burgher, not a double-breasted, comb-over NASCAR booster. One Polish lady has a site where you can browse her collection of about 1,400 caps while listening to "House of the Rising Sun." I have several she does not have. She has many that I do not. Unlike her, I get my bottle caps mostly from the sidewalk, because I don't drink beer. So, you see, the nothingness I cherish dovetails with the valuable goods discarded by others.

I love it all. I love *you*, for what you do not love, what you throw away. There's a sad paradox in that. I love you for your lack of love for what I love.

I have to say that my pride in this label collection, and my determination to keep it up, are balanced by my annoyance with it and my sporadic resolve to give it up, even throw it out. By now it has swollen to such large proportions that no one would ever have the interest or time to explore it all. I have seen people—friends—visibly repelled by it, as if it were a monstrosity, a huge boil or wen, gruesomely fascinating, but still disgusting. I wonder if those guys who save air-sickness bags or string on enormous balls have a similar experience, or the true hoarders who save every newspaper, every piece of junk mail, every oil rag, every unused bus transfer. I myself find it terribly unwieldy. Individual binders seem always to be on the verge of bursting at the hinges, forcing me to find a way to split the contents into two books, which then presents the question of where to make the division.

It did not take long to realize that the earliest pages, which I had punched for the three-ring binder, were tearing. So I started placing the pages in plastic sheet protectors, but then I discovered a wide range in the quality of those. Some would get brittle or yellow or stick together. They tear, they crease, and they feel . . . like plastic. Was that what I ever wanted? Where are the polyurethanes of yesteryear? In youth, we imagine that materials will last forever. In middle age, we experience the first tears and fraying at the edges. The colors go flat, protection brittle, and a whiff of acid hits the nose. Some collected things will obviously endure for decades, while others seem just minutes from the grave. Ephemera happens.

Markets manage life itself to a remarkable degree, but times of stability, like the stagnant end of a marriage, give way to wild fluctuations, when all those labels acquired by midlife—husband, father, doctor of fine arts, and professor—seem like arbitrary signifiers. Once your goods get packed in the Ryder truck, where do they go to get better? For six years, at midlife, my depository was a spacious townhouse in forbidding Santa Barbara, fifth circle of real estate hell. I could afford this yes-no place because it was so ugly, with cottage cheese ceilings, cheap carpeting, a gas station over the fence. And yet, for the first time since I made environmental sculptures as an undergrad, I could design my life, *ab ovo*. An important motto from those days as an art student was, "We Don't Make Art, We Administer It." My new home became the ultimate office of life, a place where I could manage the material facts of my life as an artist, and the collections figured prominently. How would I manage this wealth, my thickening life?

The bigger the collection gets, the harder it is to keep. The bigger the collection gets, the more completely it represents me and my history, and the more I feel oppressed by it. The bigger the collection gets, the more extraordinary and "valuable" it is, and the more I mourn the thousands of hours spent assembling it. I love this collection and hate it, and I keep it because it expresses me. It is a poor collection wishing it were rich. It is a celebration of material culture wrapped around a contempt for material culture. It is a burgeoning collection full of emptiness. It is a collection of nothing.

I am sorry to express such ambivalence about, let's face it, my life. Most collectors celebrate their collections and celebrate themselves by means of the collection, no matter what they collect. A shelf full of glass eyeballs or Betty Page figurines or Brownie Instamatics becomes a treasure house, culmination of a romantic quest. No doubt the collector of Pez dispensers or barbed wire or prison uniforms must have suffered and struggled during the years of accumulation, and perhaps the sacrifice required to obtain a prized possession might have enhanced that suffering, but the collection finally stands purified of all history. Out of the restless activity of life it creates timeless wonder, the world of prison uniforms or whatever. Why can I not make that leap? Why does my collection seem so laced with unhappiness and the immediate self?

My collection is the picture of middle-aged me. To collect is to predicate middle age. The novice collector has that gnawing desire but only a few things, then more and more as the years go by. Still, there are spouses and children and employers to diffuse the energy. The desire persists, like a low-pressure zone, drawing moisture, and the pace of acquisition gradually builds. Collecting never satisfies that desire but rides over it, like wind on waves, lifting whitecaps and small-craft warnings. At a certain point it becomes clear that a perfect storm is blowing. It strikes in middle

age. At that point, there is an electrically charged mass of collected material, enough to shock a noncollector, and the lightning
is ferocious. Many will drop material comforts, pets, even their
children at this point and run for cover. The true collector sees the
storm as an opportunity, a magnetic moment, to draw cyclonic
energy into the collection, as an oak tree draws lightning into
its roots. The collector becomes a force of nature, with familiar
thingamajigs all whirling in the air, tending to the rich array.

Or something like that. Once the rest of life—the normal
challenges like getting an education, finding a mate, establishing a
career, planting a garden and an IRA and some children—has been
accomplished, then the collecting takes center stage. A collector's
passion, in its infancy, can be almost embarrassing, when you have
only, say, five shot glasses, six pieces of antique lace, or four Ro-
man coins. Best not to show anyone then, certainly not the kids,
or to make the claim that you are a collector. In any case, you
have more important things to do, like trying to stay compatible
with your wife and in love with your job, or is it the other way
around? Later on, though, once those important things have become routine, your personal passion becomes both more obvious
and insistent, and now with your spindly legs and slack neck you
look a little silly.

Collecting is hardly the only way to become a clown in middle age. Look at the golf course, the yoga class, the pet show, the
political rally, the contra dance, and you'll see middle-aged clowns
who could have been collectors (and maybe some are), but at least
they find a time to put down their clubs, strip off their leotards,
treat the dog like a dog, turn on NPR, and put their feet up on the
ottoman. However, the collector will never not have the 400 pig
figurines in the front yard or the window full of snow globes or a
cellar full of expensive wine or stuffed zebras up the wazoo. So,
the particular sort of buffoonery demonstrated by the middle-aged
collector involves an immense amount of stuff suddenly intruding
large, as when, in *I Love Lucy*, a door bulged open from some lu-
dicrously expansive disaster concealed inside. In middle age, all
collectors take on the pop-eyed, manic look of Lucy.

Now, if only my inner door would bulge with modern firsts

or classic guitars or Negro League memorabilia. If only I had Disfarmer originals or Grateful Dead bootlegs, Stickley tables or thoroughbred stables, I could perform this middle-aged clown role with some dignity, but instead I have nothing, in excess.

Six years ago I began seeing a therapist and learning something about my own pathology, my wounds, my imperfect healing, my sharp edges dangerous to others. My joy, unfortunately, felt like sadness, and my good fortune like dust, and it took a while to begin clearing out the lingering guilt and shame (like heaps of old newspapers) to get down to the solid oak furniture of my life. I had hoarded so much of bad feeling that it took two years of therapy before I even mentioned my collections. It turned out that my therapist is also a prodigious collector and is married to an even more prodigious collector (this I found out only after *six* years in therapy). Freud was a collector, too. He looked, as my therapist does, for valuable artifacts from the past—a material extension of the work they do professionally. The difference with me is that I take discarded remnants from the present—from the trash—and treat them with the same care, if not the same pride. A psychosexual tangle surrounds this collection (and me), which I have at last taken time to sort out. Call it my self-love, at once ironic and excessive, unique and commonplace, open-ended and delimiting. I make a good patient, which is a little sad.

I can look at my label collection as a first-class achievement, or I can look at it as a river of pain. I can view the collection as a mental block or a marvelous fantasy, breakthrough or disaster. I deserve much more than a mountain of aging labels, and at the same time I am enormously blessed to have even that.

Since my divorce I have been in several relationships, lasting from a few months to three years, and I have met or dated a number of women in the intervals. Always it has been a puzzle when to bring up the fact that I am a collector, and more recently when to bring up the fact that I have been writing about this fact. Middle-aged women are especially on guard against being "collected" (of course, there are men who do such things), and the notion of showing up eventually in a catalogue of sorts holds no appeal at all. (John Fowles wrote an especially creepy novel called *The Collector*, about a butterfly collector who kidnapped a woman so that he could feel what it would be like to have a perfect, live specimen of beauty, pinned, as it were, to his bed. This is one book about collecting I have *not* collected and would never even mention—except, apparently, in a published piece of writing about myself.) To keep my collecting concealed, as I often do when dating, makes the disclosure all the more loaded, and yet to mention it at once necessitates a lot of explanation at a time when I am striving to explain the collecting to myself. Furthermore, the oddity and magnitude of my collection suddenly throws everything else about me out of proportion. Eyes widen or roll, some of the women bolt, and I realize I am on the verge of becoming this week's *Sex and the City* anecdote, the guy who actually plucked an empty Orthogynol box out of the wastebasket after the tube's contents went somewhere else along with me. Partly to stave off this laughable rendition, I have cultivated other ways of thinking about the collection that give it an aspect of an artistic or academic project.

On a personal level, the collection speaks of love and its loss, self-worth and self-hatred, and the awkwardness of my own connection to other people. On the universal level, the collection speaks of the riches and excesses of an era of late-twentieth-century, late-capitalist life. It testifies to the remarkable liberty of a middle-class academic to satisfy his hungers in diverse, luxurious, laughably mundane, and occasionally even exotic ways. At the same time it begs the question why that liberty was exercised to these ends. What was so good about the Wolfgang Puck soup, Soho cream soda, or Saint Aubin cheese? My conspicuous consumption is on record, though not conspicuously till now, and it is testimony to late-century gluttony—my taste in high relief. Stroll through my collection, and you'll know you're not in Soho or the Upper East Side.

Middle age is like a one-person show—an opening, at which you are seen for the first time as more than a glimmer. You are you, locked in as a brand name. And the critics *will* be there. All your hard work has brought you to this point, which is the time when they (or you) first draft your obituary. The past has made this moment standard, and the future will be laid alongside it to measure. It is best to be clear about your Statement of Purpose by the time you reach middle age, because it's more than likely that the world will just replay your singsong sound bite, rather than think you through anew.

I spiel on about how the white paper to which most of the labels are affixed works like the white walls of a modern art museum, so that each gummy label seems an iteration of or a comment on Jasper Johns or Andy Warhol. The labels are prints, many made to a high standard of craft, and they operate in a complex, coded system, sending thousands of messages and asking the viewer to buy, just like many works of art. Think of those Dutch paintings, showing a table of fruit and flowers, with perhaps a skinned rabbit hanging on the wall behind. Those paintings send a signal about the purchasing power of the burgher who owned them. My labels, too, reflect the Horn of Plenty, and they too have rarity and elegance. I could and did actually buy a Reggie bar.

I talk about how the collection helps us see the world freshly and recognize rarity and richness in the things of common life. Though once they were common and cheap, some of my labels would be as difficult to replace (with an original) as a Cimabue altarpiece. Who out there actually owns an early 1980s Glamour Puss Fish and Liver Flavor canned cat food label? (Yes, fish and liver.) Mine might be the unique example of this ordinary, unusual label in the world right now.

Here my date might perk up. "How much is it worth?" she might wonder of a treasured scrap of paper, since that is the question begged by most collectors, and yet, how much easier it would be for her to pose that question if, say, I coveted Superman comics or Depression glass. The other question that looms is, inevitably, "Where do you put it all?" If I heard that, then I was already behind in the game, and my reply ("I'm a great believer in compact storage!") would surely sound defensive and desperate. I wish my collection could be tucked into a corner of my heart or a velvet jewelry box, but then my house would feel even emptier. My collection is me, but it is also other, and so we are compatible, if not happily married.

Once the garage of middle age is packed up and then un-
packed in a wishful future, with its own capacious garage, the
day goes on, only now there is less time to get it right the next
time. Early middle age verges on later, and middle always worries
that tomorrow might prove the end. Middle is a place, a time, an
evaluation, always uncertain where it stands. What goes where
and when is a question that keeps arising in dating and mating
and making new relationships. You want to find vertical stripes to
conceal your bulky obsessions, those notebooks of tuna labels and
the funny boxes of potions to slather the gray out of your beard.
At the point of dating, one does not want to bulge at the canned-
seafood-label line, and even having too many books of modern
poetry, as I do, might seem worth concealment—as does an excessive quantity of recordings of Schubert songs, or even some few
pieces of once-polished scrap metal from one's adolescence. Such
things require too many words of explanation, at just the point
when neither of you particularly wants any words at all, there having been enough of them before. Ah, youth. Periodically, I took
stock of what was most presentable about my collecting, at least
to find any gentle entry point to what was surely going to seem a
little overwhelming. Or a lot.

So, in order to divert her hand from the can of Mace, I might
begin by showing my superb collection of envelope linings. It
seems that many people fear that if they send a check or some
other document through the mail, this will surely be noticed by
a nosy postal carrier or larcenous neighbor, and so envelopes are
available lined with some dense pattern to prevent anyone holding them up to the sun and reading the contents. Those are envelope linings, and I have a very large ledger book containing 2"
× 3" cuts from those envelopes. The book is neatly maintained,
each page containing a grid of five rows and five columns of envelope linings. After the first few pages, which came in random
order, I organized the pages according to category: stripes, florals,
hatch-marks, trademarks, solids, airmail specials, and so on. The
effect now is like a sample book, demonstrating the wide array of
possible envelopical linings, and the album is beautiful, colorful
and elegant, if I do say so myself. Everyone who sees it says, "I

never imagined there were so many different kinds." (There are currently over eight hundred distinct envelope linings in the collection.) No one exactly covets this sort of thing (I found *no* Web site for envelope linings), but when people look at this collection I can know that I have something rare and extraordinary, even eye-opening.

Am I there in all my collections? Did I manage, through all these years, to collect myself, such that I could, one day, find the album where I could affix myself, these pages here, my metaphors of middle-aged me? Given sufficient construction paper, the child should make the man. Experience is the library paste, and the result should be worthy of an open house with cookies and a report card good enough to show one's lover. When I talk to my middle-aged dates, I find that they, too, have their assembled things, keepsakes if not collections, figures of a fully developed experience. A young person can live with barely a simile, out of a backpack or a car, but later comes the lumber of life, and soon we are as dense as Donne, heavy with conceit. My metaphor weighs tons.

I am a thing among my things, and together we accumulate, without taking final form, and will continue to do so until the day I die. Then what? Once in a while, I ask myself the terrible question, where will it go? A collection, in its middle age, goes beyond being an offshoot of the collector. It takes on a being of its own, like an adolescent child. Suddenly it defines its own terms and has adult conversations with the world. The collector might even come to seem like the bygone parent, an outmoded vehicle by which the collection gained its origin and early impetus, but which can now be safely jettisoned. Still, the collection, much more than the typical child, will be dutiful to the collector's wish for it.

There have been times when I have thought my collection should go to the Smithsonian Institution, "the nation's attic," as it is sometimes called. On the one hand, I predict that the Smithsonian would not accept such a collection, so low is its utility, so doubtful its aesthetic appeal. On the other hand, I hate the thought of it going into someone's attic, even "the nation's." The institution would have its own "need" for my collection, and I feel confident that their need would be different from, if not opposite to, my own. While I would love to be a key contributor to a "Bacon Boxes of the 1980s" exhibit, I think it's more likely a few of my things would be used as set decoration for a "World of Ronald Reagan" exhibit. The collection as such, coherent, tangible, and currently open to browsing, if you ask nicely, would be mostly out of reach.

No, the collection should go to my children—if they want it, if they can stand it. They are my smallest collection, but rapidly growing, always packed full of life. I know already they will inherit my stuff, and in a sense they already have gotten a lot of it. (Where will they put it all, everything we are?) They have borne my angst, weathered my storms, absorbed my capacity for self-doubt and anxiety. They have also seen that I am hopeful sometimes. At least at the ages they are now, twelve and sixteen, they tell me they want the collection, and in fact they say they want to continue it. My dictionary collection (a volume packed full of the tiny pictures found in dictionaries) is one that has especially caught their attention, and just as I was finishing it, they each briefly started one of their own, but they didn't keep theirs going, and keeping it going is the essence of collecting. Ordinary life seems too meaningful and fun to them to waste it with curiosa, and I heartily encourage that attitude.

I imagine that, if it survives, my collection will subside into general utility, mementos of material culture, but while it is in the hands of my children its utility will be a mystery, and one they might enjoy exploring. What could they find in it? They could find traces of my time, my times, my effort, and my collecting sensibility. With a little searching, they could find themselves and their times and their coming into the world, in the form of cereals they had eaten, soup they had supped, binkies they had bitten, movies they had seen, scrunchies they had worn. But why would they want to make this encounter? Having outworn the scrunchies and spit out the binkie, they have gone on, like plows, ripping up the material soil and leaving their seeds behind. Life marches on, while we collectors trail behind, with a shovel and a sack.

At this point, I have relatively little access to the material wake of their existence, all the mood rings and skorts they put on, the toothpaste they spit out, the taffy that tugs at their fillings. Once in a while they bring me something cool, like a box of animal crackers shaped like a New York taxicab or Riz Krispies from Paris, towelettes from Beijing. Mostly, though, my collecting blends in with my job as a realm with which they cannot connect. They don't need my history. My love, which they have, will do.

One day, my children and I took all the cartons of cereal boxes to the mainstage theater in my department, and we laid them all out in a giant quilt. It covered more than 1,700 square feet, and at the end the kids counted the whole collection, and it came to 1,579 boxes (as of June 18, 2002). To deliver, assemble, photograph, repack, and return the collection took about eight hours, and much of it was hard work, but there was a joy to it also, for them as well as for me. This was the first time I had ever fully "aired" the cereal box collection or counted it, and it looked great, a brilliant tapestry of eye-catching graphics. A number of the people I work with, faculty and staff, stopped in to admire the array, and they all seemed to find some wonder in it, some forgotten flake or cool O. Ruthie had just turned thirteen, and Eva was nine. They acted like curators, answering some of the FAQs ("How many are there?" "Where do you put them all?" "When did you start saving them?"), and offering their own opinions about the most and least appetizing. So much of this cereal they had eaten, and then forgotten, oddities such as OJ's and Strawberry Shortcake, Count Chocula and G.I. Joes. We all participated in the marketing calisthenics of this late-twentieth-century morning food. By way of the collection their unusual father connected to the world in a special and rather tasty, toasted way. From this point of view the prospect of eventually owning the collection would seem delightful, a welcome inheritance.

The possibility remains that they will come to see this collection as something they did not want but had to have, as a burden and a trial. We all acquire things from our forebears, both material and immaterial, some of which we can use, some we cannot. At fifty, we think of seventy-five, and we think of twenty-five, and we split the difference, as best we can. The ratio is worth the pen-and-paper work, divvying up a life. I hope the kids will find something, not nothing, in what I leave to them. I hope they will find joy somewhere in all this stuff, or in this story, which repackages that stuff, or in the moving beyond it all into their own collections and recollections. Collecting has helped me to know the larger pattern in which my life is held. In the words of Keats (sort of):

> The voice I hear this passing night was heard
> In ancient days by emperor and clown:
> Perhaps the self-same song that found a path
> Through the sad heart of Ruth (and Eva), when, sick for home,
> She stood in tears amid the alien Corn Flakes.

When we repacked the cereal box collection we changed its organization. Now there is an entire carton of Life, another of Raisin Bran, two of Wheaties, two of Quaker Oats. The collection had become known, and to know is to order. We dreamed up other ways of ordering them, such as chronologically (using the expiration date) or from most to least healthy, according to brand or grain or principal color along the rainbow's spectrum. Pops could talk with other pops, puffs puffs, and chex mate chex. Out of the chaos of a garage in Claremont, my children watched something that was nothing achieve form and become known, a man who could sing of it all: "Corn, we're glad you were born."

When the Middle Is the End

Kim Larsen

Be absolute for death; either death or life
Shall thereby be the sweeter. Reason thus with life:
If I do lose thee, I do lose a thing
That none but fools would keep: a breath thou art,
Servile to all the skyey influences
—Shakespeare, *Measure for Measure*

Laurel put a meal together for my family and me a couple of weeks before she died. The main dish was a Tuscan soup—beans, pasta, tomatoes. Delicious. There was bread and a salad and wine. I saw a note she'd jotted to her husband, the word *wine* followed by an exclamation point. The apartment was littered with such notes, not all of them concise. Pen to paper was her mode of communication now that she no longer possessed a tongue—it had been surgically removed six weeks earlier in what would shortly prove a vain attempt to root out the cancer encamped at the base of the organ. Laurel's handwriting was nearly illegible, a forward-slanting scrawl, and we all marveled to see how expertly her seven-year-old daughter, Anya, deciphered it. More remarkably, sometimes Anya could blithely interpret her mother's attempts at speech. To anyone else Laurel's words were unintelligible—guttural starts followed by featureless nasal incantation. The will to speak still drove her, but it was useless. Anya's uncanny ability to even occasionally understand her mother represented some kind of umbilical magic. That they both took it in stride increased the dazzle of the little girl's feat.

It had been Laurel's idea to cook us dinner. She'd suggested it in an e-mail. "Are you sure?" I replied. She was sure. It would be normalizing. What could be more normal than Jim, Abe, and I sharing a meal with Laurel, Josh, and Anya? We'd done it routinely, at their place or ours, since the kids were born, two months apart, nearly eight years before. The missing tongue, of course, meant that Laurel would not be consuming any of the food she prepared that night. Her sustenance now came from a nutritionally calibrated brew that found its way to her stomach through a tube she attached to a peg that had been surgically implanted in the side of her belly. "Sure," I told her, "we'll come. What time?"

She laughed that night (her laugh was intact, accented but unmistakable), explaining how irksome yet amusing it had been to give up the taste-testing authority to Josh as she'd prepared the soup. Garlic and basil aromas floated from the kitchen. Laurel, in lipstick and a slinky blouse, sat bent over her writing pad, telling a funny story. Or rather, an unspeakably sad story about which we all chose to laugh. Flares of euphoria crisscrossed my ribcage. With Laurel's tongue had gone her pain. Now her face was unclenched from the months of physical torment, her eyes unclouded from the morphine intended to blunt the pain. This return to brute serenity felt, absurdly, like a favor to me. For months I'd pawed and prodded at the closed shell of her agony. The tongue extraction had little to no bearing on her prognosis—specialists in Boston had advised her not even to bother. But, with Anya in the mix, the vaporous hope for recovery the glossectomy held out was enough to compel Laurel to go through with it. In the end, pain eradication was the best and only reason for the procedure. It brought her back, if only briefly. It cracked open the shell, a revelation inside.

Here's a memory I could do without: Spring 2002. I'm standing on the corner outside P.S. 321, Abe and Anya's school. Nearby Abe is playing suicide, the disconcertingly named wall-ball game adored by him and his grade-school pals. An ice-cream truck pulls up, and Abe beelines over. We wait briefly for our turn at the window. The next thing I know I'm locked in a scream fest with the ice-cream lady. I do not recall what prompted it beyond my own inability to deflect some trifling yet undue exercise of control on the woman's part as she processed her line of customers. Here's what I do remember: warm spring sunshine on a bustling Brooklyn avenue; Abe, still without an ice-pop, staring at me; passersby, many of them familiar to me (and I to them) from the schoolyard, glancing over; and me at the center of an explosion of rage and epithets. I did not come to blows with the ice-cream lady (thanks solely, I'm convinced, to her containment in the truck), but the spontaneous fury unleashed between us comes back to me now like a fisticuffs scene in a comic strip.

Ten minutes earlier, at pickup time for the kids, I had seen Laurel. I knew she'd visited the doctor that day to get results on a mouth biopsy. I stood among the clutch of milling parents and nannies as she approached. I looked at her questioningly. Her eyes said nothing, but she shook her head sharply in one direction, more slash than shake, which told me several things at once: bad news, can't discuss it, I'm disappearing down a rabbit hole. Then the kids spilled out, swamping us with their tumult and after-school harangue. This happened often as her illness dug in, bits of news and half-news obliquely conveyed, swallowed and diverted by the presence of Anya and Abe, but also by Laurel's fluctuating reserves of strength to cope with the body blows of increasingly dire updates from her doctors. Sometimes she had to talk about it, and sometimes she couldn't bear to try. Short on tools and inspiration that spring afternoon, I had manufactured the scene with the ice-cream lady to provide external dimension to my own inchoate bewilderment and disbelief.

At the start of the same school year I'd stood in almost the same spot chatting with my friend Marian. We'd both just dropped our kids off at their second day of school—Abe in first grade, Marian's son, Aidan, in kindergarten. For weeks we'd been exchanging phone messages but hadn't had a chance to talk till now. So we lingered for half an hour or so, catching up—summer, kids, work. It was Marian's wedding anniversary that day: September 11, 2001. She and her husband, Dave, had a lovely afternoon planned. A sculpture show at the Whitney Museum followed by dinner at a lakeside restaurant in Central Park. In fact, she said, she was going now to meet Dave for coffee—he was due off his overnight shift as a firefighter at the local squad. Would I like to join them? But I couldn't, my car needed moving. Before parting we made plans for the six of us, Marian's family and mine, to meet two evenings later for a picnic in Prospect Park.

On my drive home an onslaught of fire trucks careening down Fourth Avenue forced me to the side of the road. At the coffee shop, Marian waited for Dave, who never showed up.

Was Prospect Park ever so crowded as it was on September 12? All of Brooklyn, it seemed, had helplessly made for its embrace. The Long Meadow, a shallow oblong bowl, gathered us in. And who can forget the weather, that hyper-real blue sky with its morphing, chemical-laden cloud staining the northwest quadrant? When Jim, Abe, and I first arrived and peered down from the meadow's rim, we saw blankets and picnics occupying every last bit of shade beneath the trees; children playing pickup games of catch and tag and volleyball; bicycles sluicing the paths—and all of it gilded in the fairy dust of September sunshine. The idyllic scene was in fact a giant wake, though the dead had only begun to be counted. We waded into the crowd. I spotted Laurel with a friend on a distant path.

The day before, after I'd parked and gawked with some neighbors at the burning towers (a bird's-eye view across the river from atop our slope), then raced inside to flip on the news at the moment of the south tower's collapse, then paced and wrung my hands, literally, and concluded that the only action available to me was to pick up my son from school, I'd telephoned Laurel. Phone connections were spotty, but finally I got through. Did she want me to pick up Anya too? Laurel was at work in Manhattan, and I knew, or thought I knew, she'd be frantic. "Oh," she said lightly, mulling things over, and then, "Yes. Why don't you." She was waiting for Josh, who was making his way down from his office in midtown to hers in the east 20s. They planned to walk back to Brooklyn together. "I'll call when I get home," she said. We hung up, and I marveled at her phrase, "when I get home," so casually tossed off. Would anyone get home? I was home already, but the fact did not console me, because my husband and child were elsewhere. Jim was unreachable, stopped (dead?) in his tracks between home and work, on a subway that tunneled beneath the World Trade Center, and Abe was at school. The air outside my window plumed with pulverized debris. Planes had tanked and towers had buckled and monoliths were ablaze in Washington. The radio and TV, both churning in my bedroom, flung indistinguishable rumor and fact at the walls of our tiny apartment. There was no telling what else the day might hold. But this much I'd been promised: Laurel would call when she got home.

An e-mail from her to me on February 15, 2001 (she was about to start a new job): "I'm feeling sadly desperate about making the most of my time with Anya. All my anxiety about starting something new gets reduced to giving up time with Anya. *I'm crazy.*" And then later in the same e-mail, in response to my suggestion we take the kids out to eat at a local restaurant: "Coco Roco sounds good to me, although I'm not enjoying eating much since I had a little chunk taken out of my mouth. I've got something under my tongue that may be a mere sore or may be something a tad more serious requiring removal. The procedure has left me a bit sensitive in the mouth and also a tad unsettled." Tally it up. One "not [. . .] much," one "little," two "mays," one "mere," two "tads," and one "bit," all in three short sentences. An equivocating declaration, but the beginning of the end.

On September 11 Laurel did not yet know she was dying. Cancer was a possibility but far from a certainty—a recalcitrant sore or a benign growth was as likely an explanation for the mouth blemish. Once the chunk was removed, focus turned to the healing process. Doctors, monitoring her mouth, were never quite satisfied. But it took months for them to recommend further action. Finally, in October, she was scheduled with a mouth surgeon for a more invasive procedure. I know there must have been shadings to those months, upticks and downticks in levels of alarm for Laurel as she embarked on her mouth's saga, and I'm certain I attempted to keep tabs, to get the "all clear" she was hankering for as soon as she got it herself. But now those months are blank for me, and I wonder about them. Not so much because I feel I let her down, though maybe I did, but I wonder what she knew or felt or intuited during that half year when the cancer had dispatched its emissary but had not yet declared war.

When, exactly, did Laurel get brave? That's not a quality she projected, generally. You might even have called her timorous. Certainly that's what she called herself—shy, insecure—though I never bought it entirely, at least not the shy part.

I first met Laurel in the late '70s, in the East Village, when we were in our early twenties, both of us recently out of college. I waited tables at La Fregata, on St. Mark's Place, a studiously Bohemian café with regulars who sat for hours discussing Foucault or the Sandinistas over café au lait in bowls the size of paint cans. Laurel worked a block west at St. Mark's Bookshop. In those days the shop occupied two levels of a lovely, whitewashed, almost Moorish-looking storefront on the north side of the block, between Second and Third Avenues. It had columns and delicately carved architraves and a twisting set of filigreed iron stairs down to the basement level, where shoppers had to duck to clear the doorway. The store maintained a byzantine inventory system in which a color-coded note card filled with tracking information was inserted into each book before it was shelved. When the book sold, the card was removed, dated, and stacked. Twice daily the stack was sorted and each card reunited with its rightful volume, plucked from back stock, whereupon the book was reshelved. Long before I knew Laurel, I knew her spidery hermetic handwriting (a precursor to the slap-dash variation that emerged in the months before she died). She was queen of inventory, it seemed. Almost invariably, while browsing at St. Mark's, whenever I picked up a card that had fluttered to the floor from a volume in my hand, Laurel's handwriting winked up at me. I knew it was hers because I'd seen her apply it as she sat downstairs in her Levi's and tank top, leaning with an elbow on the elevated checkout counter, a cigarette in one hand, a pen in the other, tending to her mounds of paperwork.

I was terrified of Laurel. She was unapproachable. To people she did not know, or did not care to know, she emitted an incandescent force field of contempt that I was still too impressionable to ignore. She was striking, very slim, with small, pert, braless breasts and a diamond-shaped face dressed in masses of long dark curls. She had a prominent, elegant nose, etched lips and static, watchful brown eyes. The basement, her domain, housed volumes of history and philosophy, as well as the two categories of books with which, I would learn, she was besotted: politics and women's studies. I was intensely aware of Laurel whenever we occupied the same room, which was fairly often because I went to the bookstore all the time. I treated the place as if it were my club, wandering in to browse, to meet friends and talk importantly about the latest issue of *Bomb*, to ogle local literary stars, to read for an hour on a tucked-away stool, and sometimes, when I was flush, to buy. I spent most of my time on the main floor, which housed literature, but I was no stranger to the basement, and whenever I descended, there Laurel would be, examining a Heinemann catalog, turning a bell hooks title face out to encourage sales, coolly recommending an I. F. Stone collection to some punked-out grad student as the perfect birthday gift for his girlfriend. I don't ever remember Laurel smiling in those before-I-knew-her days, but I remember observing a cone of intimacy spring up when she spoke to friends or coworkers, and I remember how it made me feel: skeptical and envious.

Sometimes Laurel would turn tables on me and drop by with friends for an espresso at La Fregata. She'd order in the voice she reserved for outsiders with whom she had no choice but to communicate: airy and high-pitched, with faintly formal locution, as if she were reading from a script she didn't quite believe in. Almost daily—for a year? two years?—Laurel and I orbited in each other's universe without either of us ever once acknowledging the other.

Then one day it changed. I came home to my tenement apartment on First Avenue to find Laurel and three other women whooping it up in my living room over cigarettes and beer and raunchy gossip. I had taken on a temporary roommate, Helen, a Brit, and it turned out she and Laurel were friends from Laurel's spell in England several years earlier. Helen was vivacious, magnetic, a wide-eyed teller of can-you-top-this? tales about people, some mildly famous, and their foibles. (Helen, twenty-three and precociously well connected, was launching a career in radio.) When I walked in she was in the midst of one such story, involving an encounter she'd had the day before at the home of then *Village Voice* columnist Alexander Cockburn. I don't remember the details, I'm not even sure I heard them, but her friends were awash in laughter. Even Laurel. *Especially* Laurel. Her face was a contagion of goofy glee, her body helpless and wobbly. She pawed at the air and begged for mercy. I stared. Look who was in my living room. Look who was laughing. What I found here in my first unscripted encounter with Laurel was the very quality, years later, I came to love most in her. She had a capacity for pleasure and abandon that on any given day, in any given moment, could outbid the bristling guarded eye she reflexively turned on the world. When the room had subsided, Helen introduced me to her friends. I rose to the occasion, or tried to, offering genial hellos and nice-to-meet-yous. Laurel smiled and handed me a beer, but true to form, neither of us let on that we recognized the other.

By the time I got back to Abe's school on the day the towers fell, my veins were flexed with anxiety—where the hell was Jim? Not knowing was intolerable. I walked down the hall toward the administrative office and ran into Anya with a classmate and the classmate's mother. This mom had also called Laurel to see about retrieving Anya from school, and Laurel had asked her to let Anya decide where she wanted to go, with us or with them. I had made plans to take the kids to join another friend and her two boys; when Anya heard this she opted out of the boy-fest and chose to go home with her girlfriend. I proceeded to the office to put Abe's name on the pickup list, then trailed to the auditorium, now a makeshift holding pen for fretful parents waiting for their kids to be relinquished. After only a few minutes Abe was at my side.

"Hi, Mom," he said, as if it were no big deal for me to pluck him from class at 11:00 a.m. on the second day of school. I'd been told by some other parents—erroneously, it turned out—that the school's principal had informed everyone in the building, via the PA system, of the morning's events. So the first thing I did when Abe appeared was kneel down and hug him and ask him if he was scared.

"Why should I be?" he wanted to know.

"Because the towers fell down," I said.

"What towers?" he asked.

"Didn't Ms. Phillips tell you?"

"Tell me what?"

"Do you know why I'm here to get you?"

He shrugged and demanded, "What towers fell down?" as if my reason for being there were another subject altogether. So I explained to my six-year-old that airplanes had hit the World Trade Center towers, which caused them to crash to the ground.

"Oh," he said. "But they're not here. They're there." He pointed toward the stage at the front of the room. "Or there?" he pursued, pointing in the opposite direction.

"There, actually," I said, nodding in a third direction, vaguely toward downtown Manhattan.

"But we're *here*," he said, stamping his foot for emphasis. "Why should I be scared?"

"You shouldn't be scared," I said. "Maybe a better word is *sad*." I was winging it. "Because I think a lot of people got hurt."

Hours earlier, only the night before, Abe and I had stood under a shop awning in Tribeca, taking refuge from a downpour in a storm. Abe had gone for a checkup, and we'd just left the pediatrician's office. From where we stood, the Twin Towers were in full view, several blocks south. They looked like stage props, put there expressly to dramatize the storm. Sailing bands of cloud enveloped them, sliding up the walls, then peeling off at a certain story in ghostly, illuminated billows. Rain spangled the air and lightning hectored the tips of the towers, which stood there and took it, like a couple of stoics.

As Abe and I reached the front door of the school, we bumped into Jim, who fell into my arms. For over an hour his subway had been held at the last stop in Brooklyn with doors closed and information unforthcoming. Finally he and his fellow commuters were apprised of circumstances and released. With cell phones out of commission, Jim was unable to reach me, so he walked the couple of miles from downtown Brooklyn to Abe's school to see about picking him up.

Both Laurel and I were in our late thirties when we had our babies—Abe arrived the day after my thirty-eighth birthday, Anya two months before her mother turned thirty-nine. Yet despite these fairly late runs at motherhood, we both had easy pregnancies (though Laurel had endured a couple of false starts when conceiving) and delivered without complication. We both moved to Park Slope in our last trimesters of pregnancy. We both were passionate urbanites, in love with New York and its elastic culture, where we could live our approximate lives without fear of penalty or demotion (other than forms we imposed on ourselves, of course). And our pre-baby lives *were* approximate, lashed, especially in our twenties, to ambitions we were both too stubborn to relinquish but too timid and pragmatic to launch effectively. Hmm. That last bit may more precisely describe me at the time (waitressing followed by bookstore work and freelance editing to support episodic bouts of fiction writing) than Laurel. But I know she came to regret the ten long years she stayed on at St. Mark's Bookshop—despite her *grand dame* status there and despite the seriousness with which she executed her bookstore tasks, and despite the platform it gave her to pursue her progressive causes: filling the periodical racks not only with *Dissent* and *The Nation* but also with obscure broadsides from or about guerilla redoubts in Nicaragua and deracinated villagers in El Salvador. She could simultaneously ring up books and plan actions with her activist pals.

I remember browsing in the store once and hearing her ardently discuss plans she had for an extended trip to Nicaragua. As it happened I'd just returned from a month in Mexico. Inexplicably I felt emboldened to mention this, including a detail about the Salvadorans my friends and I had hooked up with briefly in Puerto Escondido, a scruffy, tourist-friendly fishing village not far from Acapulco on the Pacific coast. The Salvadorans were sons of landowners, and for some reason—well, the reason is my own stupidity—it did not occur to me that Laurel would look askance at the subjects of my anecdote. The guys were in their late twenties. Guillermo was gallant, mild-mannered, and soft around the middle. He walked with a pronounced limp, his souvenir from a childhood sidelined by polio. Juan, on the other hand, was a tall, strapping, mustachioed swimmer (competing on the national team!)—he could have modeled for a romantic Pancho Villa illustration. Juan was loyal to and solicitous of his friend, but he also was chatty, energetic, and vain—determined, I quickly learned, to impress us. The trip north from El Salvador had been Juan's idea. They had piled into a Volkswagen Beetle and, after a day or two, stopped on a whim in Escondido, where they found me and two college friends sitting on the beach under thatched umbrellas drinking beer. Then, because the deceptively warm, turquoise, tranquil-looking sea was beset with an invisible riptide that had carved a steep cliff into the shoreline and threatened to swallow bathers whole if they so much as dipped a toe, the Salvadorans invited us back to their hotel, which, backing onto the beach, was much posher than ours, *and* it had a pool—which is how I learned what an accomplished swimmer looks like as he butterflies down a swimming lane. But I didn't tell Laurel any of this. All I told her was the story Guillermo passed along as we sat watching Juan traverse the pool.

The week before, acting on an anonymous tip, Juan's father had set out to find a corpse by a stream in a remote corner of his farm. What he discovered was the body of his foreman, the individual who had managed the farm for many years and who lived in a cottage on the property with his wife and a slew of kids, the eldest of whom had been Juan's boyhood playmate. The body was naked and decapitated, the head placed faceup between the legs; the genitals, also severed, were stuffed into the mouth. I had never heard a story like this before. I had no idea where to put it. I did not ask for context because it scared me too much. Guillermo had said something about escalating acts of sabotage against landowners, but that this level of brutality had taken them all by surprise. Was the foreman a rebel, killed to scare off like-minded cronies? Or was he a docile servant to the ruling class, murdered by activists to rouse other docile servants from their slumber? What did the mutilation signify? What did Juan's father know? Was he culpable? And what about Juan himself? Even if I could have formulated these questions at the time, I would not have posed them. The sheer horror of the story filled every crevice of my curiosity.

Juan motored back and forth across the pool like a muscle-bound wind-up toy, then he emerged sleek and dripping, full of ideas about local excursions we all might take. My friends and I spent a couple days with the Salvadorans, cramming ourselves into the back seat of their Volkswagen to explore remote stretches of coastline.

I had to butt in to tell Laurel the story of the grisly murder, to impress her—to say, effectively: you're not the only one with Latin America bona fides. You think you'll come back from Nicaragua with a story to top mine? She listened, and blanched appropriately at the gruesome part, but then proceeded to pepper me with questions I couldn't answer. Politics hadn't sent me to Mexico, but rather timing, hedonism, and a sore need for distraction on the heels of a cataclysmic end to a love affair. My response to Laurel was meek and tractionless. She narrowed her eyes and pulled on her cigarette. Months later, Guillermo looked me up, having stopped in New York on his way to France, where he was scheduled to spend a season learning the finer points of goose-liver pâté production (his family had decided to diversify their farm revenues). Specifically, he would train in the art of "goose noodling," the process by which geese are stapled through the webs of their feet to the ground, then force-fed through tubes inserted down their gullets, the better to leaven their livers for A-list pâté. The night we went out, Guillermo shuffling next to me on a cane, I carefully avoided St. Mark's Place.

Jim, Abe, and I spent the afternoon of September 11 with our friend Kristin and her two boys (her husband, Don, was accounted for and making his way by foot from the Upper East Side). They lived in downtown Brooklyn, on State Street, a residential thoroughfare of handsome brownstones on one side and the parking lots and back alleys of municipal buildings on the other. The street is only a handful of blocks from the Brooklyn Bridge, which vast portions of Manhattan were using as a footpath to flee devastation. Our little group hung out in front of their house sipping lemonade and watching the world stumble by, dusty and sweaty and some barefoot, in suits and carrying their shoes. The weather was theatrical, so brilliant the streets looked stage-lit. Abe and Cole chased balls and each other up and down the block. Kristin bounced her infant son, Leo, on her hip and rocked him in the stroller. The day felt suspended, dissociated, drugged—eerily not unpleasant as the first blush of catastrophe seeped through our veins. At some point Jim took Abe and Cole to a nearby playground and Kristin and I walked Leo in his stroller to get him to nap. When we circled back to their block, Leo finally snoozing, we found the street momentarily quiet, no Manhattan refugees trudging by. Then, out of the mist—except of course there was no mist, it was a crystalline day, but my memory has imported mist—a firefighter appeared. In full regalia, all suited up and draped in hardware, he lumbered toward us on the sidewalk. We went silent and stepped back to give him room. His head was bent, his eyes were fastened on the ground, and every last inch of him was coated thickly in dust. He was the iconic September 11 fireman, but we didn't know this, for he had not yet been introduced to the world. However, we could see that he was traumatized, consumed by freshly imprinted horror. We were entranced. We stared at him walking away, toward his tiny picturesque firehouse, the one on the next block. We looked at each other, briefly dazed, then our thoughts leaped in unison:

"Dave!" one of us said.

Dave, Marian's husband, the firefighter, the one whose wedding anniversary it was that day. He was dead, had been so for several hours. In a few months' time a fragment of his jawbone would be presented to Marian as proof. I told Kristin what I knew, that I'd seen Marian in the morning and that she was heading off to meet Dave to celebrate the day. We went inside to phone her to see how far they'd gotten with their plans.

On September 12, when I caught sight of Laurel walking in Prospect Park, I did not call out her name. She was with another friend, and they were strolling on a path that circumnavigated the Long Meadow; I knew we'd stumble upon each other eventually. In point of fact I was not overly eager to see her. Our relations were in a trough at the time, a depressingly familiar trough. Laurel periodically lost faith in me, in my friendship, and this was one of those periods. We had spoken the night before. I'd phoned to see if she and Josh had gotten home OK, to make sure Anya had fared well through the afternoon, to tell her that Dave was "missing" (invoking the euphemism of the day). But the other reason for phoning, that is, the irreducible urge to trade in the currency of wonder and disbelief generated by the day's events, that reason was not much satisfied with Laurel. Her tone was practical, as it had been earlier in the day when we'd spoken while the morning's chaos was at full tilt. Practical, and even a little skeptical, as if to say: "Don't make too much of this, Kim." Not to deny the significance of the day, but to revoke my claim on it.

I had failed her, recently, and I didn't know how. Not a clue. We were prone to this, as if to fevers, wherein Laurel withdrew the consolations of friendship but not the demands, and I debased myself trying to set things right—as if crude Pollyanna force could restore equilibrium (it couldn't). Why didn't I ever call Laurel on this, tell her how opaque and burdensome and finally unfair her sensitivities were? Because I was afraid of her. The time or two I came anywhere near doing so backfired horribly. Laurel felt so at odds with the world, so misperceived and unaccommodated in it, so awash in unspoken grievances, that when she did take a stand, she was unshakable. In this she baffled and even repelled people at times, her formulations coming across as mercurial, willful. Kristin put it this way: "Laurel is hard to negotiate with." Kristin spoke from experience, since she and Laurel shared a babysitter for their kids and thus found themselves negotiating arrangements (or attempting to) all the time. I appreciated the apt simplicity of Kristin's observation. After all, friendship is an ongoing series of negotiations—for time, sympathy, loyalty, love. When Laurel was at her most vexing with me, it helped to think that the rough going could be attributed to her poor skills as a negotiator, not to some chilling determination she might have to rewrite the codes of friendship.

On the afternoon of September 12, Laurel was freshly annoyed with me. We had planned for me to call her that morning so we could arrange to meet with the kids in the park—and I did. But I placed the call just past noon, no longer technically morning. I can imagine Laurel standing with her elbow bent, peering at her wristwatch, waiting for the stroke of twelve. "Figures," I hear her say as the hour hand lines up behind the minute hand. She does not reach for the phone to call me, because it is more satisfying to stew about how unreliable I am. When I do phone, minutes later, no one picks up, because Laurel and Anya have already made for the park (Josh is at work, in Manhattan, the only Brooklynite I know to venture across the river that day). "Damn," I say, glancing at the clock. When we cross paths an hour or two later, each of us in a clutch of friends and acquaintances, the kids hard at play, she avoids my eye. I do not apologize for my late call, because bringing it up will infuriate her. I venture a boilerplate comment about the eerie disconnect between the wide-angle view on the park and close-up shots of its human inhabitants; a bucolic paradise settled by stunned, twitchy vagabonds. "Really?" Laurel says, skeptical again. "I don't see it that way." She was not about to give me an inch.

Labor Day weekend, 1995: Laurel and I sit in my little green Neon, laughing uproariously. Anya and Abe, aged five months and seven months, are belted into their car seats in the back. The car is parked at a shopping center in Hudson, a river town in upstate New York, a short drive from the borrowed house in which we are staying for the weekend. Laurel and I and the babies have come up a few days before Josh and Jim, so it is on this cool and overcast afternoon that we find ourselves out shopping, anticipating our husbands' arrival. The trunk is loaded with groceries, and we are all set to pull out, but I haven't yet started up the car. I can't because I'm laughing too hard. A mischievous shopping cart has made off with our senses. Discarded by another shopper, the cart has rumbled to life and adjusted its angle. It is unmanned and rolling—purposefully, it seems, and self-propelled—on a trajectory to bash another cart (the one we just unloaded and abandoned), as if determined to settle a score. Laurel and I are done in by this unexpected glimpse into the inner lives of shopping carts. Laughter consumes us.

I remember Laurel's vivid face and the weather and the variation from routine represented by the rural setting and our reliance on my car and how that variation somehow reinforced the grooved repetition of mommy life. Mommy of a young child especially. An infant in particular. First baby, no less. Two such specimens propped and harnessed in the backseat; two eighteen-pound bags of bones, useless and voracious, passively (or not) sucking up every last measure of energy in a room. Laurel and I arrived almost simultaneously in the land of Mother Love, where the heart rezones because its old boundaries are meaningless. Our children scooped the love right out from between our ribs. So what could we do but swan around in our mother roles, fumbling, bored, enraptured—the usual—and fill our babies' days with what we hoped was adequate compensation for the miracle of their existence? Still, the demands of the role, and even the accumulating rewards, were wildly disorienting.

At some point, that day in the parking lot, Laurel and I remember ourselves, and then the babies. We turn to check on them. They are examining us. Anya and Abe have four of the most glorious eyes ever to look our way—Anya with her big black liquid orbs, Abe with his shimmering blue marbles. The sight of the two of them peering magisterially over the seat at their drooling, hiccuping mothers triggers a relapse of dementia in us. We laugh all over again, and the babies don't seem to mind. Laurel and I are so mutually attuned to the clang of motherhood that this unhinged interlude feels almost like a form of prayer, an appeal from both of us to a clarifying higher order.

And yet I believe Laurel's template for friendship involved a kind of mirroring that I could not live up to. Of course mirroring is the stuff of friendship, a reason it sustains us. Friendships intensify according to the degree to which we find ourselves buried in our friends—even (especially?) if the self we find seems altered. Laurel and I, having grown so close during the migrations of pregnancy and early motherhood, having groped in tandem through those difficult splendid years, had unearthed some pretty deep wells of recognition between us. It mattered that neither of us had a full-time job when our babies were young—we passed so many damn hours and days together. And it mattered that we had improbably coincident trajectories: from unremarkable Long Island childhoods to defiant (but not too) Long Island teen years to liberal (and liberating) New England college years, to books and politics (in Laurel's case politics and books) and the East Village, to husbands and Park Slope and babies. And it matters too that the more resonances are teased out of a friendship, the harder it is to bear the dissonances. Even at our most intertwined, when I was as grateful as she for the refuge of our friendship, I worried that Laurel expected something from me that wasn't mine to give: an uncompromised reflection of herself.

But Laurel wished for this in all aspects of her life. Her obstetricians were a group of hip female Soho doctors with feminist leanings and a battery of midwives to back them up. My doctor, pretty much chosen for me by our narrow health coverage at the time, was a very young, very short, very earnest guy with a paunch and a yarmulke and a penchant for gag neckties. I was perfectly happy with him, and said as much to Laurel, but she was aghast at my misfortune—or rather my placidity in the face of it—of having to entrust my obstetric care to a non-initiate. Laurel was reluctant to walk down ugly streets—hey, so am I, but her efforts to avoid them sometimes carried the scent of a moral mission. No matter how interested she was in a topic covered in a magazine article, she would not read it unless she knew the author or someone she trusted had recommended it, she explained, for fear that the writer's politics would offend. She found it hard to forgive her parents for supplying her with a childhood and a set of expectations that were more in line with who they were than with who she was. Annoying, of course, but almost universal—and if you think about it, what else can parents do? It's key to growing up—reconciling the difference, if there is one, between who you're raised to be and who you aspire to be. One time, when we were all leaving their apartment building, four-year-old Anya delightedly pointed at a powerful floodlight a story or two up the wall on the neighboring synagogue, and proclaimed how much she loved the light and the dramatic shadows it threw. Laurel differed. "Anya!" she squealed. "That light is ugly! It's garish! How can you like it?" She was not so much angry as perplexed and concerned. I could see what Laurel meant about the light, but Anya saw something too, and it dazzled her. Laurel was so distracted by the possibility that her daughter might be attracted to an unsightly object that she forgot to notice Anya engaging in a pursuit to which Laurel professed to be singularly devoted: autonomy, Anya's especially. If there was one mistake her parents had made that Laurel was not going to repeat, it was deciding for her daughter who she should be.

So I did not feel singled out by Laurel as a target for her irritation. I merely elicited a customized variation, and sometimes, perhaps, an extra-heaping dose. In the early years of our children's lives there might have been the illusion of unrippled reflection between Laurel and me, and then as the years passed and the light changed and the kids grew and the illusion crumbled, maybe she felt betrayed.

On the night of the day we laughed in the parking lot, I made a bottle of breast milk for Anya. The babies were just starting to eat solid foods, but the bulk of their nutrition still came from nursing. Due to a physiological quirk Abe was born with, I had to produce a lot more milk than he technically required. In his first year of life he had an underdeveloped glottal muscle—the muscle in your throat that keeps food from upending out of your mouth when you stand on your head, or even tilt it, immediately after eating. The deficiency was not medically significant—our pediatrician assured us that the muscle would develop by Abe's first birthday, and indeed this turned out to be the case—but it did cause Abe to "spill" a good deal of the milk he consumed. I don't mean vomit; there was no peristaltic component. It did not distress him. He would sit smiling and giggling after a satisfying snort at the breast, seemingly oblivious as the undigested milk welled up and out from his toothless grin like gin sloshing over the sides of a martini glass. But it did mean he was hungry all the time, and that my breasts were pressed into overdrive. I had stacks of little milk baggies in the freezer that I'd pumped and stored for Jim or the babysitter to use whenever I was out of the house. Laurel, on the other hand, produced plenty of milk for Anya directly from the breast but never had much success on the pump (not uncommon in nursing mothers, this volume disparity between mouth and pump extraction). That night in our borrowed house, a sprawling, delightfully ramshackle, nineteenth-century colonial filled with shadowy, cavernous rooms, I hauled out my electric breast pump to perform the nightly ritual. The babies were asleep, and the mommies had uncorked a bottle of wine. Optimistically, Laurel plugged in her pump, too.

We sat across from one another in plush upholstered chairs, sipping Syrah and pumping in unison. We were by now accustomed to the rhythmic, clinical deformity of the breast as it submitted to the pump's will, and in my case to the initially reluctant drip-drop-drip of the milk, followed by the "let-down," as it's known in the trade—the streaming release of mother's liquid calories. Laurel, gamely installed at her machine, watched my bottle fill, ounce by ounce, then glanced down at her own meager output.

"Not fair," she said, tossing back a mouthful of wine. I shrugged apologetically.

"Can Anya have one of those?" she asked, pointing at my bottle but not yet turning off her machine. Laurel had a busy week coming up, taking care of some consulting obligations for a non-profit she used to work for *and* beginning a master's program in public health; she needed some backup bottles for Anya.

"Sure," I told her. "There's plenty."

It was a casual request, easily granted, but the moment felt subversive, too. Despite the centuries-old wet-nurse tradition; despite the universality of the substance in question; and despite the improbably modern, progressive aura of mother's milk, I had to shake off the default notion that mine (which tasted like melted vanilla Häagen-Dazs, Jim and I agreed upon sampling it) was not transferable. It was, of course. And I did.

Sometime in October 2001, Marian had a wake for Dave at the Montauk Club, a swank Victorian mansion that leases out for functions, up near the park. No trace of Dave's remains had yet been recovered, so an empty coffin, flanked by honor guards, dominated one side of the huge drawing room. The place was packed with mourners, except for a buffer zone around the coffin, which in its emptiness felt powerfully inhabited. Laurel did not know Marian well, but well enough to want to pay her respects, so she joined Jim and me at the wake. From the moment she arrived I could see that she was uncomfortable—not an unusual condition for Laurel. She was finicky, easily put off by a person or a scent or a circumstance. I instinctively tried to shield her from situations that might rub her the wrong way. Stupid of me, and counterproductive, because often my interventions succeeded only in making things worse, or in transforming me into the object of her displeasure. She sensed my meddling reflex, I suspect, and resented it. Once she said as much: "You manage me. You manage our friendship. Why can't you just be in it?" This observation was spot-on and unexpected, so much so that I nimbly responded with the assertion that I had no idea what she was talking about. Silly me to think that my maneuverings were deft. Silly me to maneuver at all. I don't want to overstate the matter; Laurel brokered her own encounters with the world. It's just that sometimes, in ways subtle and, on occasion, not so subtle, apparently, I attempted to steer her around people or events that I thought would be nettlesome for her. She was too smart and far too sensitive not to notice. I failed her here. I should have tried to explain that I never set out to manage her, but did so as a last resort, because her prickliness was such a bummer, and I wanted to avoid it. Then she might have had the opportunity to point out to me that *her* prickliness was not *my* problem (debatable, but worth considering). Or she might have said something else entirely. I guess that's why I never spoke up. I was afraid of what the outcome of such a discussion might be.

That night at the wake, Laurel walked in and looked hesitantly around. The room was appointed with flowers and photo collages of handsome Dave from all the various phases of his life. Firefighters, dignified masses of them from all around the country, milled about in identical formal attire. We civilians, family and friends and neighbors, gaped teary-eyed at the photos. Five-year-old Aidan, Dave and Marian's son, a gorgeous, floppy St. Bernard of a boy and the only child present, buzzed heedlessly back and forth through the crowds. Edgy officials skulked among us, giving their attention to important-looking communications devices. Mayor Giuliani was due to arrive at any moment. Reporters jotted notes on pads. A line had formed. Do you call it a receiving line at a wake? It was long, and Marian stood at the head of it along with Dave's mother and other close members of the family. Jim and I mingled with guests, exchanging sober pleasantries, and then we joined the queue. That's when Laurel arrived. We beckoned her over, but, after meekly surveying the room, she pointed a finger to indicate that first she wanted to look at the photos. In a few minutes she approached us. Tears stood in her eyes. Her face was tentative. She asked me questions about the goings-on, as if I were somehow in charge. She glanced around uneasily.

"What's this line for?" she asked.

I gestured toward Marian.

Laurel shook her head, and then: "How does she do it?"

"What?"

"Any of it. All of it," Laurel said.

"You mean get up in the morning?" I asked.

"Basically," she said. "But this. The public face. I couldn't."

"She's remarkable," I agreed. In the god-awful collision of public and private spheres that was Dave's death (and its aftermath), Marian was forging a role for herself.

"I barely know her," Laurel said, apropos of nothing in particular. She looked distracted. Staring at a fixed spot on the wall, she gave up on our conversation. I felt responsible. The line inched along. And then, after who knows how long, just as we were nearing our goal—Marian—Laurel put her hand on my arm. "I can't do this," she said, and bolted.

Laurel's official diagnosis did not arrive till March 2002, though months before she'd been informed that her mouth lesion was "precancerous," and that they'd have to monitor it closely. There was no reprieve in this, just the start of a gloomy vigilance. I recall discussing it with her in my car, upstate again, this time in Red Hook, cresting a ridge to greet a magnificent autumnal view of the Catskills. "Let's focus on the good news," I said. "You don't have cancer." We both pondered my useless remark in silence. Of just about anyone I knew, I thought, Laurel would be least prepared to cope with a cancer diagnosis. Her sense of personal justice was so minutely calibrated, her sensitivity to minor inconvenience acute. Cancer was colossally unjust; a major inconvenience. I was almost as afraid of how she would take the diagnosis as I was of the diagnosis itself, though it's hard for me to admit this now. In any case, Laurel proved my worry profoundly misguided.

I was in Congo on assignment for a national magazine when she submitted to the surgery that pinpointed her cancer. I had been scheduled to travel some months earlier, in October. My flight was booked for a week to the day after the United States started bombing Afghanistan. A Sunday. I heard the news, then sat in my bathroom and wept. I can still feel in my bones the terror of that fall. The next day I called my editor and told him I could not fly to Congo because of the timing; it felt freakishly risky. For some reason I thought he would understand, but the news made him very unhappy. This was the first time in my life I was afraid to travel, and by all means the first time I was jettisoning an important gig. The assignment would involve traveling to an impossibly remote corner of the Congolese rain forest to report on an initiative in place to reverse the dramatic loss of wildlife to poaching in the Congo Basin. Politics, guns, gorillas, scientists, egos. A bracing assignment, to say the least. I told my editor I remained passionate about the project and hoped we could postpone, not cancel. He sighed. The story's photographer had no qualms about keeping to the schedule. When I said something about how being the mother of a small child no doubt added to my sense of peril, he said next time he'd be sure not to hire a mother. For months the project was dead, but then in December we revived it. Off I went, finally, in March, while Laurel prepared to go under the knife. On the day I got back to New York, some weeks later, she was about to emerge from the hospital. Within hours of her release she sent me an e-mail, instructing me to tell her all about my trip.

From the moment I learned that Laurel had cancer, I worried that I would fail her—fail to intuit her needs; fail to meet them; fail to comfort her; fail to fathom her despair; fail to summon or convey sufficient compassion; fail, simply, to do enough. And it wasn't just a matter of the obliterating weight of the diagnosis, or what I thought I knew about my friend's ability to cope. It just so happened that my own life, my family's, was upside down at the time.

Jim and I had sold our co-op apartment on Prospect Park and contracted to buy a brand-new house going up in another section of the neighborhood. The ensuing construction delays—the ones everyone warns you about and for which we thought we were braced—had begun to reveal themselves for what they were: harassment. Shortly after we'd sealed the deal, the developer decided he hadn't charged enough for the house and embarked on a campaign to discourage us, to get us to back out of the contract. Stoned-out thugs (nominally guards) menaced us when we approached the property. Jittery Russian-Mafia types (nominally construction foremen) sidled up with suggestions-cum-threats about how it might behoove us to rethink our plans to occupy the house. We surrendered thousands upon thousands of dollars to the developer for fit-and-finish upgrades that were never procured, let alone installed. A contractor we'd privately hired found human excrement deposited in the master bedroom closet when she showed up one day to do some work. I could go on.

Meanwhile, having sold our apartment in anticipation of the move (the date for which kept receding), we were renting it back from our buyer, month by month. But the buyer got fed up and evicted us before the new house was ready, whereupon Jim, Abe, and I moved into a tiny dismal sublet on the top floor of an iffy brownstone overlooking a highway ramp. We told ourselves we'd be there for a month, but we wound up staying for a year—with almost all of our belongings in storage. That's where we were for 9/11. We were still there for the bust in the technology sector, which had gainfully employed Jim, a software developer; he was a partner with a start-up—until he wasn't anymore, sometime that winter. And that's where we were when Laurel was diagnosed: at the mercy of a merciless building developer; sleeping on an airbed; warm clothes lost to storage as winter bore down; primary breadwinner unemployed and reeling; Congo trip on, then off, then on again—and all of it suffused in clammy post-9/11 dread.

Even without the distraction of her health, Laurel would not have joined me in scanning the skies and airwaves for signs of another terrorist attack. It was not in her nature. Her passions and instincts were roused much more to anger over U.S. policy than they were to fear over the crosshairs of fate. This, despite her lavish identification with the idea of victimhood. Or perhaps because of it. After all, by definition the United States was not—*is not*—a victim; being fearful would suggest otherwise. But I speculate.

Laurel's fierce political predilections may have buffered her from that season's freefall of civic anxiety, but it was some other kind of ferocity that equipped her to face the year gearing up to overtake her—and her alone.

More than a decade earlier, having arrived back in New York after living in Japan for several years, I stopped into St. Mark's Bookshop and came face-to-face with Laurel: ultraslim in snug Levi's and a mane of hennaed curls, long tapered fingers shuffling a stack of inventory cards. No cigarette, though; instead, a pencil was trapped between her teeth. I thought I felt a jolt of the old charismatic disdain cross the space between us, but I must have imagined it. Because when our eyes met, she said: "Kim! How are you? It's been such a long time!" Thus commenced the next phase of our relationship.

We chatted amiably and at length that afternoon. She told me she was slowly disentangling herself from the store—now she worked there just one day a week. She had edited a collection of feminist essays for Schocken Books and was employed part-time by a nonprofit that created health education materials for women in developing nations. She was organizing a conference in Zimbabwe on reproductive health, and in a couple of months she would fly there to help run the event. How extraordinary. I had plans to be in Zimbabwe at precisely the same time, to continue some research and writing work I'd started there the year before. The coincidence was an ideal premise for friendship, and in the weeks and months that followed, Laurel and I met frequently for drinks or dinner, discovering that the basis for friendship went well beyond happenstance. I liked her mixture of passion and re-serve. I liked the stories she told from her life, her diligent sifting for meaning. I liked her patter on men, books, and politics, in that order. And I liked the pure interest she took in what I had to say, as if I might influence her thinking. Which is funny, because Laurel was so damn opinionated, yet the opposite was true, too. She had a kind of craving to factor in the world around her—to understand it better, but also, I think, to find her place in it.

Laughing again, in Zimbabwe. Laurel and I are eating piri-piri chicken and sipping South African wine at an elegantly lit restaurant in the posh northern outskirts of Harare. We have washed up here at the end of her weeklong conference, much of which I attended in a kind of mascot role. Feeling stalled and discouraged with my own work when Laurel came to town, I was ripe for distraction. So she folded me into the conference routine; kept me busy pressing flesh, sizing up position papers and dispensing per diems. Because I could and because she was happy to have me there. Coffee in the morning and scotch at night. Laurel in an ink-blue linen dress, hair fetchingly up, tendrils escaping, pencil eraser tap-tap-tapping on her tooth. The smooth efficiency of the conference, its invigorating hum of focused, collaborative work, somehow reset my compass for the duration of my time in Zimbabwe. Laurel had rescued me from despondency. She was my angel of mercy.

Even before she lost her tongue, Laurel's ability to speak came and went during her illness, depending on treatment. The healing process that followed certain less drastic surgical procedures meant days or weeks without speech, and her rounds of daily radiation in the summer of 2002 turned the simple acts of sipping water or saying hello into painful ordeals. One day Laurel e-mailed me to ask if I would mind scheduling a haircut for her and then escorting her to the appointment, so I could be her voice and explain to the hairdresser what kind of cut she wanted. It struck me as a good sign that she was still making room for pedestrian vanities of this sort. I booked her with a guy I'd been using, Mornay, a stylish blond South African possessed of a brisk, confident approach with the shears. When Laurel sat down in his chair I explained that she couldn't speak due to illness. This threw him, briefly. I did my best to convey her wishes, which she'd outlined on paper ahead of time. She didn't trust haircutters, claiming that few understood her soft, springy corkscrews.

She was in bad shape. Her radiation treatment had ended a few weeks back, but the pain still raged. Probably it was dawning on her that the cure had failed (soon her doctors would say so). She looked so frail in Mornay's chair. She'd always been thin, but now it was awful, bones jutting everywhere. Yet her lovely brown eyes were lovelier than ever, dominating her face and radiating woe. Mornay examined her hair thoughtfully, rubbing locks and strands between his fingers. When he felt ready, he raised his scissors and sought Laurel's assent in the mirror. She nodded. I excused myself to run next door for a coffee, takeout. "Do you mind?" I asked. She blinked her permission. I was gone for three minutes, tops, and I came back to find Mornay blithely snipping away. Laurel sat erect and still. But as I drew near and could make out her face in the mirror, I saw tears sliding down her cheeks.

"Laurel?" I said. Her eyes met mine in the glass.

"What's wrong?" Her expression didn't change, but more tears slid. I asked Mornay to excuse us and fished out a notepad from my pocket.

"What?" I asked, producing a pen. She refused the implements and wiped her tears.

"Is the cut okay?" I ventured. She half-smiled and shrugged, as if to say, who cares?

"Is it the pain?" She shrugged again and flicked her hand, clearly wishing I'd forget about it. Then it dawned on me.

"Were you scared? Is that it? Without me here?" She fluttered her eyelids affirmatively. Sorrow flooded my veins. How could I have left her there, even for a moment? She was helpless. The notion struck me like a blow. Helpless? Laurel was forty-six years old—not a baby, not elderly—in the thick of it with a seven-year-old and a demanding job and a pile of unread books by her bed. The reassuring ritual of the haircut would not haul her back from the distant planet that disease had rocketed her to. I felt useless. Laurel jabbed her thumb toward Mornay, and vigorously hooked it back to point at her head—a command for him to finish his work.

Laurel's illness rescued our friendship. Second-guessing and cross-purposes had come to dominate our relations. More than anything, at a certain point, it was Abe and Anya's camaraderie that glued us together—Laurel pretty much said so. This made me nuts, but I felt powerless to improve matters, and so did she, apparently. Then, with her diagnosis, just when I was convinced I would fail her once and for all, some kind of grace settled upon us. Communication restored itself; lucid, murk-free, targeted communication. Laurel did not ask for much, but she accepted whatever I had to offer. It was a beautiful arrangement. It made me want to give more— though she did not do all the taking. She never lost interest in news of my life, following up on its particulars each time we met, bucking me up when my Congo story ran into legal snags, and suggesting ways Jim and I might inflict mortal comeuppance on the madman controlling our housing situation. I brought her milkshakes, which for months were all she could eat. Sometimes, when she couldn't speak and couldn't eat a thing, I came by for half an hour just to sit and hold her hand. She seemed to like this. Her mind was seething, with matters practical and otherwise. She encountered a Jeff Buckley recording of Leonard Cohen's stirring, inscrutable "Hallelujah," and for weeks she gnawed on the lyrics, which touched on grace and agony and the one word left on someone's tongue. She convened a group of friends, including a rabbi, to discuss the lyrics, then invited us back, as if itching to post dispatches from the realm of spiritual wakefulness. An avid secularist, she was surprised but not put out to find herself in that realm.

Laurel was a guide in the last year of her life, inviting others to walk with her as far as they cared to go, pointing out the marvels and monsters along the way. Her hair-raising struggle—physical, emotional, spiritual—did not shut her down; on the contrary, it opened her out. She made new friendships and immeasurably deepened old ones, even as she prepared to die. She was searingly frank on the subject of her own death, speaking about it long before anyone around her could do so. She wouldn't force us to dwell on it, but neither would she permit us to promptly avert our eyes. The pact was implicit: She would not give up on life so long as we would not ignore death. She held the two opposing ideas in her mind at once and did not go crazy. This spectacular feat of balance, of willed sanity, feels oddly commensurate with her chronological age: forty-six and dying. The middle years are all about establishing balance, conceding the fact of life's horizon and tilting, almost imperceptibly, in its direction. The brutal conversion of Laurel's midlife to its finish seemed to elicit a counterthrust from her, in which she magically summoned the wisdom of all those unlived years, and put it to work.

Frequently, as her condition worsened, I saw Laurel watch Anya enter a room or concentrate on a task. We had long ago learned to change subjects when the kids barged in, but sometimes Anya caught her mother off guard and Laurel did not have time to rearrange her face. On these occasions Anya seemed irradiated, scorched with meaning as she went about her little-girl activities with Laurel looking on. Sometimes Anya felt her mother's eyes bore through her.

"What? Why are you staring?" she'd ask.

Laurel would shake her head to snap out of it. "You're beautiful, that's all," she'd say with her voice or a pen. Anya would roll her eyes.

Several times Laurel grabbed my sleeve and frantically gestured toward Anya, as if appealing to me to do something, anything, about their looming separation.

Once when Laurel was in the hospital and Anya was at our house for the night, the kids finished dinner and bolted upstairs to play. I puttered in the kitchen until their silence pulled me up after them. Here is what I found: Anya lying on her back on the couch, eyes closed, head in Abe's lap; Abe squinting down at her, resting a folded washcloth on her brow. I tilted my head inquiringly. "She's got a headache," he explained in a quiet voice. The tenderness of the scene—her trust, his attentiveness, their independence—demolished me.

The day before Laurel died, we sat in her living room. Her breathing was noisy, gurgly—fluid had accumulated in her lungs and infected them. She was taking extra care with something she wanted to say. When she finished writing the note, she handed it over and watched me read. It asked me to promise that I would always keep Abe in Anya's life.

"Yes," I said, "I promise."

She grabbed me by the collar and brought us nose to nose.

"Are you trying to tell me you mean it?" I asked.

She nodded.

The night Laurel cooked us the dinner she couldn't eat, after she ladled the soup and cut the bread and tossed the salad and poured the wine, then toted her nutrition contraption over to the table and hoisted up her blouse and plugged in the hose to the slot in her belly; after she shrugged wryly and jotted on her pad: *Bon appetit!*; after I excused myself as casually as I could and fled to the bathroom to reason with my reflection in the mirror that if Laurel could do this, then so could I; after I checked on Abe and Anya, who had eaten their dinner earlier and were now curled up together on Josh and Laurel's bed, mesmerized, watching *The Parent Trap*; after I returned to the table and tasted my soup, which was delicious and seemed to blaze a trail for more soup to follow; after Jim and Laurel discussed some of the things he'd investigated for her about text-to-voice technology; after Laurel mused on her notepad about the possibility of taking the kids back to Tuscany and renting another villa, as we'd done when they were three; after we cleared the plates and lapsed into silence and said goodnight because we were tired; after we got home and I flung myself into bed, I wondered aloud to Jim:

"What will become of her?"

In a matter of days, we knew.

My Mother, My Sight

Allan deSouza

It happened twelve years ago on a deserted Brooklyn street, the wrong place at the wrong time, except that I lived around the corner. Two men jumped out of a car, and one ordered me at gunpoint to get down on my knees. I can still feel my face pressed against rain-dampened concrete as a semiautomatic is pressed to the back of my head and my pockets emptied; waiting for the shot, wondering what the bullet will feel like, how long the pain will last.

With the gun at my head, knowing I'm going to die because that's what they're yelling at me, *you're gonna die muthafucker, I'm gonna blow your fuckin brains out muthafucker,* a part of me still holds onto the comforting belief—at this point, what else do I have?—that if I play nice, do what they say, *good muthafucker, nice muthafucker,* they won't pull the trigger, because there's no reason to. Reason. It's a faith I've never invested in before, and though it might be really short-lived now, as might I, reason and obedience seem not such a bad trade-off for staying alive.

Even as it was happening I remember thinking: if this were the movies and I were the hero, I would twist round, slap his gun-hand away, drop-kick him in the groin, punch him in the face, and pick up the gun where he had dropped it. If it were the movies and he the antihero and I the bad guy, he would shoot me whether I complied or resisted. This wasn't the movies and there was no script to follow, and that was perhaps the worst—not knowing what would happen next. When they made me kneel on the ground with my ankles crossed and my hands on my head, I knew that they had been watching *too many* movies and wondered which script they would follow. An image of the TV show *Cops* came into my head,

and its jingle—*bad boy, bad boy, what you gonna do?*—rang in my ears.
It was so irritating that, instead of a scan through my own life, my
last thought might have been of a TV show. I had watched it a
couple of times as part of my introduction to America: it always
seemed to be white cops chasing down black or brown suspects,
or called to intervene in domestic assault cases. A black woman,
weeping and her face bruised, sheltering a couple of screaming
kids, reluctantly hands over a knife to the police as a black man is
handcuffed and led away. A posse of Latino kids is—in the show's
parlance—*assuming the position*, flat out on the ground, legs spread,
hands behind their heads, and there's one kneeling, ankles crossed,
fingers clasped behind his head, answering questions as three cops
stand around him, batons drawn. And suddenly the whole thing,
the picture of myself kneeling on a deserted sidewalk with a gun
pressed to my head, seemed so ludicrous that I wasn't scared any
more, because it was like being on TV.

The fear descended later, as did the mental run-through of
the different possible outcomes. And both—fear and rerun—have
stayed with me.

Soon after, I moved, taking literal heed of that directive "Go west,
young man." Born in Kenya, at age seven I had migrated with my
family to London, then as an adult moved by myself to New York,
and now again to Los Angeles, chasing the sunset until if I were
to go any farther west, it would become east. From England, my
parents had taken one step back east, one step closer to their prior
colonial histories, and had settled in Portugal.

After two years in L.A., when I was age thirty-eight, my eyes
began misbehaving. A few times while reading, a paragraph of
words on the edge of my peripheral vision would suddenly lift
up and scuttle off the page. By the time I blinked and looked directly at the vacated space, the words had raced back and plopped
down again, watching me with defiant innocence. Other times I
had seen spiders in the corners of rooms where walls and ceiling hugged. Fat, black, hairy creatures. They dangled on invisible threads, waving their infernal legs in taunting motion. When I
looked up, they disappeared into cracks in the walls that sealed up

immediately behind them. I hoped that they were not real, that it was just my imagination playing tricks. But if so, what would that mean? I had read once that seeing imaginary spiders was an early indication of psychosis. And by then it was probably too late to reverse it. So, what was I losing? My eyes or my mind?

I tried to ignore the spiders for as long as possible, but then the world began to disappear. It wasn't noticeable at first, and I don't know when it began; the change was so gradual, and my adjustment and acceptance of it so complete, that I noticed it only when I woke up one morning and looked out the window and saw that it was foggy. I should have known then, of course, this being L.A.—smog, yes, but fog? When I looked around my room and the fog seemed to be also inside, I realized that the change was in me.

The doctor has a name for my symptoms—which is an enormous relief—but no explanation for their occurrence—which worries me again. Cataracts, he says, though he has never seen them in anyone so young.

"I might look young," I say, "but apparently I see old."

He just looks blank, and asks if I've suffered from malnutrition. Even though I'm from famine hot spots of the world, I want to say, I experience more of an existential hunger.

"Head trauma?" he asks. There's so much going on in my head that is traumatic and traumatizing, but I don't think that's what he means. He's referring only to the physical. I think back to being kicked repeatedly in the head during a racist attack in London barely a decade ago, or getting stoned (in the biblical sense) when I was a teenager—the side of my head next to my right eye swelling up like a golf ball. This happened also in London; perhaps I was too often in the wrong place, but if your family history and childhood experience are routed through three different colonies and their colonial powers—Goa under the Portuguese, India under the British, and Kenya, again British—then being in the wrong place and at the wrong time too easily becomes habitual.

My imitation of a golf ball must be the kind of instance the doctor is asking about, but it seems to me too pedestrian. He wants a direct correlation between the effect and a cause. He wants one-plus-one to tell the whole story.

I want to know *why* it makes two. I want a more expansive, more encompassing reason. I want to know the moment or a series of moments in my life when my eyes began to retreat from the world, or refused to acknowledge it. When my eyes felt they had seen enough and, in protest, began to cloud. When my eyes drew a boundary line and the rest of my body, not as sensitive or as perceptive, blindly stumbled across. And the eyes, dragged across with the rest of me—in defiance and not a little spite—refused to do their designated work. These to me seem much more likely, much more satisfying explanations of what has stymied my vision.

The doctor sticks to his version. The only unusual factor, he says, is my age; otherwise it's a simple procedure to correct, he tells me, almost routine. Remove the clouding lenses and replace them with permanent plastic ones. I would just become a little more inorganic. A little less biodegradable. They'll do my right eye first, the eye I've begun to think of as the wrong eye. If that goes well, they'll do the left eye, the eye still left to me.

Nurses gather round as I lie on the operating table:

"Oh, he's so young," they chime, "much too young for old people's illness."

I only look young, I think again, automatically, but that visage of youthfulness has infected my own self-image so that this example of many instances of my body's deterioration feels like it's happening to someone else. "Middle age," that condition that I associate with my parents, is still alien to my conception of myself. Me? I'm just getting started.

Much too young, I'm thinking, as the needle pricks the skin on the back of my hand and the walls begin to undulate, just like a dream sequence on TV. My eyeballs collapse into their sockets, my eyelids fluttering over them like garrulous mouths. I squirm against the sudden panic, trying to keep my eyes open, trying to hold onto the world. It feels that life is slipping away, and I want it back. The darkness curls around, sniffs, licks, and swallows me whole, just like a fog. The nurses' hymnal oohs and ahhs soothe all resistance and, sheathed within the fog, I lose all cares. My brain is comatose but my tongue is wired, babbling in . . . , well, babbling in tongues.

"Don't talk; we're starting the surgery."

The growl—patriarchal, in a thickly bearded way—reminds me of the story of an angel smiting a man mute for refusing to believe God's word. Then all words, my own and others', all thoughts, all sounds vanish as I feel a flitting inside my wrong right eye, as if God himself is tinkering with it. It doesn't hurt; nothing hurts and I let myself float upon the strangeness of the sensation, so close, divine almost, inside my head, next to my melting thoughts.

The surgery doesn't work. My eye rejects the implant. It's still in but has shifted a millimeter off my pupil, giving me ghosted vision and creating haloes that a religious devotee might envy. I can see more sharply now through the still wrong, though partially righted right eye, but everything has its double; the world now exists for me in duplicate.

With both eyes open I can see a single image, though it seems to move toward and away from me as if my eyes were magnets of opposing polarity, pulling and pushing what they behold. What does it mean when one eye sees two images and two eyes see a single but oscillating one? I know it's a trick played by my brain, a psychosomatic overriding of vision, but I don't know what it *means*.

Your eyes are the wrong shape, I'm told, we'll have to wait and see how they readjust. Why did this happen, to *me*, I ask myself, wondering what might be the right shape for eyes. It isn't that I feel sorry for myself. There has to be a reason, and not the banal ones the doctor suggests. And I think I know. The clear image is the present, and the ghosting is the past. I can see through time. It makes perfect sense to me, a physical validation of what I already know from experience: born into a colony, and later living in the colonial mother country, I saw myself outside history since it never seemed to be of my making or made by anyone that seemed to resemble me. I experienced time not as a linear sequence but as fragmented, a compression of lost pasts and disputed presents (pasts imperfect and presents tense), in attempts to invent possible futures (futures perfect?). It's too bad my new vision has to take this particular physiological form.

My errant—or perhaps I should think of it now as enriched—sight continues to play tricks, switching from a double image to blurriness to relative clarity with each blink. These constantly changing visions make it impossible to tell which are more accurate, so that I can't tell if what I see *is* in fact what I see, or if it is somehow mutated by how I remember it. I can't be sure, but I feel that my memory is overcompensating for my lack of perception. Nothing quite matches, like I'm looking through those old 3-D glasses, but my eyes can't put the red and green images together, and they just switch back and forth, back and forth. Between the past and the present, present and past, neither one quite right. If I am inserting images from the past, how would I know what has changed? Or how?

The doctor explained as you might to a child that when the eyes can't fully see something, the brain steps in and fills in the details. After that, I learned to sit back and watch my brain at work.

Now, at forty-eight years old, seeing and hindsight—if this makes sense—have become for me watchable activities, almost cinematic. If the screen could be halted for a moment, if a sample slice of retinal tissue could be cut, then it would be a time frame, or rather, framed time. A picture frame. A slice of history.

Is that how memories are archived, by a superthesaurus, one word or one image leading to a multitude of others? Until a virus infiltrates, amnesia sets in, and the appropriate image can no longer be recalled, or when dementia sets in, and the appropriate image can no longer be recalled for the appropriate moment? Is my memory a dusty, musty, Kafkaesque maze of gray corridor, leading to more corridor, to more, with countless cells lined with shelf upon shelf containing stack upon stack of shoeboxes, themselves bursting with slides, glossy color prints, a few Polaroids, and some torn black-and-whites, maybe even the odd faded sepia-tone?

I suspect that my memory consists largely of these blocked-off, unaccessed areas. Here in L.A., on the other side of the world from my childhood, it might explain my desire to slow time if not halt it, to retreat from the accumulation of more memory, to clear some internal geography so I may retread or perhaps intrude into these closed zones of my own past.

Now that my vision is retreating under the Southern Californian oversaturated, blinding light and blurring into its own games, my memory seems to be clearing, becoming more focused, exercised by increased use. Perhaps it's in compensation. A seesaw between perception and recollection.

I'm also balanced now on the seesaw of middle age. From this vantage, my past and future are of equal duration, though with each new day the one will accumulate as the other diminishes.

That first eye surgery was ten years ago. Since then, there have been others, including one for a torn, detached retina. My memories of the detachment are again primarily visual and, paradoxically, of visual excess, of too much seeing. The first indication of trouble was seeing blood scroll across one eye, not in a mirror but across my field of vision. I'm inside my head, watching my eye as though it were a screen or a gauze bandage, and the blood soaks across it in panoramic splendor. For some moments I'm distracted by the sheer beauty of the spectacle, then remember beauty doesn't equal good.

After the reattachment surgery—and after each surgery it's like waking up from death: startlingly sudden, disorienting, as if ejected from a void—another visual memory is of lying flat on my back, my head immobile so that the air bubble keeping my eye inflated does not dislodge. The eye is bandaged shut, but my brain rebels against this restriction. With one eye open I can watch what is happening around me, while my brain fills in the blank space of my bandaged eye with riotous hallucinations, giving me a kind of psychedelic split-screen vision. It's like being back in art school, taking an experimental video class. I'm able to keep myself happily entertained for hours at a time.

Another memory followed laser surgery to remove scar tissue in my eye and to correct strabismus—the crossed eyes of popular mirth; though one advantage when teaching was that students didn't know when I was watching them. One disadvantage was that they didn't know when I was looking *at* them—me? they would mouth, pointing to themselves, then at the person next to them. Following the surgery I was strapped into a chair to have my cornea stitched. Though it had been numbed, watching a needle coming at my eye was unnerving, to say the least. I couldn't help wriggling as I fought the nausea, and again I was admonished. The surgeon told me to keep still, explaining that I had no pain receptors there and therefore couldn't feel anything. It was another example of the one-plus-one-equals-two approach. In his scenario, there was no place for imagination.

Since that surgery, my eyes have more or less stabilized. I still play eye ball, switching emphasis from one eye to the other, still enjoying the visual differences as though they were happening through and to someone else and I'm just watching them second-hand. One favorite amusement is a variation of that old ventriloquist trick: while drinking from a cup I look directly with one eye into the cup, and with the other eye watch the room. I can then superimpose the two images so that the room looks like it's underwater. Not only do I conflate time, I can now conflate space.

These different abilities to step back from my own vision have become automatic, fueled by the fact that I am a photographer. A professional viewer. The act of photographing something locks it into my brain, makes it more real in ways that mere vision—not even my creatively enhanced version—ever does. At the same time, the camera, and then the photograph, insert themselves between reality and me, so that things don't feel as if they're quite happening to me. I may be a professional, but I'm just an observer. And vision, like the camera, is a tool, a means to an end. The once-probable scenario of losing my eyesight never frightened me. But that was before.

Before my mother died three years ago, my last days with her were spent describing photographs I had taken the week before in Kenya, our birthplace. I was there to work on a photographic commission, but the trip was also my first visit back since leaving thirty-eight years before and, therefore, was burdened with expectation, with wondering if I might find the past "the way it really was."

When I arrive, I experience none of the eagerly awaited feelings of coming home. At first I think it's probably tiredness from the long journey, but it's more than that. The dusty roads, the small stores (The Planet, The New York Café, Scarlet Beauty Parlor . . .) with their hand-painted multinational logos of Nike and Kodak, cola cans and cigarette packets, the detritus of globalization; all these bear the worn familiarity I've experienced driving through the dilapidated outskirts of any number of cities. I feel that I could be almost anywhere in the world and am disappointed at this lack of the specific, at the disappearance of the local. I'm also disenchanted that Nairobi doesn't match the vividness I had ascribed to it within my memory and imagination, even as I know how illogical it is to expect the city to fulfill my image of its past.

It's only later, after a week or so of what begins as acclimating but in fact becomes a kind of tearing, like a seam coming apart, that I experience jolting sensations of déjà vu, that I'm not quite sure where, or more accurately, *when* I am. I feel that the past and present have indeed become conflated, or that I have stepped outside of time. I go for daily walks at the Nairobi Arboretum, a sprawling city park that I already know from the photographs my father took there of my mother, my siblings, and myself. We had to stand at patient and long-suffering attention in front of various flowering shrubs that maximized the saturated colors of the then-new slide format. My father had a seasoned eye for detail and carefully posed us; I have one slide of us arraigned before the camera against red-orange blossoms that matched my sisters' dresses. Now, as I walk these same paths, random details pop with sudden clarity, like the early-morning smell of earth after rain, a flash of color that must be a bird though it moves too fast to really tell, the fleeting, honeyed light before night descends. Described later, these impressions sound already nostalgic, but when experienced they feel like ruptures in time—not exactly observations, nor the usual processes of memory where images are recalled, pulled from an archive, as it were, and compared to a present. These are physically tangible, more re-experiences than re-memberings, with long-dormant synapses sparking again, external events firing internal shifts. That's what it feels like, that it's my very body that oscillates in time as it's being reshaped by what's around me, the past returning with a hot shiver. And it's not as though my father's photographs have come to life; on the contrary, I've moved past them as my own memories have become vividly and directly fused with the present.

These shifts are further layered by having received, within a few days of my arrival, an e-mail that my mother is in the hospital, though the seriousness of her condition is downplayed. She has had breast cancer, but only two months ago was told she was in remission. I'm told not to worry. I know that my mother hates hospitals and that she wouldn't be willingly admitted, and consequently I do worry.

I also start to see things through her eyes. Of course—especially given the particularities of my own sight—this is an imagined, almost fictive vision, because how else can one see through another's eyes, especially with someone as complexly imagined as one's mother? Perhaps I should say that I start to see *for* her, accumulating visual material that I can share with her later.

I photograph every detail of her brother's house, which is where I am staying. It's a rambling, ranch-style building with numerous scattered garages and sheds and any number of cars in various stages of (dis)repair. There's a tiny pond at the back, where they once found a crocodile (so I'm told), but now it's a watering hole for all kinds of transient animals, especially birds. I spend hours photographing the garden, but mostly I photograph the inside of the house, especially the kitchen. The kitchen is the only room that I can actually remember from our own house in Nairobi, and the mix in this kitchen of jars of Indian spices, African ingredients like maize meal, postcards on the walls from family and friends abroad, rows of hanging utensils, and the trays of vegetables and tropical fruits remind me both of our old house and of my mother's kitchen now in Portugal. It seems to me that the kitchen is mostly where we recreate our sense of home—let me rephrase that: the kitchen is mostly where we prepare our *taste* of home—and it is the place to which I am most drawn.

Ironically, though it doesn't occur to me at the time, the photographic series I am there to work on are later titled *The Searchers* and *Not at Home*. Though their references are to cinema and to tourism, the titles could equally apply to my own situation.

I process my film in Nairobi so that I will have the prints to show my mother. I want evidence and proof of where I have been and what I have seen, but when I get to Portugal to be with her, I have to describe the photographs, because she has been rapidly losing her eyesight and has now become almost blind.

For as long as I can remember, people have said that I look like my mother. If only they knew how true this was: I have inherited her eyes, in how they look and in how they see. The experience of my own changing eyesight might have prepared me for this first hospital visit, but at the same time I think that *nothing* prepared me for it.

The cancer has returned and has spread to her lungs, eventually causing her racking convulsions. Nothing prepares you for this. At the same time I do what people generally do around the sick and dying. I pretend normality. I sit at her hospital bed. She asks questions, clearly remembering the places I describe. Though I'm at first dismayed that she can't see how these places look now in the photographs, we're still able to share the pleasure of her memories.

There's the still-standing Kenya Fish Company in downtown Nairobi, its peeling walls revealing multihued layers of paint, probably right down to the time when my mother worked there; the Holy Family Cathedral where we went every Sunday in emulation of its name, its dour concrete interior barely lit by the narrow slivers of stained-glass windows; the Khoja Mosque that we as kids fantasized about since it seemed so much more lively, so much more *exotic* than our place of worship; the rolling Ngong hills on the outskirts of the city where the white families used to live in their "English-style" timber-frame houses and flower gardens. These more than anything, in their recreation of the "mother country," invoke for me the now-anachronistic colonial past.

I had remembered all of these places, places that reverberated through my and my siblings' periodic reminiscences. Encountering them again made them seem smaller somehow, less mythical, even disappointing that they weren't the fantasy places of our imaginations, their ordinariness not even worthy of postcards. As we drive around Nairobi, I can't help thinking how unattractive the city is compared to my (selective) memory of it. It's dusty and grubby. There are too many ugly gray facades, much of them from the 1960s Brutalist style of concrete slabs. Vast stretches of shanties, some the size of what anywhere else would be large towns, spread like wounds across the city. And yet this desperation is met with an equally strong resilience: the flowers and blossoming trees that seem to be everywhere, the Maasai herdsman who drives his cattle through the heaviest traffic knowing that he was there first, the schoolchildren loping along despite the weight of their backpacks, the canoodling couples.

And there's something about the meld of African, Asian, Arab, and European, in architecture, in clothing, in food, in language, that feels immensely reassuring. My early ears were filled with the sounds of English, Swahili, Konkani, Kikuyu, and Hindi, with no doubt a smattering of other tongues that I had no names for. There was something about the casual nature of this mix that made me feel, even as a child, profoundly part of the world, an immersion from which I felt lifted out only when we migrated to England.

There, drawing became my solace. I drew animals obsessively, but only the African animals that I already knew. It was my way of holding onto the past, but perhaps a way that drew me back only into myself.

Now I tell my mother about the animals I encountered at the arboretum: the hornbills with their improbable beaks and massive bulk that shook the trees each time they took off or landed; the elegant bee-eaters that at first I saw only as flashes of darting color; the Sykes' and vervet monkeys that maintained a constant racket from the trees.

I tell her about the *matatus*, the careening taxi-buses, each one individualized by painted scenes: elephants, lions, sunsets, portraits of Michael Jackson; and painted slogans: "Real Men Don't Beat Their Sweethearts," "Here Comes Your Papa," "Make Peace Not War," and "Best In Africa."

I look for information in each photograph as I describe it, even though the descriptions are routed through my own childhood memories. My descriptions are an attempt to bring together the past and the present, but mostly they are an attempt on my part to bring peace, if not to my mother's body, at least to her mind.

At this point, I'm refusing to accept that she might die, and think that our conversations will put her in a more positive frame of mind. What I'm secretly hoping is that positive thinking is part of the battle, that my mother will mentally "relocate" to the place and time she has always thought of, and still thinks of, as home, the magnitude of which I've only recently come to understand. Understanding this, I also begin to suspect the extent of how distanced she has felt from her life since leaving Kenya. Maybe what I believe is that by closing the gap, bringing her at least mentally back home will also bring her back to *this* life. Healing the dis-ease of dislocation will, I hope, galvanize another kind of cure.

"The fog's coming, the fog's coming back," she says, and clutches my hand in panic. I don't know what the fog is, and think maybe it's the morphine kicking in and that she can feel her lucidity, the remaining contact with the world around her, with *me*—ebbing away.

Ten, twenty, maybe thirty minutes later, she squeezes my hand slightly as she wakes from sleep. She smiles weakly, the fog has lifted. I don't know what the fog is; the nurse says it isn't caused by the morphine. When I ask my mother, she just says, "It comes," as if that's all I need to know.

When my mother said that the fog was coming, she described it in visual terms, that the fog prevented her seeing. I knew what the fog had meant for me, but since she was nearly blind, I didn't know what it meant for her. I understand it now as a fog that obscured her inner vision—that complex amalgam of memory, imagination, and projection. Without access to the externally visual, my mother was dependent on this visualization. The fog, then, was an internal blindness. I can only imagine her dread as this last refuge, this place where memory takes physical form, this place where the self resides, was being obscured.

It made me realize that the reason I hadn't feared my own physical blindness was because of my reliance on this internal vision.

I remember photographs even as other memories fail. It is the photograph—and my enduring faith in its veracity—that I have held onto as proof. And for many years I have had the proof, the many photographs taken by my father, the tangible evidence of our life in Kenya: the parking lot of the Holy Family Cathedral, my First Communion—the tropical sun casting hard-edged purple shadows and setting my white shirt, shorts, and socks ablaze. With close-cropped hair, my most striking features are my ears, which stick out from my head like amphora handles. I look terrified, faintly absurd in my white finery, like a diminutive waiter at a fancy hotel, and those flapping ears ridicule any claim to dignity. How do I remember that day? It doesn't matter. Though I had felt saintly, proud, pure, it was my word against the camera's proof. And that's no contest. The photographs taken that day, presenting to all eyes a frightened creature, sweep other remembrances aside.

And yet the recent return of memories in such physical, bodily ways has accumulated and layered meaning beyond the simply visual. As a result, my faith in the photograph as ultimate repository of memory is, if not shattered, at least shaken. Now, when I look at the two-dimensionality of photographs, I wonder how much else is lost along with that third dimension. Or perhaps I'm merely reexperiencing my earlier disenchantment: the failure of a photograph to match the vividness I have ascribed to it within my memory and imagination.

Part of me is thankful that my mother could not see the photographs I had taken, in case she was disappointed by the ordinariness of the scenes. And in case her own memories were deflated by this evidence of the mundane.

I don't tell my mother that I couldn't find our old house in Nairobi, or that no one would take me to the neighborhood because they said it was now too dangerous. I remembered the tourist name for the city, Nairobbery, and the urban legends of tourists' hands chopped off to get at watches. While such tales grew more grotesque at each telling, I was also told that Nairobi was a crossroads for guns going to and from the various conflicts in Somalia and Sudan, an unneeded reminder that wars don't stop at national borders.

The memory of the house where I grew up is now even stronger for my not having seen it, and I realize that memories don't require a geographical return to their place of formation. In fact, they require its opposite. Memories feed off distance. This sounds like a contradiction of what I said earlier about the physicality of my memories, but those memories returned in such bodily form precisely because of my long separation from them. This leads me to speculate about what else is lurking, disembodied, and still awaiting reconnection.

Mother doesn't ask me about our old house, and I wonder if she also doesn't need the evidence, in case it usurps the memory.

When I ask her about her childhood, she smiles. I'm not sure if it's a smile from the pleasure of remembering, of being led away from her hospital bed, or whether it is a smile at my transparency in trying to lead *her* away from it. She tells me things I've never been told before, things about herself, about the small towns where she lived as a girl, how she and her brother would roam the dusty streets and play with the small animals they would catch. I feel that I'm finally beginning to learn something about this woman who has kept her past secret for as long as I can remember. It is only as an adult that I've come to think of this secrecy as a failure of communication or as a barrier between us.

Later, when I ask others about what Mother has told me, they tell me none of it is true, that during the years she was talking about, she had been sent away to boarding school in Goa (had I counted on my mother to be a guarantor of truth?). Did she simply forget, did she imagine alternate lives for herself and over the years come to believe them, or did she deliberately lie, manufacture a history that she thinks I want to hear, to lead *me* away from her hospital bed?

It might be that, even at this point, my mother couldn't bear to reveal herself, but later I think that the idea of irrefutable history matters less than the importance I give it. What might equally count is a shared pact between my mother and me to *believe*. Or that history is conditional upon what we need to believe, so that we can believe in each other.

While I am attracted by this proposal, by its potential to conflate history with imagination, I am equally disturbed by what actual histories it might allow to remain hidden.

By now, my mother's death has passed into fiction. This is not to say that it hasn't occurred or that I am any less affected by it. Fiction, after all, can be a more encompassing way to understand occurrence, not a way to deny it. (I have the photographic evidence of my mother in her hospital bed and, later, in her coffin, but these are hidden away, a too-real proof that I don't need and don't want, yet a proof that I can't bear to destroy.)

By fiction, I mean that what I have written about my mother has already been distilled through memory, and that parts might be imagined. I wake in the mornings remembering conversations with her, or imagining different ones, or—as with dreams—waking up not knowing which have actually happened. As the days pass, it becomes less and less important to know which are which or to separate one from another. I realize that I'm doing the same thing as my mother did, not so much fabricating history, but seeing it as a weave of possibilities.

There is no return to the way "it really was." I think my mother knew this but was paralyzed by its implications. I think she longed for a different kind of life, for an "elsewhere," and since she couldn't imagine a different future or at least was never able to act upon that possibility, she had only the image of a lost past to ground her. For her, there was only return, even though she knew equally well its impossibility.

I wonder about how my mother negotiated her own difference; she emanated it as a palpable sense of dislocation. She was never fully present, part of her was always elsewhere, in time as well as in place. Since that elsewhere no longer existed or existed for her only within memory or imagination, a part of her—with no ground to stand upon—was never able to come fully into being.

My mother wanted the sum of her past to add up differently, for one-plus-one to generate multiple outcomes. I'll never know if her imagination allowed her access to those possibilities— although her variable narratives suggest that it did—but if I am at all my mother's son, and if I am to amount to more than only appearing like her but to actually *see* like her, if I am to put myself in her place, then I have to learn how to prevent the fog from returning.

There's a stake now in everything I do, there's a weight and a gratitude to life that I never had when younger. Perhaps, at least for me, it took the possibility of losing my vision, the possibility of losing my life, the fact of losing my mother to create that stake. As we get older, common wisdom has it that we become more conservative, we become more fearful since we have more to lose and a greater understanding and appreciation of what there is to lose. I tell myself, whether I believe it or not, that each day that I have vision and life is a gift, a bonus.

My mother died the day after my forty-fifth birthday. This year, three years following her death, was the first time I felt reasonably comfortable marking my birthday. Friends were invited for tea, and many brought flowers, beautiful bouquets of yellow roses, lilies, daisies, and sunflowers. It was July, and the yellow evoked summer days, bringing their light into the house.

Later, my partner, my teenage daughter, and I shredded the flowers, carrying the bags of fragrant petals to the beach at Santa Monica, near where we live. At the peak of the Ferris wheel on the pier we flung out handfuls of the petals and watched them flutter radiantly, like butterflies, like sunshine down to the pier, onto the beach and into the ocean. My mother might have outwardly disapproved, but I think she would have secretly loved it.

It's been a long time since I've felt this way, but I'm now looking forward to my next birthday, even as it means getting one year older. Mostly, I'm looking forward to celebrating it with those around me, and also to now sharing it with my mother.

Through the Looking Glass
Keeping Up with Alice in Her Teens

Ellen McMahon

Alice is twelve. She has tremendous round green eyes. Her hair, which is dyed a dark maroon, falls in ringlets around her face. She is wearing a big silver chain (I think it's a dog collar) and a string of bright, multicolored, plastic, heart-shaped beads that fit snugly around her neck. She is tall for her age but weighs only about ninety pounds. Her tight orange T-shirt and a pair of super-baggy jeans, with legs twice as wide as their tiny waist, emphasize her delicate frame. We are stopped at a red light. She says, "Mom, I love my life."

As I sit down to form this essay out of my journal entries from Alice's teen years, our house in Tucson is strangely quiet. A few days ago Alice, now eighteen, left to work as a waitress on Cape Cod for the summer. She's planning to return in the fall, but this house will never again be home for her in quite the same way. My husband, Matt, also moved out a few days ago, a mutual decision to separate after twenty years of trying everything we could to stay together. This place that he and I have made spacious and comfortable over the last six years by constant renovation and addition, now houses only our younger daughter, Della, who is thirteen, and myself. She's busy with friends and when she is home she's usually lying in her bed, talking on the phone, watching TV, painting her nails, and sometimes drawing pictures of stylish outfits or funny animals—all at the same time. I have the physical and mental space I haven't had in the eighteen years since Alice was born, an opportunity to reflect on the whirlwind of the last five years.

Alice has just turned thirteen, and Della is eight. We are lounging on Della's bed on a lazy weekend afternoon. Alice begins to talk about the pressures of starting middle school. She is laughing and crying alternately, sometimes simultaneously. She tells us about a friend who lost her virginity and thought it was so cool that she blabbed it to everyone. Instead of being impressed, her friends thought she was slutty. The next day the same girl was kicked out of school for smoking pot in the locker room. Alice says she saw some really big kids push a little freshman boy from Russia up against the lockers. She moves on nervously to a true-story cop show she saw on TV about some white teenagers who killed a black kid their own age.

Today I dropped Della off for a week of overnight camp. Alice is fourteen and has become moody and sullen. I'm looking forward to spending some time alone with her while Della's at camp. Alice and I lie on my bed for two or three hours and talk about what it's like to be a woman. She confides in me, "I'm flirting with two boys. I have a giant crush on one of them, but it's fun because I feel like I'm in charge, like I have power over them." Almost overnight she's gone from being a shy little girl to a bold and cocky young woman, a femme fatale. It scares me because she sounds like me at her age, so cavalier but so driven by the desire for the attention of boys. All of a sudden, she seems to know everything there is to know about sex. I worry about where she's getting her information.

I gave birth to Alice when I was thirty-five. When she was hitting puberty, menopause was taking the ground out from under me. I've heard that during this midlife milestone the unsettled psychic issues from a woman's adolescence return for a final reckoning. I know mine got right up in my face, demanding my attention in the form of insomnia, migraines, and exaggerated mood swings. I felt as anxious and insecure as I did when I was fifteen. I knew if I hid from my psychic demons they would have their way with me for the rest of my life. I knew this was my chance to face them straight on and that if I learned the hard lessons they had for me, I'd be more comfortable in my own skin as I aged. My dominant demon is my self-doubt. From my undergraduate days as a biology major to my current position as an art professor, I have kept this demon at bay with my excellent memory, and a large part of my confidence was based on my ability to recall names, places, dates, and numbers. My sudden inability to remember even what I had done a few minutes before, and in particular where the hell I just put my keys, caused me to question my intelligence and my value. I think adolescence is a similar challenge, a turning point, a time to let go of beliefs that don't work anymore and to test new ones, a crucible of identity formation. For five years for better or for worse, as our hormone levels dipped and surged, Alice and I formed and reformed ourselves in relation to each other.

Matt, Alice, Della, and I are at my mother's beach house on Cape Cod with my mother and three brothers, for our annual summer vacation. Alice, at fourteen and a half, is dressing more provocatively than usual—or I'm just noticing it now—because my mother and brothers are shocked by her appearance. She is grumpy and rude, especially when she comes home from spending the night at her friend Nita's house. One morning Nita's mother calls to tell me the girls took a bottle of wine and drank it together the night before. When I ask Alice about it, she confides that she started taking beer from our refrigerator earlier in the summer, drinking alone in her room to help her sleep. I listen respectfully, glad that she has told me. I talk it over with Matt, and we decide that we need to clarify the rules: she is not allowed to drink. While I'm at it, I'll make sure she knows that she's also not allowed to have sex, smoke cigarettes or pot, or take any other kind of recreational drugs. She will lose phone privileges and clothing allowance if we catch her breaking any of these rules. Alice doesn't like to talk to her dad about things like this and says she feels ganged-up on if we talk to her together, so I'm usually the one that delivers the parental position, the bad news. She will be angry. I need to preface it by saying how much we love her.

It's 4:30 a.m. I'm awake worrying about Alice, nervous about talking to her. I keep thinking this is my fault for not paying enough attention or spending enough time with her in the last few years, always so distracted by my work and my own problems.

Later that day I ask Alice to join me in the upstairs bedroom so we can have a talk privately. I clarify the rules as planned. I expect her to argue, to be indignant and blustery. Instead she rolls over in a fetal position and buries her head in the covers. She gives me the silent treatment for almost an hour. I wonder if she's testing me, seeing how much time I'll give her. Finally it occurs to me to ask her what I can do to make her feel more loved. She begins to cry. She replies, "How can I make Nita feel loved so she doesn't go after the boys so much?" I think about myself at Alice's age, the first time I ditched my best girlfriend for a boy.

That night while the whole family is gathered together over dinner, my younger brother David is jumping around on one leg, howling, and frantically swatting the air. He's doing an imitation of himself working in his organic vegetable garden being attacked by mosquitoes. I laugh until my stomach hurts. After dinner he hears about Alice's drinking and asks me to go for a walk with him. Tears come to his eyes as he says, "Alice is probably someone who should never drink." He cautions me not to have any alcohol or prescription drugs in the house. He is still suffering the long-term effects of these substances, which he began using at Alice's age. Three of his friends have died from mixing drugs and alcohol. His voice shakes as he says, "Just tell her you don't want to lose her."

My youngest brother, Peter, is also concerned about Alice's drinking. He was the one who dragged David out of harm's way repeatedly when they were teenagers. He tells me, "We're all deserting her."

My brothers have left and the summerhouse is peaceful. Della and I walk to the bay to see the sunset. Bright pink and orange clouds are reflected in the water. A black skimmer flies by along the water's edge, silhouetted by the vibrant sky.

The next day we fly back home to Tucson. The first morning home I wake up at 4 a.m. once again with not enough sleep, a headache, and a sore neck from a nightmare. I'm counting my hot flashes. I had thirty yesterday during the trip home. You might think the suffering brought on by my hormonal fluctuations would make me more compassionate toward Alice, but instead it makes me more impatient and self-involved. In spite of my condition we have a good family dinner. I lie low and enjoy watching how cooperative and respectful both girls are with their father. Alice was out with friends before dinner, and she looks stoned to me, but maybe she's just spaced out from the heat. I'm less in a panic about her since we've gotten home. I want to have a talk with her about the difference between experimenting with and depending on drugs and alcohol. I will stress the genetic component of dependency and make sure she knows how many people in our extended family struggle with addictions.

Ninth Grade

Alice is beginning her first year in a large public art magnet high school. I'm trying to follow Matt's lead, which is to make reasonable rules for our daughters, give them consequences if we catch them breaking them, and don't take any shit. I like the idea and wish it could be that simple. He is a captain in the Tucson Fire Department. He works ten twenty-four-hour shifts each month, so he is gone one-third of the time and sleep-deprived for another third. We are involved in a massive home remodeling project. He is doing the majority of the work himself, so most of the remaining third of the time he is doing hard manual labor.

I know intellectually that boundaries are necessary and even comforting for teenagers, but I have trouble enforcing the rules when Matt's not home. I'm afraid if Alice knows there'll be consequences, she'll stop telling me about the things that are worrying her and hide more carefully what she's doing. I believe that the more I know about her life and her friends, the more effective I can be at protecting her. My friend Anne thinks this is superstition, like that ritual of last words, "be careful" or "be good," when your child leaves the house. Then if something terrible happens, you can live with yourself because you did what you could and you said the magic words.

Anne, my friend Leslie, and I have gotten together regularly over the years to share the ups and downs of mothering, and as our trust has grown, we've added many other aspects of our lives. Our daughters introduced us when they were three years old and became best friends in preschool. Since then we have become like a big extended family, spending holidays and vacations together, so our daughters are more like cousins or sisters. But now they are in their teens, their personalities are getting stronger and they are diverging. Leslie's daughter is focused and self-disciplined, an excellent student who works out every morning at 6:30 a.m. before school. Anne's daughter is cheerful and easygoing, a cheerleader and a synchronized swimmer with an irresistible smile.

Anne is a neuropsychologist who spends her workdays evaluating people with various forms of brain damage. Her responses to my situations with Alice are always right on target, a perfect combination of clinical interest and compassion. Leslie is an industrial engineer. She doesn't share Anne's objectivity and psychological expertise, but I know I can always depend on her for support. Somewhere in every conversation about our kids, Anne reminds us that their frontal lobes aren't completely hooked up and won't be for several years.

A month into ninth grade, Alice seems chronically more or less angry with me. Her case against me is clear but mostly unspoken: I've let her down, bought her things to make up for neglecting her, been late to pick her up a million times, and made her feel less important than my work, my phone calls, my deadlines, my meetings. I need to win back her trust by listening, engaging her in constructive activities, setting and holding clear boundaries, doing what I say I'll do, showing that I believe in her, helping her feel good about herself. I overwhelm myself with my high expectations. It feels impossible and probably too late. This is the dark side of my supermom subculture. Am I overly invested in my children's successes, too busy and proud to let them falter and learn for themselves?

Alice is studying Stoicism in school. I've been prodding her for days to do the essay on morality that's due tomorrow. She's procrastinated for weeks and is now passive and hopeless, torn between wanting me to rescue her and wanting me to leave her alone. I'm tired and discouraged, hating myself for not making morality an integral part of her upbringing.

At 3:00 a.m. I'm still awake, furious at Alice. I feel like a fool, like a victim. I worked so hard to get her into the art magnet high school, and if she gets bad grades or gets in trouble, she'll be kicked out and have to go to the neighborhood school. If that happens and she doesn't have her art classes as an incentive, I'm afraid she'll drop out. This speculative scenario is my justification for devoting my life to the futile activity of trying to control her. She spends hours on the phone and doesn't start her homework until the middle of the night. She gets so little sleep she's walking around in a trance. I'm afraid she's going to get run over crossing the street. I can hear her, still awake, banging around in her room. I get out of bed and go in to tell her I'm sorry for nagging her so much this evening. It's frustrating to see her so stressed out, so involved in taking care of all her friends. How can she be so compassionate and so overly responsible for everyone but herself?

I'm totally confused. If I can get back to sleep, I will consider it a miracle.

At almost fifteen Alice has her first boyfriend. Last year he was the heartthrob of her entire middle school, completely out of reach. Now that they're in high school, he's noticed her in a big way. He is exquisite. Tall, lanky, and soft-spoken. His eyes, skin, and knotted hair are all almost the same soft golden brown. He plays jazz saxophone, works with his dad, who's a fine woodworker, skateboards, and, I suspect, smokes a lot of pot. He spends a fair amount of time at our house and has dinner with us often. Alice seems to like this, and I'm glad that she's not ashamed of or embarrassed by us. I need to appreciate this before I tell her that I'm uncomfortable about how much time they're spending in her room with the door closed.

Alice is going to Italy and Greece with her art history class this coming summer. I'm thrilled because I went to Greece when I was her age. I suggest I could volunteer to go as a chaperone. She assures me with only a look that this will never happen. I interpret her reaction as solid evidence that I've failed so far as a parent. I come down with the flu and rent the movie *Magnolia*, watch it and cry off and on for the rest of the day, consumed with regret.

My brother Peter is visiting for Christmas and has designed a loft bed for Alice made out of plumbing pipes, which they have built together. It floats magically up near the ceiling in the corner of her room attached to two walls so only the ladder touches the floor. He, Alice, Della, and I have just returned from a nice but tiring day trip. I am in the kitchen making dinner. Alice and Della are in the bathroom. I hear a dull thud and a blood-curdling scream. I practically kick down the door in the half second it takes for Della to unlock it. Alice is passed out cold, draped into the bathtub, which is filling with water. I drag her out of the tub and she comes to. She is crying and her whole body is quaking violently. I get her out of her wet clothes, into a dry nightgown, and put her in my bed with a hot water bottle. She has a fever and a headache and is still trembling. Peter lies down on his side beside her and tells her a soothing story that he makes up as he goes along. Della climbs into bed behind him and puts her arms around his neck. The next day Alice is fine. The doctor has no explanation: he says that sometimes teenagers just pass out.

The hardest thing about parenting is watching your children suffer. Like most parents I did everything I could to alleviate Alice's suffering when she was young. She was born prematurely and stopped breathing several times in the hospital. I'm sure almost losing her in those first weeks has exacerbated my vigilance and protectiveness. Now that she is fifteen she is growing impatient with my buffering, determined to get me out of the formula, ready to work without a safety net.

People say that Alice looks like Clara Bow. She does love the look of the thirties and has seen all of Clara Bow's movies. She has figured out how to do amazing things with makeup, exaggerating her eyes to look twice their size, her eyelashes so lush and long you can't believe they're real. She's plucked her eyebrows down to tiny fine lines and shaped them so she looks perpetually surprised. Her hair, now dyed black, makes an elegantly snarled frame around her little heart-shaped face. Her skin is so pale and translucent that a network of tiny blue veins is visible just under the surface. She buys all her clothes at thrift stores, cuts them up, then tacks them back together Frankenstein-style with crooked hand-sewn seams of silver thread. Because of her appearance I don't want her to ride the city bus or walk around by herself. I need to tell her to tone it down, but I'm dreading it. I know from previous conversations that she'll take it as a personal rejection, a stifling of her artistic expression.

She identifies with Catwoman, the obsequious secretary who transforms herself, mostly by way of her homemade cat costume, into an ultrasexy, powerful avenger. Maybe Alice's flamboyance is partly a response to being stared at all of her life, her way of taking control of being looked at. I know she would get more comments and come-ons from men if she dressed more normally. As it is, I think people are so flabbergasted they're speechless. I wonder if being out in public is as exhausting for her as it is for me when I'm with her. Come to think of it, she never looks at the people watching her. Like a movie star, she fixes her gaze slightly above the crowd. I'm the one who sees people's expressions as they look back and forth from her to me.

Alice has stayed up all night customizing a pair of tennis shoes to wear to school today. They are covered with hundreds of tiny plastic objects, party favors, photographs cut out of magazines, little drawings and paintings and scraps of mesh and metallic fabric. Each one has two big googly eyes in the front that move and click when she walks. Her humanities teacher is so impressed she makes her take them off and pass them around the room so everyone can get a closer look. Alice says she hates school, begs me to let her stay home, and is flunking French because it's her first class of the day and she's almost always late. But on parent-teacher conference night her art and humanities teachers' faces light up as they say, "So you're Alice's mother." They rave about her, tell me she's the life of the class, so articulate and engaged. It's hard to believe they're talking about the same person who refused to come with me to the conference, who's brooding in her room behind a slammed door.

By chance Alice is placed in a black-and-white photography class freshman year because the required technology classes are already full. She produces a series of self-portraits taken late at night in her room. She transforms herself with clothes and makeup into an array of glamorous, dramatic, and usually tragic characters. In one series she is covered in glitter, looking over her shoulder into a broken mirror. In another she has thick black stripes painted across her eyes and mouth. One morning as I wake her up for school, she opens her bedroom door covered from head to foot in multicolored feathers that she glued all over her face and body the night before. After the photo shoot in the wee hours of the morning she was so tired she just curled up in her feathers and went to sleep. Unfortunately, she neglected to close the large can of rubber cement, so it gave off fumes all night in her room. This inspired yet another lecture from me about the hazards of art materials that, I know, fell on deaf ears, maybe too hard to hear through her almost chronic headache that was probably worse than usual that day. These pictures result in her being chosen as "Photographer of the Year." Some of them are on display in the high school showcase for the entire year. They create quite a buzz, and this, coupled with her shyness, contributes to her mystique and her celebrity.

Alice wants to go and see a band at an underage punk club downtown. She calls me at work. We argue about whether it's a safe place for a fifteen-year-old and whether it would be OK with her if Matt just took a look inside the place when he drops her off. She tells me this would be totally humiliating and completely unacceptable and she just won't go then. She also says she won't go if she can't stay overnight at her friend's house after the show. This makes me suspicious.

This and other things. She doesn't or can't sleep at night, so it's almost impossible to get her out of bed for school in the morning. She has also added brightly colored and patterned kids' Band-Aids to her highly customized look. She puts them on her arms, back, and legs, combined with big stars that she draws all over her arms with black markers. Recently, after seeing *Girl Interrupted*, she burst into convulsive sobbing, baffling Anne's and Leslie's daughters, whom she was sitting between in the backseat of my car.

She's so overwrought, I concede about the concert and the overnight. The next day when I pick her up, the sleeves of her shirt are rolled up and I see the cuts on her arms. I pull the car over in an empty parking lot and ask her about them. She says she cut herself while we were talking on the phone the night before and I was giving her crap about the concert. Not only can I not protect this child from harm, but also according to her I am the cause of her self-inflicted injury. I say she has to go to therapy. She says she won't. She swears it is the first time she ever cut herself and it will never happen again.

I call Anne to get the name of a good therapist for teenagers. It's hard to talk about Alice cutting herself, but I know Anne can help. She tells me cutting is a reaction to extreme stress, not that unusual in teenage girls. She tells me that adolescents often have what are called depersonalizing experiences where things seem unreal to them, sometimes their bodies feel numb. Cutting is one way they bring themselves back to reality, focusing more oceanic stress and anxiety to one point of pain.

I make an appointment with the therapist Anne recommends; hoping Alice will change her mind. She refuses to go; I go alone to get some advice. The therapist is not as helpful as Anne, but she says that if I force Alice to go to therapy it probably won't do much good. She suggests that I read *Reviving Ophelia* and *Parenting Teens with Love and Logic*.

Over the next few months, things seem to be calmer, but Alice is still exhausted all the time. I take her to a new female pediatrician who comes highly recommended. I'm hoping to get some advice about dealing with her headaches and her insomnia, and I'm even hoping she'll say something helpful to Alice about the scars from her cutting. Instead the doctor is distant and recommends Alice learn relaxation techniques to manage her anxiety and insomnia. Alice is angry and silent most of the drive home. Finally she snaps, "Why couldn't she just give me some sleeping pills?"

A few days later Alice is in her room tangled up in her covers, her flailing arms and legs straining against the sheets, sobbing and moaning. I go in to ask if she's all right. She freezes and says only two words, "yes" and "leave." As soon as I leave the room and close the door, she starts wailing again.

Alice broke up with her first boyfriend several months ago. She says that it was because he wanted to get more serious than she did. I also suspect he was a little passive for Alice, who likes intense emotional engagement. "I just didn't feel comfortable going out with someone more beautiful than me," she told me with a fiendish little smile. One day after school in the early spring she meets a boy at the mall. His name is Malcolm, he's eighteen, out of high school and has a large eye tattooed on the back of his neck. After telling me this, she wants to know if I'm going to let her go out with him. Matt steps in to say we need to meet him and see three forms of ID so we are sure of his real identity before she gets in a car with him. He explains that this is so we have somewhere to start if she disappears. She seems resigned, so we assume she's agreed to these conditions. A few days later she arranges for Malcolm to pick her up at school. He takes her by the pet store where he used to work so she can hold the snakes, and then to dinner and the movies. She calls twice during this time to reassure me that she is with girlfriends and everything is fine. At the end of the date, she boldly has Malcolm drop her off right in front of the house, and is busted. At Matt's urging we ground her for a week.

Things have quieted down with Alice grounded. Tonight she and I come home to the empty house together. Alice wants to go in her room to take a nap. I'm disappointed because I was looking forward to spending some time together. A couple of hours later she emerges, and we watch *The Adventures of Priscilla, Queen of the Desert*. After the video we talk about some theory I'm reading about gender and identity. She tells me one of her female friends is bisexual. I understand why girls her age find same-sex relationships more appealing than dealing with the urgency and ineptitude of teenage boys. She says she herself wishes she were a man so she could be a drag queen. I can also understand why performing femininity would be more appealing to her than having to take on the whole package.

One Saturday morning in May on my way out to yoga class, I notice someone in the bathroom. It seems too early for the kids to be awake. I go to the partially closed door to say I'm leaving. I hear a faint "Don't go" and open the door to find Alice lying on the floor, her face a pale light green, curled around the toilet. She says in a whisper, "I need you to take me to the hospital. I'm sick. I've taken a lot of Tylenol." I call 911 and explain what's happening. I hear the ambulance before I even hang up the phone. When the medics arrive, one kneels down beside her and asks, "Were you trying to kill yourself?" Alice looks surprised and confused by his question and says no. When we get to the hospital they say it's too late to pump her stomach, but she is admitted for several days to get a treatment to block the Tylenol from destroying her liver. Later she explains that she stayed up late watching a movie about a drug-addicted model and when the movie was over made an oil painting on the inside of her bedroom door. She got a headache so took a handful of Extra-Strength Tylenol and went to sleep.

It's Sunday, Mother's Day. I indulge briefly in feeling sorry for myself that motherhood is such a burden for me to bear, but the feeling is quickly overtaken by a wave of gratitude that Alice is alive today. Alice is still in the hospital, and I spend the day sitting by her bed. She looks so little in her hospital gown, so young and vulnerable without her makeup. She needs to come home to a calmer household where she can talk about how she feels, and what she thinks, and can get help making better decisions about herself.

There is no doubt that this near-death experience has changed her. She's clearly grateful to be alive. I think she is surprised by the fragility of life and also impressed by her physical resilience, her ability to survive this. She is even more of a celebrity when she returns to high school, and she handles it well, with a new kind of confidence. She credits the whole experience for getting her over her shyness.

A few days after Alice is released from the hospital, she, Della, and I are in Mexico with Anne and Leslie and their families. Every year since our teenage daughters were in preschool together we've rented a big house on the beach for a weekend in May. I am feeling sad that Matt's not here but also looking forward to the solitude I can have in my room. I'm thinking about how I need to make a closer connection to him so we can parent more effectively. I'm having a relaxing morning reading in bed to the sound of the wind, the waves, and the shore birds. Alice comes into my room to get some sunscreen. She's wearing a bathing suit that reveals a cluster of Band-Aids on the outside of her left thigh. She shows me what they're covering, three almost four-inch gashes made a few months before, that have become thick angry scars. She sits on the edge of the bed, and we both cry. I feel it is traceable back to me being too critical, expecting too much, not listening to her or seeing her for who she is. My heart sinks into my stomach. I feel nauseous as I imagine her slicing so deeply into her skin with a razor blade, how much the cuts must have bled, what she went through to hide them from me, from everyone.

I'm grateful that Anne and Leslie are there, because they love Alice and I can share my worries openly with them. Leslie tends to agree with Matt and my mother that I give Alice too much freedom and that it is hard on her. Maybe they're right and she would do better if I were less tolerant and gave her more structure. I wonder if she should be on anxiety or depression medication or even in a residential treatment program. But I don't think any of this will work with Alice. My resistance to their advice contributes to my sense of parenting in isolation and probably makes them less sympathetic when things get more out of hand.

Back at home from the weekend at the beach, I try to establish a dialogue with Alice, hoping to learn something about the underlying problems that are motivating her self-destructive behavior. She tells me, "You're unstable. I don't know how you're going to react. You don't respect me or trust me. You get mad and you're rude to me."

The psychiatric residents who evaluated Alice when she was hospitalized for the Tylenol overdose required her to see a therapist. She hates going and seems to hold me responsible, giving me the silent treatment to and from her appointment in the car each week. The therapist recommends Alice go to a psychiatrist for an evaluation to see if she would benefit from antianxiety medication. After a short interview with Alice, the psychiatrist asks me to join them in his office. He tells Alice that he can prescribe something that will help her sleep and feel less anxious, but it will reduce her intensity, maybe her creativity, and definitely her all-night art-making sessions. A couple of days later she says out of the blue, "That was scary, what he said." Alice knows that making art is integral to how she negotiates the world, so the drugs he offered are not an option. I agree with her decision but must admit how much I love the idea of a pharmaceutical silver bullet, a chemical cure for her suffering and my helplessness in the face of it.

Two months later the whole extended family is at my mother's beach house for another summer vacation together. I'm worried about Alice. She is still sullen and withdrawn, miserable about being with the family and separated from her current romantic interest. One warm sunny morning when we're all getting ready to go to the beach, Alice pulls me aside. "Mom, I need you to help me with a photo project, but you can't interfere or ask a lot of questions." Though I'm looking forward to a day on the beach, I see this as a rare opportunity, because she actually wants to spend some time with me, so I agree to her conditions. "What kinds of writing can you do?" she asks. I write samples on a piece of paper, and she decides my writing is good enough. We go to the upstairs bedroom, which is small, airless, hot, and humid. She brings some black markers and a notebook of her writing and tells me where on her body she wants each one of the words and phrases to go: *life* and *death* on the bottoms of her feet; *something poisonous, delicious, forbidden* on her lower back; *I was dying but inside her I lived* on her stomach. She takes various poses and directs me as I take the photographs, several rolls of black-and-white film over the next few hours. She's wearing a pair of little-boy Spiderman underpants, but she wants to look discreetly nude in the shots. For moments I detach enough to be utterly absorbed in my job as photographer, but most of the time I alternate between feeling like she's taken me hostage and like I'm invading her privacy in some way that a good mother would never do. There is another feeling that makes my chest ache, that she would trust me enough to have me help her like this. We take a break and I see our reflection in the mirror. I am facing it, agitated and exhausted, at the edge of my maternal capacity. She is facing me with her back toward the mirror, looking over her shoulder, blowing a big bubble with her gum, on top of the world. I am holding the camera, so I take the picture. Later that evening before dinner, Alice is leaning proudly on the kitchen counter, scantily dressed, still in her body writing. The rest of the family is unusually quiet. My mother raises an eyebrow, shakes her head, and bites her lip.

Alice gets all the pictures developed and sends a bunch of them to her crush back home. In the fall she makes prints from some of the negatives in her photography class. For Christmas she presents me with an 8″ × 10″ print of the picture I took of us in the mirror, which she's put in a chipped, light pink, thrift shop frame. I prop it on my bedroom dresser and look at it often over the next several months.

I've been photographing my daughters since they were born. They love to dress up and pose, and both have a striking rapport with the lens. I entered graduate school in visual art, when Alice was ten and Della was five. I began to see my images of them as exploitative, voyeuristic, and sentimental, so I turned the camera on myself, the ambivalent maternal subject. The images in my final thesis exhibition were all of myself, my head wrapped in baby undershirts, covered with slide projections of my daughters' writing and drawing. I also made drawings of baby bottle nipples, as a stand-in for the mother, being distorted and transformed by the pulls and pushes of life with children.

My decision to stop using images of my children in my work coincided with Alice's self-portrait project, and now she was asking me to photograph her as part of her work. But the spontaneous image I took of Alice and me together in the mirror represented something about my experience of mothering her more effectively than any of my previous work; something that may have been obvious to others, especially to my mother, but remained mysterious to me. I decided to write my story of what happened that day to accompany the picture of us in the mirror. I titled it *Alice's Idea*. It was a turning point for me, as writing became an important part of my creative practice.

Sally Mann, a well-known artist, created controversy by exhibiting and publishing erotically charged photographs she had taken of her children. She defended them as innocent and natural depictions of unself-conscious youth. I was struck by an offhand comment she made in a videotaped interview, that she has almost no memory of her own childhood and that perhaps she is reenacting scenes from her own forgotten childhood in her pictures of her children.

Am I doing this? Am I recreating the chaos of my childhood in the way I'm raising my daughters, setting the stage to repeat the struggle, this time as the parent? And most importantly, am I hiding behind my daughters, telling my story through them? Would it be more honest to talk about my cutting, my adolescent sexuality, and my dishonesty?

Should I be writing about the night my cousin Tessie and I made delicate cuts with razor blades into the tops of our wrists in a pattern still visible on mine as faint white scars, how we ran through the high-power sprinklers on the golf course behind my house, among the sweet, wet, rotting piles of grass, letting the diluted blood run down our arms, how it felt like a ritual, a celebration, thrilling and empowering? It was around this time my mother let me go and stay with Tessie and her family for a few weeks in the summer. She was one year older than me; curvy, with thick black hair and purplish blue eyes that my mother used to say were as deep and sexy as Elizabeth Taylor's. Tessie teased her dark, coarse hair into a big, hard lump on the top of her head. My hair was fine and light compared to hers, but she showed me how to tease it so high in the front that I could fit five little clip-on bows in a vertical stack. She was tough and fearless. We walked the streets of Union City, New Jersey, in the dark, and went to a double feature of *The Head* and *Horror Hotel*.

I remember my mother asking about the Band-Aids on my hands the next morning after Tessie and I had run through the sprinklers. I lied (cat scratches) and didn't want to show them to her. She didn't insist but probably suspected they were self-inflicted, because I do remember a lecture about how the top of the wrist is even more deadly than the underside, where people usually slit their wrists if they're trying to kill themselves. I never did it again, but a few years later I started a nightly routine of drinking red wine from the big bottle that always sat on the kitchen counter, and I practically stopped eating. The wine, the empty stomach, and the two or three dance classes a day, that's how I got through high school.

Tessie was a Merit Scholar, her IQ one of the highest they'd ever tested in the state. She went to a private girls' high school and wore a navy blue uniform with a pleated skirt and a white blouse. One day in her senior year, she didn't come home from school. Weeks went by, then months. Occasionally her mother would get phone calls, an almost inaudible mumbling voice that sounded like it might be her missing daughter. It turns out she went to Mexico with her heroin dealer. When she returned she was unrecognizable, and she has lived in a haze of prescription drugs ever since. My family has more than its share of stories like Tessie's, and I'm determined not to let Alice's be one of them. My bottom line: keep her from running away.

Tenth Grade

Alice is chronically sleep-deprived and so wound up socially she can't focus on her homework. She starts to make a halfhearted effort, then the phone rings. She talks for a long time to six or seven people every night who seem to always be in crisis. Then it gets really late and she's overcome with dread and panic because her work's not done. Even when I'm sitting there helping her, she'll focus on her schoolwork for about five minutes, then she's talking about her hair or what she should wear tomorrow, something she has to dye, cut, alter, or customize. I'm trying my best to provide a quiet time with no phone calls every evening so she can get her work done. I'm reading in my parenting books that I should set up opportunities for her to experience the pleasure of meeting her responsibilities, because it will build her self-esteem.

It's September and I'm taking Della and two of her friends to a funky little hot springs resort in New Mexico to celebrate her eleventh birthday. We're crossing the Continental Divide, and the desert is so vast I can see into Mexico to the south. To the north there is a train so far away it looks like a toy, two bright yellow engines and a long string of cars in blue, brown, and orange against the parched earth. It's 105 degrees and the air is so dry it makes my skin tingle and the inside of my nose burn. The sky is immense, brilliant, and bright blue. In my headphones Willie Nelson is singing a version of "Everybody's Talking at Me," the theme song from the movie *Midnight Cowboy*. I think about my father. We called him Ace, a nickname from his football-playing days at Princeton. He loved road trips, his wide, short, tan arm holding onto the steering wheel of our turquoise Chevy station wagon, the other arm leaning on the open window, his white shirtsleeve whipping in the wind, some loud static-y baseball game on the radio, a cigarette hanging from his bottom lip, the wind sending ashes and sparks onto us kids in the backseat. Willie is wailing with abandon in my headphones about skipping over the ocean. My father, once a successful psychiatrist, ended up on the streets, homeless. I was in my early twenties, living in the West, so I didn't see his deterioration on a daily basis. I know he was in jail once for stealing a muffin. During one of his lowest periods, I had dinner with him while visiting Boston with Matt, when we were engaged. My father was crashing at someone's loft in the warehouse district. He wore a red and white handkerchief on his head and was missing several teeth. All of his possessions fit into one paper bag, except his dog, which he named Willie, after Willie Nelson, his role model at that time. We bought my father dinner at Durgin Park, one of our old favorite family restaurants. I didn't have much appetite for the prime rib, mashed potatoes, and corn bread I loved so much as a child. I felt guilty about not telling him Matt and I were engaged, but I thought he was too unpredictable to invite out to Tucson for the wedding. I was afraid once he got there he might never leave. As we were standing on the sidewalk outside the restaurant saying goodbye, he told me he never felt more free.

At fifty-one I feel sick a lot of the time, probably a combination of exhaustion and my current imbalance of hormones. I just drag myself through my days feeling irritable and persecuted. It's obvious to me that the female body was not designed to be raising teenagers in its fifties. But I'm one of the first generation of women who grew up believing we could have it all, and many of us do, but at a price. Some established their careers first, didn't plan to have children, and then in their thirties and forties changed their minds. Fertility and reproductive biotech businesses have flourished with their promises to middle-aged women that it wasn't too late to have their own biological babies. Other women who had children first, or took a break to have kids, have had a harder time getting into competitive professional positions. Like many of my friends, I did it all at once. This involves a lot of rushing around and feeling guilty about shortchanging both family and career. When my mother comes to stay with me, she can't believe the pace I keep. When I was teaching full-time and working on an MFA, with a five- and a ten-year-old, she asked me why I didn't just raise my kids first and then get a university teaching job when they were older. If only it worked that way.

For Alice's sixteenth birthday her friends give her a baby chameleon. It's so tiny she names it Buggy. I feel run-down but still make a nice birthday dinner for her and a few of her friends. At her request I serve a bottle of red wine. Alice drinks more than half of it in big, hearty gulps. She becomes brassy and overconfident. It's the first time I've seen her really drink, and it scares me to see in her the serious drinkers of my childhood.

I'm helping Alice clean her room. The song "The Origins of Love" by Hedwig is playing. Referring to the lyrics she says, "Isn't that a great idea that making love is like trying to get two halves back together that were split apart?"

This makes me nervous. Trying to encourage a more practical perspective, I offer that maybe love is actually when you see that other person you desperately hoped would complete you for who they really are in spite of all you wanted and needed them to do for you.

I'm cleaning the house, which is a good thing, but the speed and ferocity with which I'm cleaning is how I'm currently trying to manage Alice's dropping grades and lack of interest in her homework. My teen parenting book says don't rant, rave, and rescue, don't get into a battle you can't win, don't forbid anything you can't control, or you will lose their respect.

Alice is sixteen and I'm saddened by how automatically and easily she lies, frustrated that I can't control her, can't protect her even from herself, let alone from outside forces. I can't even get her to drink enough water to relieve her frequent headaches. When I tell her she can't do something, she just hides it more effectively. I know she's smoking and drinking, involved in some kinds of sexual activities, and I suspect she's taking a variety of recreational drugs. She sleeps all day on weekends and may be sneaking out at night, but I'm too exhausted to wait up to catch her. She is also bright-eyed, graceful, and smart, cautious and self-respecting. Occasionally when she passes me in the hallway or we find ourselves in our tiny bathroom at the same time, she pats me on the back lovingly like she understands my life is hard, and that it's at least in part because of her.

We're almost through Alice's second year of high school, and we're arguing regularly about chores, homework, and her freedom to do what she wants. My whole family seems to resent me for trying to control them. I think it's time for some good therapy or maybe a trip to a hot springs resort. I decide to get some regular appointments with a therapist that my HMO will cover. She is starting a support group for women and invites me to join. One night I ask Alice to stay with Della, who's now eleven, while I go. She doesn't want to do it, but I insist. When I get home I hear from Della that they sat on her bedroom floor together and burned the fingertips off Della's Barbie dolls.

The next week Alice is supposed to come home in time to watch Della again so I can go to my support group, and she stands me up. When she finally gets home, I overreact, scream and yell, and all my resentment about other things comes up. I start by grounding her and end up changing my mind and apologizing for not listening to her side of the story. I know the resentment buildup is a problem. I need to say no in the right places and stop feeling like a victim. I'm confused because when I talk to Matt and other adults it seems obvious I should be more firm, but when I'm talking to Alice I agree with her that I'm strict and unreasonable. How do I give Alice appropriate responsibilities and consequences? I seem to be always under or over the mark. My parenting book says to ask for her options rather than give advice, and help her to sort out the differences between her thinking, feelings, and actions. Yes, I need to learn that for myself too.

Alice is upset because Matt has said she can't go out because it's a school night and she's behind in all of her classes. She disappears into her room for an hour or so. After Matt has gone to bed, she emerges in an innocent-looking, spaghetti-strapped summer dress with tiny flowers on it, and red paint dripped down her cheeks and onto her chest like bloody tears. She tells me she put on the dress, painted her face, and lay down on her couch with the video camera propped between her feet. She videotaped herself reading a list of grievances from her journal. After a while she began to laugh, when she realized she was telling her troubles to a machine, a lens.

It's a comfort to me that she's figured out how to use art as a way to calm herself by getting some distance from the intensity of her feelings. Perhaps this is the upside of her seeing me make art about my life since she was a young child.

A few months later Matt and I spend eleven hours putting up a wood ceiling in our new living room. The kids are happy and co-operative. Some tension and sadness seem to have lifted. Alice has washed off the black stars that she's had on her arms for months, and I'm working on an attitude adjustment in myself. I'm trying for mutual understanding and respect instead of control.

The next day Matt is gone for his twenty-four-hour shift at the fire station. Alice and I start the day relatively friendly toward each other. As we eat lunch together, she tells me about her art history class. Her eyes get teary when she describes the beauty of the baroque statue of Daphne turning into a tree. Her teacher has asked her to do an extra-credit presentation to the class about the Vladimir Madonna, knowing her passion will be infectious for the other students. She dyes a slip green and puts it on when we are getting ready to go out in the afternoon. I tell her she has to change or put on another layer of clothes. She refuses, slams her door, and I hear her sobbing in her room. An hour or so later she comes out, and we talk about the possibility of getting antianxiety meds for her. We agree to go out with her in the slip as an experiment. The results are no surprise—everyone stares at her and I am uncomfortable—but it is a small step forward to see it as an experiment we're doing together rather than as a power struggle.

That evening Della, who's eleven, is talking about the look people get when they really want something. She calls it a "puppy face," and we all take turns doing our most convincing version of it. When I lie down to read to Della at night, she makes me laugh, then starts imitating me laughing. This makes me laugh so hard I can't breathe. Tonight as a joke she says, "Don't say that to me, I'm fragile." She's mocking herself, mocking her sister, suggesting the manipulation, the act that can feel so real.

It's the summer before Alice's junior year in high school. I'm trying to get her interested in college, so she'll work for better grades in high school. She agrees to visit the Rhode Island School of Design (RISD) while we're on the Cape for our summer vacation. The day we go, it's in the high nineties, humid and smoggy. The weather is making us both feel sick. After the two-hour drive we get out to look at risdworks, a little store of work by alumni. Alice sees some shredded stockings for sale, just like the ones she's made for herself. Back in the car heading toward campus we see a cool-looking girl cross the street. Alice starts to feel worse, doesn't feel up to the three-hour tour, and doesn't know if she wants to go to art school after all. I say we can skip it, and we start the drive back home. She says, "You're a good mom for not making me do it."

Eleventh Grade

I am doing most of the parenting now. When Matt's not at the fire station, he's completely absorbed in the remodeling project. I'm sure our mutual realization of how incompatible our parenting styles are underlies his withdrawal. I can't recommend my approach, and I can certainly understand him tiring of the emotional turbulence of life with Alice and me, but I can't figure out any other way to do it.

Alice is seventeen and has had a steady boyfriend for a few months. I need to face the fact that over the last few weeks she's been spending increasing amounts of time in her room with him and emerging looking less and less put together. I think about my position on this. I tell her that the rule is she comes out of her room fully clothed, looking like they've been sitting on the couch talking. I say, "Is that too much to ask for the freedom you get on your side of the door?" She laughs and agrees to my terms.

I know one of Alice's friends has been raped, and some have been sexually active for years. It's popular in her age group to have sex with several people without being in an exclusive relationship or dating. The Internet is also used by some kids to set up sexual encounters with no strings attached. One of my friends told me she answered a knock on the door late one night; it was a middle-aged man her seventeen-year-old daughter had attracted on the Internet. He drove across several states to find her in person.

I think Alice is too young to be having sex, and I have told her that, but I am also grateful that she has reached the age of seventeen without having had a traumatic sexual experience. By giving Alice the privacy to experiment at home, I believe I am reducing the risks and helping her figure out how to be sexual on her terms.

I was not even sixteen. It was 1966 and the sexual revolution was going on around me. He worked in a jewelry store in Harvard Square. I used to go there regularly with my best friend to flirt with him. One night when my mother dropped my brother and me off at a coffee house, I simply left and went to his house. He met me at the door with a gin and tonic in one hand and a hash pipe in the other. We had sex. I don't know if he knew it was my first time. I got back to the coffee house a few minutes before my mother pulled up to take my brother and me back home to the suburbs. I was proud to be able to tell my older friends that I finally did it, that I wasn't a virgin anymore. I don't remember ever seeing him again. About a year and a half later, when I had a regular boyfriend, I asked my mother to take me to get birth control. I had already had plenty of unprotected sex and had worried myself sick about being pregnant, the first sign of every period a cause of great relief and even celebration. She said I was too young to be sexually active, and that was that. After our conversation I remember sitting in the bathtub for a long time, the water getting cold and clammy, thinking about where else I could live.

Alice has been offered an empty studio to display and sell her work in the biannual downtown open-studio tours. She asks me to buy her spray paint, fabric, and other supplies. She makes a stencil of Clara Bow's face and paints it on slips and handbags she's gotten at thrift shops and dyed. She makes jewelry from nails, wire, and other construction debris she finds around the house and puts her photographs in secondhand frames. She designs and distributes flyers. She borrows pedestals and lights and transforms the raw space into a theatrical boutique.

Della, who's twelve, lectures me, "If I had a seventeen-year-old daughter, I wouldn't let her do porno." She says her friends make fun of her because her sister is practically naked in the self-portraits that are hanging up in our house. She says now they're porno because Alice is going to sell them in the open-studio tour. I'm surprised by her tone and think I recognize in it her friend's judgmental mother. Later, when Alice isn't there, Della is sobbing as she tells me, "I'm afraid Alice is going to get raped walking home from school because of the way she dresses."

Alice's studio is packed all day with artists, high school friends, gallery curators, and people who own clothing and jewelry boutiques. A curator and a new genres professor who's known Alice since she was in elementary school buy several things and ask if they can come over to see all the other stuff she has in her room. She also gets several business cards from people who are interested in her work. She doesn't follow up on any of these opportunities, but she makes $200 selling her stuff.

It's around this time Alice tells me she's ready for birth control. I take her to my gynecologist for an appointment. Alice comes out of the doctor's office looking proud. She tells me on the way home in the car, "I feel like a woman." Later she says, "Taking me to get birth control is the coolest thing you've ever done, even cooler than not making me go on the tour of RISD." She says she's especially appreciative because her friends can't tell their mothers that they're sexually active. She's gone to Planned Parenthood more than once to support frightened friends who needed STD tests and treatment, birth control, and "day after" pills. I'm not surprised when I compare notes with Anne and Leslie that sex hasn't come up with their daughters yet.

Soon after the open-studio tour, I pick up some photos for Alice at the drugstore. Something about the way the guy looks at me at the one-hour counter makes me curious. I open the package when I get to the car. Sure enough, it's retro flapper erotica that Alice and her new friend Felicity have taken of each other. I sit in the parking lot trying to sort this out. I just picked up the pictures and paid with my credit card, and I think this is technically child pornography. Could I be arrested, find myself in the newspapers, or maybe even lose my job? Sally Mann had to face the grand jury because of the pictures she took of her children. When I get home and tell Alice my concerns, she thinks I'm overreacting but agrees to be discreet with the pictures. I am worried about who is going to see them. I especially don't want her sister and father to see them. Later that night, when Matt has gone to bed and Della is watching TV in her room, Alice has the pictures spread out all over the dining room table. She's making duplicates and enlargements on the computer. I tell her I hope she's not making them to sell. She rolls her eyes and says, "Of course not; I did it to boost Felicity's self-esteem." I ask about the pictures of her. "Oh, that was just for fun," she says casually. I wake up at 6:00 a.m. the next day after not enough sleep with another migraine.

Alice has her learner's permit, and I'm teaching her how to drive. She loves practicing and asks me almost every evening to take her out. Sometimes she wants to just ride around in the car with me driving. I enjoy this time with her but feel guilty, that I should be home cooking, cleaning, or helping Della with her homework. Matt is working constantly on the remodeling project, and these evening drives provide a welcome relief from the constant roar of power tools. When Alice got her license Matt bought her a beat-up, primer-gray, 1979 Camaro Berlinetta. It's exactly the car she wanted. She can't believe the perfect beauty of the shape of the back window.

It has no heat or air conditioning, and the doors and windows are nearly impossible to open. There are also more serious problems, like a rusty gas tank that requires her to blow compressed air into a hose in the engine to get it started. She carries a small air compressor in the trunk, but it's a two-person job to open the hood, which must be at least eight feet long. Maybe her father thinks it will build her character to deal with these mechanical shortcomings. I suppose he has a point, but I think it's dangerous. Alice and Matt spend time working on the car together. I'm happy to see it, since they don't have much other interaction lately. After she has the car for a few months, she paints an indented area in the front, where a grill is supposed to be, red with little white pointy teeth, transforming it from a muscle car to something more like a cartoon shark. When prospective drag racers pull up next to her, they must be surprised to find a ninety-pound girl, dressed in vintage punk, looking like a Cruella De Vil understudy, behind the wheel. She loves the car and exclaims regularly, "Isn't this the perfect car for me?" She names it Leviathan after the whale in *Moby Dick*, the book she's reading in English class.

We're doing round-robin makeovers on Della's bed with a big set of cheap makeup I gave her for her twelfth birthday. Alice does my eyes. Della does Alice's eyes; I do Della's eyes. The phone rings.

Della says under her breath, "Pray it's a wrong number." She knows we'll lose Alice to the phone if it's for her. When Alice is back from her phone call, Della is doing my lips. The lipstick is bad, hard, and waxy—more like a crayon than lipstick. Alice tells Della, "Be careful. Mom's little lips have had to be burned and stuff." She's referring to the treatment I had that chemically burned precancerous spots off my lips. Alice has referred to me in diminutive terms before, but I am struck at this moment by her maternal protectiveness.

At 2:00 a.m. I'm startled out of a deep sleep by a loud knock on my bedroom door. It's Della telling me the police are here. Holding my breath, I struggle into my bathrobe and stumble to the front door. Alice is standing there with a guy I've never met and two police officers that seem unnaturally large in our small front room. Alice's friend has long, unwashed hair and is wearing a tight, dark blue velvet suit, high-heeled boots, and face glitter. He looks like a disheveled cross between Mick Jagger and Prince. The cops tell me they originally pulled her over for making a wide left turn. Once they stopped her, they realized she had alcohol on her breath and was out after the Tucson city curfew. Her blood alcohol levels are low, and they don't believe she's impaired, but they've cited her for underage drinking and for drinking and driving. I get dressed so we can move her car to a safe spot for the night. It's clear that I don't need to say anything. The legal consequences will be plenty.

We go to see a friendly young female parole officer at juvenile court, who offers Alice the option of being in a determent program called Teen Court. She is eligible because she is not yet eighteen, and the parole officer recommends it highly because Alice is smart and sensitive. If she agrees, she will appear before a jury of her peers who will hear her case and determine the appropriate workshops and community service for her crime. I jump in and say she'll do it. When we get back to the car she is livid, horrified by the prospect of being judged by her peers. She tells me it's the worst thing I've ever done to her.

I'm relieved when we leave town for our annual summer vacation, glad to have Alice out of the dance party scene in Tucson. While we're on the Cape, my brother Peter recommends that she rent the movie *Badlands*. It's about a guy who kidnaps a much younger girl who's infatuated with him at first but has her doubts when he embarks on a killing spree. After Alice watches it a few times, she mentions that the protagonist reminds her of her current boyfriend. She calls him shortly after seeing the movie and ends their long-distance relationship. Now, there's a tip you're not going to find in a parenting book.

Despite massive amounts of protest and dread over the summer, Alice gets to her Teen Court appointment in the fall, and for several Saturdays she goes to serve on the jury. We go to a series of workshops together where we hear other families tell their stories. I think it's good for Alice's perspective, and she is clearly grateful when she compares her situation to those of the other kids who are in much worse trouble with a lot less support. Alice works at the St. Vincent de Paul thrift shop to fulfill her community service hours. She takes it seriously and is appreciated by her boss, is liked and respected by her coworkers, and loves helping her customers. The store has a program that provides a new set of clothes once a week for the homeless people who come in. One day on the way home in the car, she tells me her favorite part of the job is helping them pick out their outfits.

Twelfth Grade

It's the first week of Alice's senior year, and Matt and I have just grounded her for staying out all night. She is angry at first but in general seems happy and relieved to be getting a break from her (social) life. Every once in a while she gets grumpy, and I know she's thinking about the dance party she's going to miss this weekend. But being grounded seems to give her permission to be a kid again. She also seems to enjoy the attention of being incarcerated, under tight surveillance.

Sitting at the kitchen counter, eating the French toast I just made her (and had to stop myself from cutting into bite-sized pieces), she talks in a businesslike tone about getting her own place in a few months when she turns eighteen. She wants to know if Matt and I will still pay her car insurance when she's not living here with us. I want to say I think it would be disastrous for her to move out now, but I keep quiet. She knows it depends on her having a job. I'm banking on that not happening until after she finishes high school.

On the Saturday night after Alice turns eighteen, she uses her birthday money to rent a room for her and her new boyfriend in a restored art deco hotel downtown. He comes to get her in the three-piece suit that his father got married in. She is wearing a 1950s pale yellow cocktail dress with a full skirt and matching high heels. She calls from the hotel room to say goodnight. She tells me they strolled arm in arm up and down the street outside the hotel earlier in the evening. I'm a little uncomfortable about the whole situation but tell her I'm proud of her. She has made it to legal adulthood and seems to be calming down a little. She has a stable relationship with someone her age who seems nice, and it even looks like she is going to make it through high school. She tells me she is proud of me too. She doesn't say why, but I assume it's for letting her be herself and letting go enough so she can grow up. I have a sense of accomplishment, feeling that maybe the hardest part is over. I feel the significance of her age, knowing this will be a year of separating for us. At the time I didn't realize it would also be the year I'd separate from my husband.

In March Alice is nominated for a high school visual arts award. To receive it she's required to put a portfolio together showing all of the projects she did as a student there. She's put it off for weeks, and the night before it is due she finally gets into it. She is making so much noise in the living room with the printer, I give up trying to sleep and come out to help speed up the process. In spite of being tired, resentful, and frustrated by how often her procrastination has led to my being inconvenienced, I'm amazed. Every page of her portfolio is a crazy-quilt collage of writing, photographs (both self-portraits and pictures I had taken of her as a child), drawings, paintings, documentation of the dances she's choreographed with elaborate costumes and sets she's designed and produced, and all kinds of interesting papers and other materials she's found around the house and in my studio.

During graduation Alice's name is called over the scratchy loudspeaker, and she walks up to get her award. She is one of only two students of the six hundred graduating that year to receive the Visual Arts Endorsement. I sit in the stands on the metal bleachers, the glaring low afternoon sun and tears in my eyes, among thousands of multigenerational Mexican-American families who are cheering and blowing big horns. Matt and I have recently decided to separate, but we are waiting until the school year is over to tell the kids. He is sitting motionless a few seats away. I want to join in with the crowd, but I can't get a sound past the aching lump in my throat. I am so proud of Alice's accomplishments, so relieved she made it through high school, so grateful she survived her teens.

Because of my social class, my time period, and my particular circumstances, I have grown up slowly along a relatively unprescribed path. This uneven process, which sometimes seems like a luxury, sometimes a curse, has been catalyzed by my daughters, partly because I've had to take responsibility for my own actions to ask that of them, but also because I want them to see me age well. Keeping up with Alice has required a kind of brutal self-honesty that I can't imagine developing voluntarily. As she has navigated the difficult years from thirteen to eighteen, I've gone through my own equally dramatic, though more internal, struggle to a new life stage.

Now almost three years after I began this essay, I've gotten over my divorce, my hormones have settled down, and Della is almost sixteen, so far, with no major incidents. Alice is twenty-one, an art major at the university where I teach, and doing well. She is a wonderful person and a compassionate friend, but it's not that simple. I think she drinks too much, and it's recently dawned on me how much I'm still trying to control her with my worry.

Maybe I was too close to see what was best for her. Instead of just seeing her as my daughter, I saw her as a peer, a miracle, an amazement, a muse, an inspiration, a subject. But as Alice and I have survived our heartbreaks and shared our recoveries, our love for each other has become richer and more complicated. I don't know if I'll ever completely shake my demon of self-doubt, but it's less important to me now, because I know from ample experience that I can do a lot wrong and things will turn out all right anyway. And this is one of the great pleasures of being this age.

Note: Some names have been changed.

My Dead

Calvin Forbes

When my mother died I was visiting friends in Kingston, Jamaica. Betty, my oldest sister, wired me, but the local telegram operators were on strike. It must have been because of the dreadfulness of the message that one of the operators decided to hand-deliver the news to the house where was I staying with my friends. I was out when the telegram arrived and have always regretted that I never got a chance to thank the woman personally for going out of her way to bring me the message that my mother had made her transition. I like that phrase, *made her transition;* it implies that the state of being alive is temporary, that life and death circle around each other, and that you can't have one without the other. This is in keeping with many cultures' traditional view of the endless cycle of life and death, birth and aging, of the ties between the material and the spirit world as well as between generations. It also seems universal, deeply human. Or, as the joke reminds us, no one gets out of here alive.

I was thirty-nine in 1984 when my mother made her transition. By then I had already experienced the death of my father in 1970 and the deaths of two of my older brothers, George in 1971 and Richard in 1974. It's an understatement to say my mother's death threw me off balance, but it was the death of my sister Betty in 1994 from breast cancer that made me stand up and take account of my life. Rather than change careers, buy a motorcycle, or get a ring in my ear when I crossed the bridge into my middle years, I was confronting the net effect of recovering from the series of deaths in my family. I no longer could put it off. I had to grow up.

As I figure it, by the time I hit middle age, suspended between youth and death, I was supposed to have some smarts about life, or at least be good at feigning it. The best thing the old can teach the young is that they too can survive the worst life has to offer and that they don't have to arrive beaten down and bitter and full of regret at the end of their life. With each death in my family I up the ante, and work twice as hard on improving the way I live my life and at building better relationships with the people I love.

I realized if I could get over my sister's death, I could survive anything. Some Sundays even now I still think of phoning Betty, then catch myself, and smile, somehow happy. No doubt this is what Shakespeare meant by "sweet sorrow." It's also one of the core messages of the blues: Broken hearts can heal and will be broken again. Most of the time. So get used to it and get on with your life. Betty and I were very different, but we shared a special bond only siblings can experience, that a lover or a friend couldn't begin to match. Betty's former husband used to complain that she felt closer to her brothers than to him. She told him yes, I am closer to them. I have known them longer.

I wonder if it's possible to know anyone, to truly understand them. No matter. What I can say with some assurance is that, with my sister no longer around, I no longer have someone who has known me long and well enough to provide the perspective I need to measure my personal growth. A mate of many decades or a good friend who has known you a long time can play this role in your life, it's true, so all is not lost. Since I have had no close friends from my childhood around me for some time now, my current relationships will have to do, but none of these, not even a spouse, can provide the safety net a sister or a brother can offer. Of course, the opposite is sometimes the case. Family can also bring you nothing but grief.

What does it mean to miss someone, to have a space in your present life that can never be filled by the living, a space that somehow can never be quite empty either? After my mother's death it was Betty I would call when I needed to touch base, to feel connected to my past and thereby to my future. I miss my brothers George and Richard, and I regret not having told them in so many words how important they were to my life. With Betty and my mother it was never a question. Much to my regret, I was never close to my father. But I am not neurotic about it. It makes me sad for the both of us that I don't miss him, yet there's no denying his influence on my life. Maybe it was a negative influence, but so be it. My father died disconnected from family when at the end of life it was all that he had, and to top that off he didn't have friends, just cronies. I never wanted to be like my father. His wasn't a good death. He had to have died a disappointed man.

Burying a sibling, burying a parent, though equally troubling, touch on different emotions. As you get older you struggle to prepare yourself for the eventual death of your parents, but the loss of a sister or a brother presents a different scenario. Their deaths, like those of your contemporaries, make you feel vulnerable, leave you wondering who's next or what will happen next. You begin to think of your own demise speeding toward you.

Luckily I had no significant sibling rivalries or jealousies to guilt-trip me when my brothers and sister died. And good also was the realization that I had resolved most of my conflicts with my mother and father by the time they died, so I didn't have anger or unresolved issues to work out when I hit my forties full stride and started slowly, very slowly, strolling through the briar patch toward my hoped-for destiny as an old man, an elder. I have seen too many people enter middle age still angry with their parents not to feel grateful for having avoided that fate.

My parents, Jacob and Mary Forbes, had eight children, six boys and two girls, all of whom became reasonably respectable adults, not an easy task to accomplish whether the family is rich or poor, and we were decidedly poor. Having that many children is a monster of a responsibility, mentally and physically. No child can raise itself, and it fell to my mother for the most part to raise us with grace and humor, because my father was busy pursuing his dreams. My mother had a gentle way about her, and she was quite able and willing to laugh at herself. There was a lot of laughter in the house despite our often dire financial circumstances. When I was a kid if my mother was angry with me, or even when she was calling me to run an errand, she would often call me by one of my brothers' names, or run down the list, from the oldest to youngest, until she got to me. I liked to tease her, and I'd say, Momma, I'm Calvin, and she'd answer, Boy, I know who you are, faking anger and admonishment. The image of my mother I still hold dearest is of her standing in the kitchen, near the stove most likely, banishing me from her sight with a big wooden spoon in her hand. The picture I have in my mind is so much better than a photograph, because I can call it forth anytime, or it can arise on its own to surprise and please me when something in my day happens to remind me of my mother.

My brother Jacob, named after my father, is the oldest, followed by James, Charles, George, Richard, and Betty, then me, and finally, Karen, the baby of the family. The story is that my parents kept on trying to have a girl until they had Betty. If this story is true, why they didn't stop at Betty is a mystery. Only a few years separate the births of the four oldest boys. Then, after a gap of several years, Richard, Betty, and I were born, all within a few years of each other. My four much older brothers were out of the house when I was coming up, so I grew up with Richard and Betty, and when I was around ten Karen made her entry. Could the waxing and waning of romance, the rekindling and ebbing of passion, explain the gap between pregnancies? I have no answer. I wouldn't have dared ask my mother such a question. I was born in 1945, the onset of the baby boom generation, at the end of World War II, though my father didn't serve in the military. He did hold down a steady job through those years, working as a chef, in Atlantic City, I believe. My father once told me that this was the last time he worked for white people. It was probably also the last time he had a regular job. My father had conflicting attitudes toward white people, typical perhaps of black men of his generation. This might help explain his ambivalence toward my civil rights activities in the 1960s. One time when I got arrested in a civil rights demonstration, he asked me why I was risking my future trying to integrate with white folks. White people weren't going to change, he told me. Yet at the same time many of his business associates were white.

My involvement in the civil rights movement provided me

with the type of an education I didn't receive in high school, because it exposed me to a world I knew little about growing up. I began to realize how not only race but also class shaped the way human beings lived. It was an eye-opener, one I still grapple with while trying to understand its myriad dimensions. I remember sitting on the steps of my house one afternoon with some of my homeboys when I was eighteen. I had just come back from a meeting and from visiting the home of one of the white civil rights organizers. He was middle-class and lived in the suburbs. I had never been inside a white person's home before, let alone visited someone in the suburbs with a two-car garage. I remember telling my friends that there are people who don't want for basic stuff, like plenty of food to eat from day to day, who can snack any time they want and never seem to worry about drinking the very last of the orange juice in one go that was supposed to last the whole week for the entire family. I said this in a voice tinged with amazement, because for kids to be able to take what they wanted from a refrigerator stocked full of food and drink was a state of being unheard-of among the folks I grew up with. Issues about class continue to be as important to me as those of race. Most Americans alive today have never experienced having to portion out the amount of food your family can enjoy until the next paycheck. Now that I am middle-class myself, I never want to take for granted what others struggle to achieve.

I grew up in Newark, New Jersey, just across the Hudson River from New York City. My mother and father came north from North Carolina during the period known as the Great Migration, when thousands of African Americans fled the South for what they hoped would be a better life in the North. When I was a teenager my father opened Forbes Food Shop, a soul food restaurant. Before he opened the restaurant he was a partner with some white gangsters in running a beach resort for African Americans on the Jersey Shore in the mid-1950s, a time when, due to the whims of segregation, there was still a need for businesses that catered to a mostly black clientele. The beach resort was called Forbes Beach. That both businesses bore his name says something about my father. His ego was always front and center, but he also saw these enterprises as family businesses, with his sons following in his footsteps. That he failed to pull this off must have nagged at him toward the end of his life. My father's wheelings and dealings were major undertakings for a black man of his generation with only an elementary school education, yet despite his many accomplishments, the quality of our lives never changed that much. While he was running the beach resort, we continued to live in the same rundown apartment building.

We always lived in apartments, none larger than two bedrooms. The apartments were in multifamily houses that were not large enough to be described as apartment buildings. We always lived with landlords below us or above us, except for the first house, the one I was born into in 1945; it had a total of six apartments and an absentee landlord who didn't give a damn about his building or his tenants.

The house at 95 South Fourteenth Street was a ramshackle dump. My mother wouldn't like that description, out of pride if nothing else, but she couldn't honestly dispute the facts. When I was a kid we used to play hide-and-seek in the hallways and hide under the stairwells during the cold months. The sidewalks were our playground during the warm months, when the front porches up and down the block would be full of friends, neighbors, and family sitting around talking, joking, the adults telling tall tales and the kids playing jump rope or stickball or hopscotch. In the winter we used kerosene stoves for heat. Air conditioning was unheard-of and electric fans were rare, so we were always too hot in the summer and were never quite warm enough in the winter. Yet I often had a good time growing up. It was bleak, but it was home; there was loads of love, both in and outside of the walls of our narrow existence. The people I grew up with, not only my family, provided me with the sense of community that continues to ground me. I had people around me I could depend upon, who cared. It was a real neighborhood, with families who had known one another for decades. I felt anchored there. Still do, though I have long since moved on physically.

Some of the families in the neighborhood were worse off than we were, namely, because they didn't have a mother as steady as ours. Experts on such matters say that children need at least one person in their life who can serve as a beacon of hope, an island of tranquility. It doesn't have to be a parent, or even a relative.

My mother was the kind of lady whose best friends called her Miss Forbes. Even the neighborhood winos and the local hoods held her in high regard and would offer to carry her shopping bags home free of charge to our front door. She had class, though her nose was never up in the air. Yes, we were poor, meaning we often couldn't afford the basics—reliable health care, decent clothing, or even enough food at times—but because of my mother's knack for making the best of a bad situation and her skill at turning leftovers into delicious meals, we never went hungry or knew how paltry the pantry actually was. I have fond memories of walking home from elementary school, ten to fifteen blocks, for lunch, to devour a yummy plate of homemade biscuits and syrup. It wasn't until many years later that I realized that this was the only food in the house and that there was no money to buy lunch at school or at the local deli nearby like some of the other kids did. We didn't suffer from comparing our lot to what was on TV like kids do today. The must-haves were a pair of Converses, and I never heard of anyone being robbed or killed for their Converses. Back then being poor was a lot easier.

The thing I hated most about living at 95 South Fourteenth Street was that the hallway lights would frequently burn out, or the bulbs would be broken or stolen, and not be replaced for weeks on end. The alley cats that roamed freely in the neighborhood would seek shelter in our hallways on cold winter nights, and you could hear them, especially the large tomcats, crying out in the night or fighting each other. Most terrifying of all, as you made your way to your own door in the dark, you might step on one of the alley cats, or they might leap out at you from the pitch blackness. It was a living nightmare. It's a wonder that today I am not paranoid around cats.

When I was in my mid-teens we moved a few blocks away, to 27 South Thirteenth Street, a three-family house, which was luxurious by comparison to the house on Fourteenth Street. For one thing, it had central heating. Best of all, it was clean and well maintained, with the landlord living on the first floor. The apartment was also slightly larger; it had a dining room, which my two sisters, Betty and Karen, could use as their bedroom. Before then, the four children living at home—Richard, Betty, Karen, and I—slept in one room in two bunk beds. In the new apartment I shared a bedroom with my brother Richard, and my parents had the second bedroom.

Home in 1970 when my father died was another rented apartment in another three-family wooden frame house on the opposite side of Newark on a quiet street with lots of trees, a few miles from where I was raised. I wasn't living at home when my father suffered a massive heart attack one spring afternoon while sitting on the front porch. He died instantaneously. My father was not the kind of man to waste his time sitting around the house on a Saturday, lazily soaking up the sun and waving hello to the neighborhood kids as they rode by on their bicycles, but that's where and how he died, spending an afternoon at home. My sister Karen found him slumped over in a lawn chair. I have always suspected he knew his day of reckoning had come and so found his way outdoors to catch his last breath of Jersey air.

A few days later the family gathered to discuss his funeral arrangements. I traveled to Newark from Boston, where I was then living. I was twenty-five years old. The living room where my family gathered to discuss my father's funeral arrangements is also the setting of one of the few photographs I have of my father. He is sitting on the couch, which was set against the wall opposite the hallway entrance. At the other end of the couch my mother is sitting. The distance between my parents, while only the length of a single couch, is telling. It's the only photograph I have of them together. The occasion is a visit from Atlantic City by my aunt Alma, one of my father's sisters. Aunt Alma is sitting in an armchair near the window, facing my parents. The colors in the Polaroid photograph have faded, but I remember how the pattern of the wallpaper contrasted sharply with the florid design of the slipcovers blanketing and protecting the couch and the armchair from wear and tear. My father is in a short-sleeved white shirt, my mother in her familiar housedress. In the photograph no one is smiling or posing.

They appear to be uncomfortable, not willing to face the camera, awkward perhaps in each other's company, or from having their picture taken. Some families have lots of family photographs. My family doesn't, much to my regret. Family photographs help future generations understand from whence they came. Having pictures of your grandparents or, better yet, your great-grandparents is a marker of sustained family relationships and suggests a state of family economic advancement as well, because the two often go together. Building similar totems of our family life would become my personal mission once I was old enough and settled enough for my family to pay attention to my opinions.

The big question confronting us after my father's death was whether he had enough insurance to cover his burial expenses. It was worrisome because in the past he had cashed out family life insurance policies to raise money for one of his business schemes. My brothers argued about money, and my brother George, who had only recently arrived home from Germany where he was stationed in the army, got into a heated exchange with my brother Charles. The army is good about airlifting servicemen home for emergencies, and George had just come off of several hours of traveling. Perhaps this helps to explain the brusque tone of his voice, and Charles's hostile response. My brother Richard was off somewhere. Richard, like the rest of us, wasn't prepared to face up to the fact that my father would no longer be dominating our lives. My mother sat quietly through most of the discussion and didn't say much until George and Charles raised their voices in anger and she had to shush them and remind them that we were family and not to be rude to each other in her house. You are always a child to your mother, so why fight it, why try to prove you are your own man by resisting?

As the child of a mother who often worked twelve-hour days, I had to learn to draw the outlines of my life from an early age. I didn't have time for teenage angst. Growing up too fast can leave you half-finished, but what saved me was the bedrock of knowing right from wrong and never wanting to embarrass my mother. I actually became a fully functional adult somewhere in my mid-twenties, when my father died. I was well on my way to being capable of taking care of myself physically and spiritually, but I had to get myself together so I could be responsible to and for someone else. This is the best definition of being an adult I can muster. After my father's death, my mother and my family needed me to help carry some of the weight that his passing had placed on our collective shoulders.

My father thought being a good man meant providing a roof over his family's heads, nothing more or less. He was a strong man, of mind and body. The thing that drove him forward was his lifelong ambition to be somebody special, to be his own boss. It was a worthy goal. But to paraphrase B. B. King, my father made his family, especially my mother, pay the cost for his wanting to be his own boss. Whatever money he made, he spent pursuing his personal ambition. It didn't trickle down to a better life for his family. He didn't spend money on fancy clothes or cars, though he always drove a nice car and never looked bad. He didn't drink, didn't smoke or use drugs. He only gambled; it was gambling that both greased the path to his greatest success and provided the slippery slope to his failure. He eventually lost most of what he won because he always wanted more and couldn't turn away from playing the odds. Even when the restaurant was doing well, he wanted something larger, fancier. All he could do was hope for a better deal at the card tables and his other semi-legit activities, like loan sharking, than what the legit banks were offering even qualified black men in the 1950s.

Jacob, my oldest brother, was in charge of making the funeral arrangements, as he would be for all of the funerals that would follow. Jacob, eighteen years older than me, is old enough to be my father. Over the years I have watched and studied Jacob's leadership and enterprise in burying the family dead. Would I one day have to perform such a task? I don't welcome the job, but if push comes to shove, as the saying goes, I could shoulder the load. Somebody has to step forward, why not me? I have nothing to prove to anybody, including myself. How do you prove you're grown up, and not a child in disguise? It's similar to trying to prove you're a human being to a racist. By opening up that window you concede power to someone who doesn't have your best interest at heart. My mother is the only person I have to prove anything to. My mother and God can judge me, if need be. So anyone else, back off.

It fell to my sister Betty to write my father's obituary. She wanted to add a sentence saying that my father had been a so-so dad, but after much debate and protest from the rest of the family about its appropriateness, if not the accuracy, Betty relented. My mother had to remind Betty not to speak ill of the dead. It was a tense moment, but the obituary was rewritten. Betty had a deep and stubborn sense of right and wrong, born of her religious conviction. I think my father's failures angered her more than they did the rest of us.

My father's death took the wind out of everyone's sails, but my older brothers had borne the brunt of his influence, which I believe had a lot to do with Charles and George's outburst. He simply had more energy when they were growing up in the decades before my birth. He was such a big force in our lives, a gale force wind, not a breeze. Now he was gone and his death unleashed a surge of dammed-up emotion, anger mixed with grief, a potent cocktail.

George's death only a few years after my father's created another opportunity for a gut check. George was the star of the family. I say this without any envy. Every large family has its ranking system, and I was happy playing my role as the slightly nerdy but down-to-earth younger brother and uncle. One of my mother's many gifts was to make every one of her children feel special. Everyone in the family, including Betty, worshipped the ground George walked on, yet I never felt second best in Betty's or my mother's eyes. George was handsome, had charm and smarts, and was so smooth in all his manners yet so modest that he personified what *cool* is supposed to mean. His friends, male and female, loved him. It was from George that I picked up what little sense of style I have. At his funeral grown men and women cried freely, willingly sharing their grief.

George was stationed in Germany most of his army career. I seldom saw him or spent time with him while I was growing up, unless he was home on leave. My brothers James, Charles, and George all joined the army in the 1950s in time for the Korean

War before graduating from high school. Jacob went into the navy. It wasn't because they were gung-ho patriotic. As Colin Powell has pointed out, in the 1950s, the army—if not the navy, which was still segregated—offered African Americans a degree of equality that civilian life did not. George was a member of an elite Ranger outfit, qualifying as a paratrooper in the 82nd Airborne Division. Everyone was proud of George's accomplishments, including his friends and people in the neighborhood. To put this in context, you have to know that African Americans were once relegated to being cooks or to other low-level jobs in the armed services. America didn't believe black people were capable of or suitable for other duties, like actually carrying weapons and behaving responsibly. So when George achieved the rank of sergeant in the 82nd Airborne, it was a notable achievement and something to be celebrated and respected. He was going to make a career out of the army and retire in his late thirties with his army benefits and most of his salary intact and be set for the rest of his life after doing his bit for Uncle Sam for twenty years.

But for some reason, when I was a teenager he didn't reenlist. He came home from Germany and stayed with us for a few months while looking for a civilian job. He never found one that paid enough and that didn't require him to relinquish the sense of pride he had worked so hard to burnish while in the army. He decided to reenlist way past the deadline, and thereby lost his rank in the process. But within a few years he had regained all of his stripes and was once again a sergeant, living near Munich, with his new German wife and their two children. No longer jumping out of airplanes, he now was running a noncommissioned officers' club in Germany. On my first trip to Europe, after spending a month on an island in the Adriatic Sea off the coast of the former Yugoslavia, I visited George and his family in Germany. We saw little of each other during my stay, since he was busy at his job, day and night. The most time I spent with him during that trip was when he drove me to the airport on my way back to the States. It might have been the single largest block of time I ever spent with him in my entire life. The drive to the airport sticks out in my mind for many reasons. Before I got out of the car, he asked me if I needed any money. I said no, that I was all right. He asked me if I was sure; I said yes. It was his way of showing me affection, how much he cared about me. He was my big brother, and even though he knew I was working, in the first year of teaching at a prestigious university, he was looking out for me. It was the last time I saw George alive. He died in a car accident on the Autobahn.

I remember reading that bad things happen in sets of three. Or possibly it's just a superstition I picked up and never discarded. I think its origins go back to World War I, when it was said that it was always the third soldier in the trenches who got shot by a sniper after a single match to light their cigarettes was passed around between soldiers. I still believe that things happen in patterns and that the only way to avoid the events already set in motion is to somehow figure out what's happening and do your best to get out of the way. After the deaths of my father and George, I began to wonder which one of us would be the next to go. But no one knows when his or her time is up; hence, the common dread. I don't think other animals worry about this like we humans do; at least there's no evidence that animals obsess about death and dying. We humans are so conscious of our mortality, increasingly so as we age. I have been close to dying more than once, and I am thankful that I am still around to enjoy growing older. Two motorcycle accidents bred in me a fear of a third, so I stopped driving motorcycles. I almost drowned twice, once as a dumb kid and later as an even dumber adult trying to attract the attention of a woman who was as graceful in the water as I was not. But I wasn't to be the third in my family to go. My brother Richard was. I was becoming increasingly acquainted with death, and not by choice.

I think my mother had a special place in her heart set aside for Richard. He was gay, for one, and my mother, though not wise in the ways of the world, must have intuited that he suffered greatly because of his sexual orientation. Being an effeminate gay teenager in the inner city during the late 1950s could not have been easy. I have vague memories of my mother having to go downtown several times to the board of education and to court hearings to seek help for him, to find alternative schooling for him, searching for ways to protect him, since he couldn't drop out of school, not until he was sixteen, when he eventually did leave school for good. Richard was five years older than me. He dropped out of high school and enrolled in a beauty academy, where he learned to be a hair stylist. Richard said to me the day of George's funeral in 1971 that he couldn't take this anymore. He was speaking about the double whammy of both our father and George dying within a year of each other. I heard later from George's first wife that George had gone out of his way to reach out to Richard when the word got back to him that Richard was definitely gay. I can only imagine what Richard might have thinking about when he made that comment about not being up to handling another death. Was he like me, wondering who would be next? Richard himself would be dead all too soon. Richard was murdered a few years later, in 1974. A man who tried to rob him beat him to death. Whether their encounter started out as sexual or not is still a question in my mind. Nonetheless, I think it's safe to call it a case of gay-bashing. Richard's death deeply affected my mother. Richard was the only one of her children still living with her at the time of his death. He never left home. It took a lot out of her to bury another child, especially since both children died so unnaturally.

My father's reaction to my brother's being gay must have been difficult for both of them, since my father's reputation among Newark's small-time hustlers and crooks was built around his being a man's man. My family, for the most part, handled Richard's homosexuality by not talking about it. Richard compromised by not flaunting his personal life and dressing conventionally, though he wore makeup and plucked his eyebrows and pressed his hair in a style more suitable for a woman. It was a delicate balance, on everyone's part, and Richard played along. None of my brothers would have dared disrespect Richard, out of fear of offending my mother. He was our brother, family.

It wasn't just Richard's death that bothered my mother; it was the way he died and the way the police handled the crime that troubled her, right up to the end of her life. To the police Richard was just another dead fag. They suggested that he had died while turning a trick, which was really offensive to those who knew him, since Richard had worked as a hair stylist all of his life and had more money than he needed. The prejudice of the police offended his gay friends too, many of whom actually did work the streets. Richard was not like that, I heard one of his friends say during the wake, with a mixture of pride and anger. Several of his transvestite friends, decked out in a colorful hodgepodge of male and female finery, came to the funeral and visited our home afterward to convey their condolences to my mother. For years after Richard's death my mother would routinely stop by the police station to ask if there was any progress in capturing her son's killer. They never caught the man who murdered my brother. I don't know if they even tried.

A few months before he died, Richard opened up his own hair salon, and he was feeling rightfully quite proud of his accomplishments. Before he could finish refurnishing his shop, he asked me if he could borrow some money to cover some of the last remaining expenses. I lent it to him without hesitation. I could tell he was uneasy about asking, and I could also see how relieved he was that I didn't hesitate to give him the money. Richard died without my ever once telling him that I loved him; he died too soon. I promised at his funeral that no one I loved would go through life without knowing I loved them. I want to believe that my brother knew the truth even though the words were never spoken. I had to learn to be more open, to not put off the showing of affection, because tomorrow may never come. While I detest all forms of prejudice and have struggled to rid myself of any bias, it would be silly for me to claim that my love for my brother helped me to understand homosexuality. He was family; he was my brother. It's as simple as that.

The giving of money or material gifts shouldn't be discounted as one of the ways to show love. It's an easy way, perhaps a trite way, but it is one way. My mother always gave her many grand- and great-grandchildren birthday and Christmas cards with a few dollars included. I hope they understood that it was the thought that counted, not the amount of cash they received, as she liked to say. One of my mother's favorite sayings was "It doesn't cost you anything to be nice." It also doesn't cost you anything to show your love.

My dead are always with me, but I don't mourn them to the point of being morbid. Over the years I have learned from my study of African traditions to understand what the dead can give to the living. Many people think pre-Christian and pre-Islamic religious life in Africa was built around worshipping inanimate objects, or a spooky belief in ghosts. Traditional African religious values have a lot in common with traditional Asian and pre-Christian European beliefs. The dead, our ancestors, are all around us, inhabiting a spiritual world cojoined to our own. And the dead continue to thrive as long as their descendants remember and honor them. I feel my dead around me all the time and have grown to welcome their protective presence. You can find some of these same concepts in many traditional cultures.

I lived from 1982 to 1983 in Jamaica, where many African traditions are alive and well. It was during a return visit in the summer of 1984 that I received the news of my mother's death. Though I don't have a copy of the telegram telling me that my mother had died, I do have the telegram Betty sent me on May 3 in 1983, three days before my birthday, when I was living in Jamaica. It says "Happy Birthday. Mommas in Hospital. Please Call. Love Betty." My mother had suffered a second stroke, the one that would eventually lead to her death. I did call home and my mother did survive, only to die the following summer.

I have a photograph of myself from when I lived in Jamaica, taken on the roof of the apartment complex in Kingston near the University of the West Indies, where I was teaching and writing after receiving an NEA fellowship. The sky is blue behind me, and there aren't any tall buildings in sight, just clouds. Kingston's few skyscrapers are downtown, a short distance from the university. My hair is long, uncombed, and nappy. And I was so thin! I have had a shaggy beard since the '60s. I once mentioned to my mother that I was thinking about shaving my beard off. No, she said, you look good in a beard. Her compliment startled and thrilled me. I started wearing my hair long and nappy, accented with a short beard, in the '60s. I always assumed she had long since rejected my look as wildly unstylish and embarrassingly militant. She had changed with the times. She always liked to remind us that she was hip. I'm hep, she'd say. In so many small ways during the last decades of her life, my mother let me know that she liked the man I had become.

I have a photograph of Betty, taken by a professional studio photographer, where she sits formally posed. She is classically beautiful, her hair carefully coiffed, her makeup perfect, and her dress modest yet stylish. The photograph dates from a few years after she finished high school in 1961, two years ahead of me. We went to the same high school. I hated following in her footsteps; it grew tiresome always being compared to my perfect sister. When the photograph was taken, she was working downtown in Newark at the Social Security office, a job she held for the rest of her life. When I look at this photograph, I ask myself why this elegant woman seemed to cherish becoming matronly when she settled into being a mother. In her last years Betty's focus was more on her spiritual growth and being a good mother and person than on anything else. Betty, like my mother, was thoroughly religious. Did she want to be like our mother, who by the time we knew her was as simple in all her ways as the gift of a drink of water?

I have no photographs of my mother from when she was young, but I have no doubt that she was a pretty woman, delicate of bone and manner. I do have a picture of my brother George from when he was in his late twenties. People who never knew George, who have only seen this photograph, comment on how good-looking he was. He wasn't vain, but he did have an abundance of self-confidence and the easy bearing of an intelligent man who wasn't afraid of his own allure but was not overtly proud of it either. George could have been a movie star, a leading man, if a black man could have dared to harbor such dreams in the early 1950s. Betty looked up to George, but she thought the world of all of her brothers. She was so proud of me it humbles me still.

Betty told me she never would have forgiven herself if I hadn't made it home from Jamaica in time for my mother's funeral. I should have been the one burdened and made anxious by the possibility of missing my mother's funeral, not Betty.

Betty emerged after our mother's death as the mainstay of the family. She died ten years after my mother, from breast cancer, in 1994. Betty did have at least one bad habit. She started smoking cigarettes in her late or mid-twenties. I don't know how much smoking contributed to her cancer. Usually people develop the habit of smoking in their teens, but I think the ups and downs of her marriage, giving birth to her son Michael, and being the adoptive mother of her husband's two children from his previous marriage, then divorcing, becoming a single mother, took something out of her. Like many parents, she feared failing her only child, her son, Michael. Not that you would have noticed any signs of distress in Betty's demeanor. Her spirit was as typically bright and affirmative as ever. I loved her more than words can say, which is a cliché, I know, yet it says it all. She died on November 13, 1994, ten days before her fifty-first birthday. She was two years and a few months older than me.

Karen probably misses Betty more than the rest of us, because Betty was her best friend, as well as almost a second mother to her. In large families older siblings typically help raise the younger children. In many ways my older brothers did help to raise me. I was raised by a village way before that expression became popular. It's one of the good aspects of coming from a big family, even a poor one. My brothers gave me unsolicited advice, clothes, money. I wouldn't be who I am today without their input.

Betty's death propelled me through my middle-age years, which I take to mean coming to the realization that you probably have fewer years in front of you than behind you. It's not that I was unenthusiastic about growing up; I was just not conscious of the process, what it meant. You have only two choices, ultimately: either you get older or you die. I was committed to the first choice, and by the time I was in my thirties I was searching for a way to live the rest of my life consistent with my values. Of course there are plenty of fifty-year-old teenagers around, and probably an equal number of people too old and set in their ways before their time, but neither of these options ever appealed to me.

I had other older male role models besides my brothers, erudite mentors like the poet Samuel Allen and his brother, the civil rights activist Joseph Allen, and William Couch, a colleague of mine at Howard University, where I taught in the early '80s. So I knew being middle-aged and an adult didn't mean you had to stop having fun and having a hunger for learning more about life. I also knew growing older didn't mean the same thing as slowly gaining some quality of maturity. I asked myself a simple question: When were you happy, when were you most at peace? One response took me back to my childhood, to my family, to my neighborhood. Yes, we were poor, but I grew up with people I could depend upon. My relationship with my sister Betty was crucial to my development. It was because of my rapport with her that I learned to be friends with women, to treat them the same way I wanted any man to treat my sisters. Betty and I were different, yet we were as close as white on rice. People don't have to be alike to get along. It was my sister, not my mother, who shaped my relationships with women. I have always been attracted to women who were close to their brothers, who felt some empathy for men.

After Betty's death I had to step forward. Her son, Michael, needed my help, guidance, and advice. It was the least I could do, what she would have expected of me. Michael once told me how much he missed his mother, and I answered him by saying I wasn't going to get into a debate about who missed her more, him or me. He knew how close his mother and I were. I had to carry on, and he had to do so as well, if for no other reason than to honor his mother's memory. Honoring the people who made your life possible is an act of love. I didn't come this far on my own, so I owe it to my ancestors to give something back, whatever and however I can.

I turned sixty-one in 2006. My father died when he was a mere sixty-three, an age too close for comfort to the age I am now for me to take anything for granted. I want to avoid my father's mistakes. His chief error was mistaking material success for personal fulfillment. It's a typical dilemma, whether you are poor or rich, famous or just your average Joe. I like the quality of life money can bring just as much as the next guy, but the bottom line is this: I want to be a better person at the end and to be at peace with myself. I believe this is what my father missed out on. But this is the death I believe my mother experienced.

My life is very different from my father's not because I am smarter or a better person. I was lucky to be born when I was, so I could take advantage of the gains made by the civil rights movement. I don't take complete credit for the fact that I am not broke, spiritually or monetarily. I escaped poverty, but the scars will always be there as well as the muscle. I once dated a woman who lived in the projects. One day as we were leaving the building where she lived, she said, speaking of her mother and her siblings, whom I had just met: "We only live here to keep it real." We both laughed. It was a good moment. It's a truth people who grew up poor, the ones who make it out of poverty, often talk about. How do you strike the balance? How do you keep it real?

Betty liked to call me a vagabond, since I moved from job to job, city to city, and sometimes even from country to country. I told myself I could settle down anytime I felt like it. Half-consciously I thought that if all else fails, since my mother was dead, and that prospect had played out, I could always go live with my sister when I got too old to wander. Betty's death ended that fantasy. I was on my own, albeit in my mid-forties. I had to build another template. It was about time, some would say. I agree.

One year, emotionally confused and broke, and a few years out of graduate school, I came home from Boston to live with my mother for a few months. My father had been dead around five or six years, my brothers George and Richard around three or four years. I think it was 1979. My mother was living with my brother Charles in a three-family house Charles and I had bought together. So I had a place I could return to, a refuge for renewal, a room of my own albeit in my mother's house.

My mother put me on a curfew; not in so many words, but whenever I left the house toward evening, she would ask me what time I was coming home, reminding me not to come in too late, because I would wake her up, or she wouldn't be able to sleep from wondering and worrying about me if I stayed out too late. I slept in the small den, on a daybed; it became my room, my hiding place. My mother was pleased to have me at home, and I was enjoying myself visiting old friends and family. The front door was a few steps away from the den, and my mother's bedroom was in the back of the house, through two other rooms, yet inevitably if I came home in the early morning, but always well before dawn, she would yell out "Calvin?" as soon as I had closed the front door as quietly as possible behind me. I was thirty-two years old. I wasn't offended to be on a curfew, to have my lifestyle curtailed by my mother, and in fact I laughed about it, still do. I respected her wishes as best I could, and went about my business, which usually meant meeting friends in Manhattan or Brooklyn. It was downright comical, classic sitcom material, never tragic. Picture a scene where a grown man is hanging out with his friends and he suddenly realizes it's near midnight and announces that he has to call his mother to let her know he's safe and on his way home so she doesn't have to wait up for him.

After a few months living with my mother I moved to Washington, D.C., where I lived for several years, teaching and writing, and in 1991 I moved to Chicago. I am glad I had that time at home with my mother. I took her to a couple of jazz clubs in Manhattan, once to hear George Benson, and she had a ball. I took her out to lunch and dinner. I set up my portable typewriter in the living room. I would shout back to her while she was the kitchen, where she usually sat watching soap operas on TV. "Momma, how do you spell . . .?" I would shout. She would patiently spell the word for me, yet typically she'd also remind me that we did have a dictionary in the house.

I could always ask for her help in resolving some grammatical impasse, such as the proper placement of prepositions, because my mother knew the finer points of grammar backward and forward. I'd tease her, for example, shouting, "Momma, where's the newspaper at?" And she'd answer, "It's behind that preposition." She was well educated for a black woman of her generation. She had attended a finishing school, a school that passed for a college for "colored" women in the South of the 1920s. She had been raised middle-class in a relatively comfortable upbringing, though she never really talked about her childhood; it was her fate, or call it what you will, to fall in love with a poor and less educated man and to have eight children with him and remain poor and beholden to him, until he died and her children could take care of her in a manner she deserved. In North Carolina her father had owned a prosperous funeral home; like most American ethnic groups, black people generally bury their dead with their own, which gave black funeral home owners a key economic monopoly. Burying the dead, and to a degree preaching and teaching, provided a steady, respectable, middle-class income for black people in the segregated South and North. In her final years my mother didn't want for anything materially or otherwise. Her surviving children made monthly contributions to her that doubled the small amount of Social Security income she was receiving.

I once asked my mother after my father had passed away how she met Daddy. Secretly, I wanted to know why she married a man who seemed her opposite. We were sitting in the kitchen, as usual, at the then unfashionable 1950s-style Formica table that was the centerpiece of the kitchen. There was a small TV at one end of the table, and an old stove near the back door, across from the sink and cabinets near the always well-stocked pantry. My mother, being a child of the Depression, believed that it behooved her whenever possible to have enough canned goods and other non-perishables on hand to feed her family for a month if need be. She sat across from me and eyed me curiously. My mother didn't like talking about the past, or talking about herself, and only once or twice do I remember her ever mentioning what it was like growing up in the South in the early twentieth century. North Carolina is where my parents first met, courted, and married, against my mother's parents' wishes. She once told me that when she was a young girl she had watched a black man being dragged down the street behind a car with a rope around his neck and attached to the bumper of the car. She told me this story because I had decided to resist the draft during the Vietnam War and had returned my draft card to the draft board. It was her way of warning me not to take white people's sense of justice lightly.

I had bought or borrowed a tape recorder with the goal of collecting stories from my mother's youth. I wanted to create a record of my family's history. I envy people who grew up hearing their grandparents' stories or, better yet, their great-grandparents'. Family stories are more important than DNA. Genes can reveal only the soil you grew up in, not the nutrients that made you possible.

Intent on getting my mother's story, I placed the tape recorder between us on the kitchen table. My mother looked at me like I had lost my mind, though I had forewarned her and asked her permission several times. Why do you want to talk about that old stuff? she asked. She frowned; I smiled, trying to coax her out of her shell. So how did you and Daddy meet? At a dance, she answered, reluctantly. What was it that first attracted you to Daddy? Well, he was a good dancer. I couldn't believe it. "You mean you married a man, ran off with him against your mother's and father's wishes," I asked, "and had eight children by him, and stayed married to him for more than fifty years, all because he could dance?" She stared back at me like I was from another planet.

The best part of hearing this story about my mother and father's courtship was imagining my mother as a young woman going out dancing. This chapter in my mother's life still tickles me. One reason I had difficulty imagining my mother as a young woman is that the earliest photograph we have of her is when she was already in her fifties, and being fifty years old back then meant being fifty years old.

Another time I popped the tape recorder down between us and asked if she had ever heard Louie Armstrong perform live. "Oh, yeah," she said. Her face lit up in a big grin. "Your father and I saw him once." Her smile told me more about jazz history and what Louie Armstrong meant to my parents' generation than I could have ever read in any textbook. My mother was born in 1908, my father the year before. They were teenagers, young adults in the prime of their lives, when Louie Armstrong was hitting his stride with the records and performances that would change and make jazz and American history in the mid- to late 1920s. My parents must have shared some good times, some laughter, some tenderness and love, before the sadness and drudgery set in. But what can children ever understand of their parents' romance, of the coupling that brought them into existence, no matter how many questions they ask? Aren't we all essentially outsiders to other people's interior lives, no matter how close we are to them, no matter how much we probe? Even now I find my parents' relationship incomprehensible. Yet they did stay together, and isn't that an accomplishment worth noting and celebrating?

I think the thirteen years she lived after my father's death in 1970 were some of my mother's happiest. I am glad she had those years. For a while she worked part-time at a local hospital, in the kitchen, of course, where the young people who worked alongside her called her Momma. She liked that and she liked her job. She didn't have to work; she had enough to live off of comfortably. All of her children except for me lived at most a twenty-minute drive from her doorstep. Having Betty and Karen and their children living in the same house with her was a comfort to my mother in her last years.

I was always the dutiful son, writing or calling, and visiting whenever I could. She would forward my mail, since I continued to use Newark as my primary mailing address. I still have a few of the little notes she sent to me, written in her neat penmanship. She always signed off by saying that all the family was well and sent their love, and she always signed her letters, "Love, your mother, Mary B. Forbes," as if I didn't know who she was. I had to have some inkling of who she was in order to find myself. The best way for me to thank my mother is to help someone else. Teaching, my community involvement, being a good friend, a good father and uncle and brother help pay her back.

My mother died before she could fly in an airplane. It was not unusual for my mother's generation not to have flown, just like it was typical of her generation not to make frivolous long-distance phone calls. Where would she have flown to? Vacation meant visiting relatives in Atlantic City, a short bus ride or car ride away. Vacations meant a change of scenery, talking endlessly with relatives before drifting off to sleep while sitting on lawn chairs on their front porch; it meant a change of routine. It didn't mean Paris or catching a Broadway show or walks in the countryside.

As far as we know, she was an only child. I suspect that my mother's birth father was white. Regardless, something happened and her aunt and uncle, the only grandparents I ever knew, raised my mother. My mother's birth mother disappeared from her life until they were both old ladies. My mother never talked about the circumstances of her birth. I didn't know until I was a grown man that the woman I had grown up thinking of as my grandmother was actually my mother's aunt who had raised her. Before her first stroke, yet after my father's death, we found out through a letter from a third cousin on my mother's side (whom I had never heard of either) that my mother's birth mother was alive and living in a nursing home in Richmond, Virginia. A few weeks after the letter arrived, my mother took a train south, with my baby sister, Karen, to Richmond, where my mother met her birth mother—as far as I know, for the first time. Soon afterward, Sadie, as she was named, died. Given my mother's upbringing, is it any wonder she placed such value on holding her family together? *Birth mother* is an awkward phrase, just as awkward as *nonbiological parenting*, but both terms reflect a centuries-old complex reality our society is only now owning up to.

Family history *is* history. Every family has stories to tell, of a family banding together, raising children, nieces and nephews, rather then sending them off to orphanages or abandoning them to the streets or to the state. Children can't raise themselves. These types of stories are not especially African American. Anyone who has read Charles Dickens knows this much is true.

I always give thanks to my ancestors, going back to the first Africans who stepped off the slave ship, survived bondage with their human values intact, and raised their children and subsequent generations to be upright people.

In order to give my father the kudos he deserved for doing his part to keep our family together, I had to be out in the world and gain knowledge of myself and how someone just like me might have lived in another time. My father tried to prosper in this country by his wits rather than the sweat of his brow, tough for any uneducated man, tougher still for an African American, then and now. We were never close. I can't recall ever spending a private moment with my father, except a time when I was over twenty-one, the legal drinking age in New Jersey, when we once had a drink together in a neighborhood bar. It was one of few genuine father-son moments I can recall us ever sharing. Did he know who I was? After I published my first newspaper article, a review of a B. B. King concert, his comments surprised me. I sent a copy to my mother, and months later when I had returned home from Honolulu, where

I had been living, she mentioned that my father had told her that I was writing about myself as much as I was writing about B. B. King. I was amazed he knew anything about me. I did indeed fall in love with the blues once I discovered the music in all its glory. To rephrase a prayer my mother taught us, I had to learn to forgive my father in order to learn to forgive myself. My father was not a stupid man, far from it. But he was a selfish man. Our family's destiny had to be reflected through him, through his triumphs.

Before I left for Jamaica in the summer of 1984, I knew that my mother was dying. I just didn't know when she would make her transition. The second stroke had taken a lot out of her. She had battled back from the first one, in the late '70s, but the second one was a monster. It beat her down, though she fought back like a champion.

I asked Betty whether I should go or stay. Betty encouraged me to go, explaining that I already had my ticket, assuring me that Momma would be okay. Before I left for Jamaica I visited my mother in the hospital, where we talked for what would turn out to be our last time. We were alone in the hospital room. She was quiet and composed, weary, not just from battling death, but from the toll life had taken on her. In time I would go and visit Betty in the same hospital during her last days. It was the same hospital where my mother had worked part-time, the same hospital I used to pass on my way to elementary school.

I took advantage of the moment to ask a question I had wanted to ask my mother for the longest time. Why did you name me Calvin? I asked. What's the matter, she said, don't you like your name? She said the doctor who delivered me was named Calvin and that he asked her if she didn't have a name already picked out for me, would she consider Calvin? I held her hand and chuckled at the sheer strangeness of the story. Who the hell was this doctor dude named Calvin, and why did he want me to carry his name?

All I could do upon reading the telegram from my sister saying that Momma had died was to flop down onto a chair as if I had been sucker-punched and stare off into space. Erna Brodber, the Jamaican writer I was staying with, stood nearby, worried, her face full of concern. We were in the dining area of the house, a sparsely furnished yet comfortable townhouse not far from the University of the West Indies, on a quiet cul-de-sac. The sun was streaming in through the front windows. After I shared what was in the telegram, Erna asked me several times, "Are you all right, Calvin? Are you all right, Calvin?"

"My mother's dead," was all I could think of saying. Then I added, "I finally have to grow up." I said this without thinking, hitting the truth on the head without realizing it. I couldn't retreat to my mother's house ever again.

I am glad I had the opportunity to watch my mother fight against the changes thrust upon her body and mind by the tenacity of her two strokes. Watching her learn to write again was inspiring. She would sit down at the kitchen table and practice writing the alphabet like a schoolgirl. She had a lot of pride. I hope to be as brave as my mother when death comes looking for me. She showed me how to die with dignity, just as she taught me how to live with dignity.

The church I grew up in and attended weekly throughout my adolescence was torn down to make room for a highway after I graduated from high school in 1963. It was later rebuilt a few blocks from its original site, but it was too late for us to reconnect with it, since my family had moved away by then to the other side of town. Betty, my mother, and Karen started attending another church. This would be the church from which my father, my brothers, my mother, and ultimately Betty herself would be buried.

The church stood on a corner lot, with enough pews to seat maybe a few hundred people; it had stained-glass windows on three sides, a full basement with a kitchen, and rooms for meetings and Sunday school classes. It was about the same size as the church I grew up attending. If it was a special service, like the one for Easter, the church could easily be packed tightly with people standing. Ushers dressed head to toe in white would be busying themselves directing people to squeeze in a little closer to make room for someone newly arrived for the service. This was Betty's home away from home. The worst thing any of her siblings could possibly say about Betty was to wonder aloud what she did for fun besides singing in the church choir. She always enjoyed singing and had sung in a girls' singing group as a teen, before she got religious.

For Betty's funeral the church was jammed to the rafters with family, friends, and people from her job and from the church where she had been a mainstay for many years. The preacher talked about how Sister Betty had been as solid as a rock, a boulder for others to lean on, how when the spirit caught Sister Betty, she would dance up and down the aisles, lifted up by the Holy Ghost. This was a side of my sister I didn't know, a sight I would love to have seen. Betty was not the boogying type, at least not in her mature years. I smiled, happy despite the occasion, looking around the church, trying to imagine Betty full of the spirit of the Holy Ghost, losing her self-consciousness as she ran around the church shouting out "Jesus, Jesus!" The church rocked with the singing of the choir, which had turned out in full force to honor my sister. I was deeply moved by the love people I didn't know had for Betty. I sometimes question whether I did enough to find better medical care for my sister. Maybe something could have been done to prolong her life. But her doctors in Newark kept saying the cancer had progressed too far, too quickly.

When the opportunity came for the family to speak, I stood up and made my way to the front of the church. I wanted to address my family, principally the younger children, my grandnieces and grandnephews. I said that after Momma had died I wondered if we could remain a family. Betty had stepped in, I said, and she became the glue that held us together. I wanted to remind them how much my family had meant to me while I was growing up, and that I wouldn't be the man I was without my brothers and sisters, and I named them one by one, recalling words of advice, money lent, kindness delivered. I said it was this sense of family that had sustained black people during and since slavery, despite what they might have heard or read. I asked that we remain a family; then I took my seat again in the pews until the funeral service was over.

I once worked at a temporary job many years ago alongside an older woman. During our conversations she constantly referred to her mother. This woman was old enough to be my grandmother, and listening to her go on and on about her mother, I realized that you never get over your mother, for better or worse. Fathers too, it's true. Ultimately what my mother gave me was her presence. I still want to please my mother and still seek her approval.

Sometimes when I fly home now, I think about how my mother would be proud to know that many years after her death, her children, grandchildren, and great-grandchildren remain a family. I think she would be proud also that I have settled into being a responsible adult, without enlisting too many yawns, at work, among friends, family, and society. I think my father would be proud too.

Tax Time

Peggy Shinner

Sighting

I go to my accountant, this accountant, because he reminds me of my father. He brings him up. I thought of your father last week, he said. He said this to me last week, when Ann and I went to see him for our taxes. He was punching numbers into the computer. We were sitting across his big, messy, mahogany-colored desk. I'm uncomfortable at this desk, spread out like a landmass between us, because I feel like I haven't yet legitimately—with my own income—entered the ranks of the middle class. At fifty-two, I teach fiction writing and martial arts, an unlikely combination that might make me interesting at dinner parties but provides little in the way of reliable income, and less in the way of job status, and my shabby W-2s prove it. But I can't claim to be anything other than middle-class either. I'm a middle-aged, middle-class woman who inherited her working-class-turned-middle-class father's money earned, first, from owning a laundromat, and later, selling furniture seven days a week out of chintzy model homes. Really? I say to Rick, soft-pedaling my interest because I don't want to appear overeager and, worse, needy. It feels like a sighting. Rick's seen my father roaming around on the edges of his memory, and he files a report. I wait for him to offer up his choice morsel. It's not that he teases me, but he doesn't deliver right away either. He has a comic's sense of perfect timing. Or maybe it's just that at the same time he mentions my father he's also perusing my interest and dividend statements—one of which is from Calvert, a socially responsible investment firm that, to my consternation, hasn't done so well lately, meaning I've squandered my father's money for the dubious idea of responsible investing and my accountant is about to nail me for it—and his recollection will unfold in good time.

To meet with him, I drive to Northfield, a suburb thirty-five minutes from my house, in good traffic, every year in early spring. Rick does my taxes, makes me penalty-proof, talks about my father. If I pay too much for him to do my taxes, as a friend once implied, a friend who said that if I went to her accountant I would pay only half of what I pay now, this is what I'm paying for. I pay to keep my father alive. The price this year is $365, up ten dollars from last. Some people go to synagogue and say the Kaddish in memory of their loved one. I go to my accountant. He's one of the few people left who remembers him, who has memories of my father separate and different from mine. Every year he resurrects a memory, and even if he resurrects the same memory, or a version of the same memory year after year, I appreciate it. His memories become my own.

Or that's what I tell myself. I'm proprietary. I reassemble all the far-flung pieces of my father, including the ones he gave to someone else, because somewhere, in the deepest part of me, I feel they are rightfully mine, even if, in another part of me, I know that that's impossible.

I was telling somebody about our poker game, Rick says, handing me back the statements. Rick, who used to be my father's accountant, used to play poker with a bunch of *alter kockers*, rough-edged self-made Jews, one of whom was also my father; they were all, at the very least, thirty years Rick's senior. Rick is rough-edged too, even though he wears expensive though casual, perfectly hung pants and matching, muted shirts, possibly Italian. He has slim hips, a flat stomach, a belt of polished leather. His tush is small and rounded. He probably works out, at 5:30 in the morning, with other overworked, type-A overachievers. Referring to some arcane, and to his mind, stupid regulation in the tax code, he calls George Bush a fucking moron.

Poker

Was he a good player? I say. Despite my effort at nonchalance, at the mere mention of my father, I'd felt a surge of tears, quickly squelched, and on his behalf, fished for a compliment instead. My father was a good player; I already knew that. Or, I knew that as a nine-year-old girl knew it, when he always beat her at gin. He would keep track of the cards I picked up from the discard pile, and when it was his turn, never toss out anything of the same suit. He was not one of those fathers who let his daughter win. Rick answers by telling me what a good player *he* was, not that I'm bragging he says, don't take this the wrong way, and then adds that my father was sharp as well. Your father knew how to play, he says knowingly, noddingly. They were the good players, and the others were pathetic. But he kept quiet, he says, because who was he, the young one, the upstart, to say anything to these guys. Your father was disgusted with them, he says, suggesting that at one time or another my father probably gave someone—Maury Zitlin, Irv Witt, Fox Williger, Lou Singer—a mouthful. I have no trouble imagining it: quick to blow up and slow to forget, my father ended up in many angry confrontations. Still, I take posthumous pride in his skill and reputation, as if the shine from his card-playing acumen has rubbed off on me and I'm basking in the light of a revered tradition.

Aunts

Relax, Rick says. I'm nervous about my taxes. Now that I organize my aunt's taxes, my great-aunt's, who this tax season turned ninety-eight, I can't seem to keep track of my own. Rick has an aunt also. Ten years younger than my aunt, this aunt has eleven nieces and nephews to look after her affairs and pay for her expenses. She doesn't have a cent. Every year we talk about our aunts, about their bilious temperaments, about the expense of caretakers, about how they, the aunts, live on and on, enlivened by their meanness. Both our aunts are sharp as tacks, which they don't hesitate to stick into you. They've moved his aunt out of her apartment, he says; now she lives in a palace, the word practically exploding from his lips. She's patently ungrateful, he implies.

My aunt lived like royalty too. This, according to my father. He used to call her The Queen. Widowed, wealthy, martyred, entitled, she sat on her throne in her thirty-fourth-floor apartment above Lake Shore Drive, watching her investments accrue interest. My father, after the furniture business dried up, worked as a cashier at a car wash. Your father called me The Queen, she told me, as if it was the nicest thing ever said to her. Now, however, twenty years later, her investments have taken a dive, and she's lost her title.

When his aunt complains, Rick says, he threatens her with the death stick. He holds it over her head. I see it materialize, a wand of great potency, making its final and glorious descent. Ann and I laugh. Where can we get one? Somewhere in the conversation I let out that my aunt's name is Etta, and he, in a triumph of coincidence and one-upsmanship, says that his is Yetta, Yetta Etis. Etta Fefferman, née Zaslowsky. Yetta Etis, née Garfinkel. Can you tell they're Jews? he says. Our names are appropriately assimilated, mine perhaps overly so. I know of one other Jew named Peggy and imagine a small society of others, '50s-born Jewish girls—their parents aggressively American—named Margaret, Megan, Maggie, Peggy, for girls who came over on another boat. As for Shinner, my father's name was originally Shinitzky, but a month before his marriage, at the urging, I suspect, of my mother, who did not want to be saddled with such a foreign-sounding name, suggestive of shtetls and head coverings and garlic, he changed it. Rick's last name is Winer.

He's still talking about his aunt. Have you ever noticed, he says, how they—he means old people—take out their keys long before they get home and jangle them in their hand? He says the word *jangle* with particular distaste. Yes, yes, Ann and I say, in a rush of recognition. Etta does that—or used to, when she went out—too. Across from me in the passenger seat, blocks (if not miles) from her apartment, she'd fish in her purse for her keys, while I looked on with mute and growing annoyance. The elderly, it seems, prepare for their arrival long before they get there. It's as if the trip is over as soon as you begin the return, and that's the part we can't stand. The foreshortening. I hate that jangling, Rick says, and in that moment we hear it: the far-off clanging of a distant gatekeeper. If I ever jangle my keys, he says, shoot me.

Finally, we go back to the taxes and Rick reassures me that I'm prepared for our appointment, I have everything he needs, and if not, if I've made some terrible mistake or omission, we'll fix it. He has pale skin, blue eyes, washed-out red hair. His trim beard is red and gray. He seems, simultaneously, younger and older than I am. In his swiveling leather chair, he could be a father, a brother, a friend. He grew up, or so I remember, in the same neighborhood as I did, went to the same grammar school, Hannah Greenbaum Solomon, was possibly even a member of the same congregation, A. G. Beth Israel. But while my house, a one-story ranch, seemed simple and straightforward, as if, by its very layout, it could harbor no intrigue, his, a two-story, red-brick Georgian, formidable and silent, was full, in my mind at least, of secrets. We'll fix it, Rick says, with a smile that suggests nothing, in that instant, is insurmountable, and I feel my anxiety, like dead skin, slough off, melt away.

Signs

Rick reminds me of my father in a physical way too. Every year he gets older. He's getting older in the way that certain Jewish men get older. I can see it, sitting across the desk, the way you can see it only when you see somebody once a year. Over the weekend a colleague of Ann's died. He'd just had surgery on his Achilles tendon, and was in the shower when he called out to his cousins. Within three minutes he was dead. Did he see it coming? Did a storm gather overhead? I can see it coming on Rick. I can see the years accruing, the fatigue setting in, the sorrows and disappointments, a certain Semitic sag of the face and chin, leavened by a sharp wit, good wine, an occasional par on the golf course, accomplished children, an Italian wife, and the fact that with Ozzie Guillen as manager of the White Sox everything has changed.

I didn't see it coming on my father. I refused to see it. It took me by surprise. I saw him once a week, and the week before he had his stroke, we had breakfast together at the Barnum and Bagel restaurant, where, over lox and onions, he told me that the day before his hand had gone numb and he'd dropped a cup of coffee, a sure sign, I knew, I knew even then, if I'd wanted to see it.

Fingers

I notice Rick's fingers. They're wound around the pencil as he scribbles some figures from the computer. They're short and stubby, like my father's, and impeccably groomed. Like his face, they look pale. Does he get his nails done? Is that a vanity he permits himself? My father had a manicure once when he was seeing Rose, and at the time I saw it as jumping ship. He was, by slapping on some nail polish, trying to abandon his class for Rose's, Rose, a woman who subscribed to the symphony and tried to break his use of double negatives. He was also dandying himself up, something, I wondered, if he'd ever done for my mother when she was alive. When he told me, with an impish shrug of his shoulders, that he'd fallen asleep at the symphony, I was pleased.

Rick puts down the pencil. He punches in a few more numbers and furrows his face as he attacks the keys. My father never sat at a computer. He counted on his fingers, he computed in the air. His fingers would paw the imaginary numbers in front of him until they reached a conclusion. Sometimes, when food got stuck in his mouth, he'd run his thumb and forefinger over his dental plate to dislodge it. He seemed to make a show of it, like his thumb was a fine-tuned instrument. He took a certain pride in being crude. My fingers, like theirs, are short and stubby too.

Gains and Losses

Perhaps Rick, certified public accountant, is like a father. The tax man, before whom every year you spread out your papers, your receipts, your tattered scribblings and calculations. You show him your gains and losses, your business expenditures, your list of charitable contributions and deductions, and with equal parts wizardry and math, he tells you what it all amounts to, how it all adds up. Look, you say, or want to say, how much I gave away last year, to the Crossroads Fund, Lambda Legal Defense, the Lesbian

Community Cancer Project, the Chicago Women's Health Center, Amnesty International, Grinnell College (your alma mater), WBEZ (your local public radio station), the National Coalition for the Homeless, Housing Opportunities and Maintenance for the Elderly (HOME), an organization for which, ever since your father died and they came and took his furniture (which the Salvation Army rejected), you've always had a soft spot. Look, $763, in spite of your limited, patched-together income, which, minor consolation, lands you in the lowest tax bracket. Not to mention (but you do, you have to, for the deduction) the in-kind donations—household goods, books, clothes, recycled birthday presents—you made to the Brown Elephant resale store. You want to impress him with your generosity, which you well know isn't generous enough. Is it generous if you're not giving anything up? You seek his approval, not as a client but as a child. Have I donated enough money? Have I done good works? Will I be inscribed in the book of life? You own a house that's appreciated over ten times its purchase price, have a lover of twenty-six years, march down State Street in protest of the war in Iraq, teach six-year-olds to punch and kick, and juggle two, three, sometimes four part-time teaching jobs; your life is an improbable mix of stability, good fortune, hazard, and marginality. Did you sell any stories this year? Rick asks, and though you did, how can you tell him you got paid with two free copies of a journal he's never heard of? You sink, crestfallen in your chair; you're a failure, you think he thinks, but he turns his blue eyes back to the computer and does his best to hide his condemnation.

My father—my real father, not Rick, the ersatz father, the once-a-year stand-in—thought I could do no wrong, as my aunt, The Queen, once said. In his eyes—by turns warm, mischievous, weary, wounded—my approval rating was 100 percent. He approved of everything he knew about me, but he didn't know everything. He didn't know, for instance, that Ann is my primary beneficiary, that down the road she would inherit what's left of the money he left me, that she would get everything I've got. That everything I've got, sixteen years after my father's death, is less than I had.

Gathering

Rick's father died a long time before mine did. Maybe he's looking for a father too. Maybe that's why he played cards with a bunch of *alter kockers* thirty years his senior, most of whom didn't know a thing about poker. None of them, singly, reminded him of his father, but together they formed a quorum. Maybe that's why he talks about my father. Together we can conjure up a father between us. We can whistle one up. An old Jewish guy, grizzled, gruff, argumentative, proud, vulnerable, savvy, who once a year makes his congenial appearance around the tax table, who, with little prodding, deals a hand or two from the deck. The fathers gather together, mine, Rick's, Rick himself, who decorates his office walls with the emblems of fatherhood—photos of his children smiling out at him, two sons and a daughter; a picture of his radiant, dark-haired wife; finger paintings, temperas, a mixed-media construction of a dinosaur in Jurassic Park; a certificate honoring him as Little League coach of the year; framed ticket stubs to a White Sox playoff game, where, I imagine, he and his kids went together—and surrounded by these ghosts and trinkets, we turn to the year's evidence and do the taxes.

Refund

Do I see it coming? Do I see the end? Not in the foreseeable future, but how far can I see ahead? I see tax season after tax season, year after year of visits with Rick. Two years ago Ann had breast cancer; a month ago we had a car accident and landed in a ditch. My aunt lives on, but she tells me she won't see her next birthday. She's been saying this for years, perhaps to thwart the gods above, and I used to reassure her, but now I know better than that. My father had a stroke on the Dan Ryan Expressway, and four weeks later he was dead. Rick is still running the numbers. Ann and I sit murmuring to each other on our side of the desk. I suck on a toffee from the candy dish. Where should we go for lunch? she says. Finally Rick looks up from the computer and smiles at me again. Good news, he says.

You're getting a refund. Great, I say, relieved and greedy. Now that I don't have to pay, I wonder if I'll get a windfall.

About two hundred dollars, he says.

Two hundred dollars?

A minute ago I was worried about paying, and now I'm disappointed, like it's not much more than loose change.

Rick rises from his desk. We gather together our papers. Maybe the White Sox are for real, I say, but Rick shakes his head as if to say he's beyond excitement. I'll mail you the forms, he says, accompanying us out of the office. He pats his hands on his pants. Call if you have any questions, but of course he means about our returns. I'm waiting, but he makes no mention of my father, and in this moment I know, as I know every year, that this is about taxes, and that Rick is my accountant, and that if we have, ever so briefly, conjured up a father, that father has been sucked back into the bottle and the bottle has been capped, and now the daughter, with her shopping bag full of the year's accounting, the promise of a modest refund, and a toffee wrapper crumpled in her pocket, has been sent back home. We shake Rick's hand. Then Ann and I head to the hallway, and for a second I feel that drop in my stomach as the elevator pulls us down.

Reuniting

Maud Lavin and Locke Bowman

The Dinner

I was angry. Locke had said he'd call me around 5:00 when he got
to his hotel. By 5:30, though, I hadn't heard from him. Impatient,
I almost decided to cancel, and had to catch myself—the feelings
were too strong for such a short wait. It was as if some pocket
of hot anger from the breakup twenty-two years before was still
there. Or maybe I was afraid and looking for an excuse to get out
of the dinner. Fifteen minutes later he did call from the hotel—his
plane from Chicago had been late. I was still irritated. A woman, I
thought, would've called earlier from the airport and not kept me
wondering. I didn't cancel, but I made him come to my neighborhood. Let him have the aggravation of running around the city.
Anyway, Carroll Gardens was a good place for a reunion, one of
Brooklyn's oldest neighborhoods, so Old World that people still
sometimes spoke Italian in its restaurants and cafés. New World,
too. At that time of year, whole blocks were decked out for Halloween. The gardens in front of the row houses were lit up with
plastic goblins and planted with drugstore tombstones, and some
emitted piped-in music, groans, and cries. Walking over to the
restaurant, I was suddenly pleased by the idea of seeing Locke. I
imagined us wandering around after dinner looking at the ghosts
and lights.

I had asked Maud to dinner on impulse. I told myself it was no big
thing—a way to fill a three-hour expanse of time that otherwise

would be spent reading in a New York hotel room; a chance to touch base with an old friend, whom I'd seen only on one uninspired occasion in the last twenty years. But the impulse came from a deeper place. What I really wanted was to see my past. Maud was my age. Went to my college. Knew me, remembered me. At forty-two and recently divorced, I was in search of friendship. Crossing the Brooklyn Bridge by cab in the mid-October night, I had a half-melancholic sensation of space—and time—condensing. Maud in her life. Me in mine. Coming closer.

I had the cabdriver let me out a few blocks from the restaurant so I could walk the last bit of distance. I was surprised to be nervous. Glad to breathe in the cold October air.

Inside, I scanned the restaurant tables through the dark. Maud had arrived first—seeking tactical advantage, I suspected—and saw me looking for her before I saw her, seeing me. Maud. Fuller, larger, draped in an elegant-looking sweater, wearing glasses with slightly imposing rims, the faintest trace of gray in her dark hair.

She'd gotten to her feet and stood by the table, not approaching me, as I walked toward her. Her standing seemed a measured gesture of respect for our remeeting. We embraced like well-intentioned strangers, upper halves only. We both looked great, we said.

We talked. Awkwardly at first. As you'd expect. She's working with so and so. No, I don't keep up with him anymore. Haven't seen him since . . . Maud let me know her life featured book contracts, lunches with magazine editors, dinners with the guy she was seeing, manuscript editing. I have a writing project too, I said, a book review for a quarterly literary magazine. My pay is I get to keep the reviewer's copy of the book. I told the story as a self-deprecating joke. Maud didn't smile. I remembered. Maud does not truck with self-deprecating humor. She expects the best from people.

It was when the check for dinner arrived that I started to relax. Maud reached into her purse, pulled out a twenty, and plunked it between us on the table—preempting my unease about whether to offer to pay. "This is for my share," she said. She leaned toward me, wagging her finger in mock severity, "I'm going to the bathroom. And I expect change from this when I get back." I watched her walk toward the ladies' room, liking her.

Over coffee she told me that she read the horoscopes daily. She remembered my college interest in astrology, how I'd bought texts and tables to chart out horoscopes. I'd forgotten that. "I read for the encouragement," she said. "They talk about love and work, things that everybody thinks about every day. So they always seem to matter. And, besides, they're fun. It's a break at the beginning of the day."

We didn't much discuss our own shared past. I told her one thing, though, something I'd meant to say to her: "I've always looked back on our relationship with fondness," I said. "We were generous and sweet to each other, even though we were young and hurt each other because of that. Our relationship is a happy memory for me, something I like about my past."

Maud has these beautiful dark eyes, shaped like almonds and shiny with intelligence. Her skin is very fair, and smooth and clear. "I agree," she said. "I've felt that way too. We were both sweet to the core—most of the time." She laughed. Looking at Maud's eyes (as clear as ever, on the other side of her glasses) and seeing the shape of her face and her soft skin, it seemed as if twenty-plus years hadn't gone by, as if we had wandered out to dinner from our college dorms. I was startled. For an instant I lost track of where I was.

It was time to go. "You've got to see the Halloween decorations around here; I'll show you." She led me out into the late evening and down First Place, where orange, black, and yellow lanterns and goblins proliferated to stunning proportions, rivaling the most garish Christmas display. Maud laughed when I said I was staggered.

"I told my mother I was having dinner with you tonight," Maud said. "She was pleased. She said to say hi."

"Your mother used to hate me."

"She didn't hate you. She hated the fact that we were having sex.

"I haven't forgotten the sex," Maud continued. "How could I? I had my first orgasm with you."

"Yes. Right." Had I forgotten that too? Maud always had known how to leave me speechless. I felt a sudden tingling itch to make more orgasms with her.

So, half a block later—another impulse—I asked her where her apartment was. "Woodhull Street, isn't it?"

"It's two blocks that way," she said, gesturing. "Here," she added, steering us in the opposite direction, "you can almost always get a cab on Clinton Street."

We walked for a bit in silence.

"My horoscope for today said I would renew an old friendship. So it's come true. I was hoping it would," she said. She must have wanted to soften the rejection. It was kind of her, and I was touched. I put my arm around her as we walked. Feeling nice, aware of her.

When we got to Clinton Street a cab came along with disappointing promptness. After I'd hailed it, I hugged her, then kissed her, right on the lips. Felt her startled by that, but not pulling back. And a moment later I was in the taxi being whisked away.

I'd expected to stay in the past with Locke. I'd thought we'd talk at dinner about the adventures we'd had in college and what had happened since that time to college friends, with the usual obligatory updates about ourselves. I'd thought we'd have a pleasant but distant time. But I was drawn in. He'd always been sexy. He was still good-looking and I appreciated that, but he was also interesting in ways I couldn't have predicted when we were younger. I knew he'd become a lawyer. I found out that now he was working for a nonprofit organization that opposed the death penalty and fought for prisoners' rights. He explained that he was free to choose cases to set precedents as well as to help individuals. Before this, he had worked his way through various lawyering jobs, including slaving away in a corporate law firm and, more happily, serving the Harold Washington mayoral administration until he'd finally come into his own, though he hadn't put it that way. But in a challenging, modest, and steady way, he could and did contribute to change. This was someone with whom I wanted to be friends. It seemed like so many of us in our forties had gotten less idealistic. Focusing of necessity on our retirement accounts seemed to have drawn our attention away from the public good. I still tried to contribute politically, to work occasionally on welfare rights issues, for instance, but I worried that I couldn't really afford to take that time away from bill-paying work. Locke, though, had managed to stick to his ideals and even earned a living making them concrete. Maybe for this reason our conversation seemed more to the point than others I'd had recently. More mature somehow. Which is funny, since mature is not how I'd remembered Locke or myself.

As for the kiss later, I felt a little embarrassed. After all, he'd mentioned that he was seeing someone in Chicago, and I was seeing someone in New York, so it didn't seem quite right. Not quite wrong though, either, as if our history gave us some prior claim to touch each other when we wanted to. Who knows what prerogatives our bodies still honor that our minds have forgotten? I admit, I was glad he kissed me. I knew Locke—or at least a key aspect of him that I'd bet was still there—and I sensed that along with that thinness (had he gotten even thinner since college?) and the asceticism of his long work hours there was that same devilish-eyed grin, the same lust, the same love of surprises. In a way, I would've been insulted if he hadn't made a pass at me. But a kiss was one thing, going further was another. My drawing the line had been quick. There was no way I was saying yes to his bid to get us to my apartment. I was not going to be a one-night adventure for Locke.

I hoped we'd be long-distance friends. I wondered if we'd been too open, and what we would say to each other now, or if there'd be one of those long silences. But Locke, who had often played it cool with phone calls at eighteen, now at forty-two apparently was much less inhibited. He e-mailed right away.

Date: 29 Oct 1996
From: Locke Bowman
To: Maud Lavin
Subject: It was nice

to see you on Sun. night. You look great (exactly the same).   I like your neighborhood. You should invest in sunglasses before they start decking out for Christmas. Let's do it again sometime.

Locke.

Date: 29 Oct 1996
From: Maud Lavin
To: Locke Bowman
Subject: You looked

great too, and exactly the same. I do not look exactly the same—I'm plumper, but I'm managing to sail into my forties with attractiveness and health intact, so I feel pretty good. And I plan, God willing, to continue to be an outrageous flirt well into my eighties. It was fun and uncanny to see you. I think we hit the nail on the head when we said that at 30 we were more different from ourselves than around 20 but now are in essence the same. Good to know we still both have preserved our kindness at the center.

Fondly—Maud

Date: 30 Oct 1996
From: Locke Bowman
To: Maud Lavin
Subject: uncanny

is just the word, I think, to describe the experience. It's more complicated than just being more like our post-adolescence selves than we were ten years ago. We've recaptured some of our comfort with ourselves (is that right?), but we've also been through twenty-some more years of living, which yields much more resonance than we had as kids. We're more there, I mean. So, I would say definitely "uncanny" is just the word. Better than a college reunion.

Don't stop flirting, Locke.

— ✳ —

I was content to leave it at that. Maud and I had separately traveled a full generation since our college days together. There's something in that. Whoever we were at age twenty, we'd now had two more decades in which to become someone new—or, more accurately, to go on becoming ourselves. This was (if you reckon by the length of a human life) a great expanse of years to have come between us. How extraordinary that a single thread of spirit continued to unite us with our younger selves. And what a humming pleasure to recognize and be recognized by an old friend. It was so much more than just a feat of memory. I was glad to have seen Maud again.

It's uncommon, for many of us, to encounter someone other than family who knew us when we were young. These are mobile times; jobs change, locations shift. Work sweeps us along and we barely look up. And yet, though we might forget this, we exist not just in space but over time. So to encounter an old friend is to be reminded of another dimension in ourselves. I was grateful.

As for the kiss, I didn't give it much thought. It had been an impulse, after all, and I had no expectation it would lead anywhere.

— * —

I called my friend Kim and told her all the details, which I tried to put in a harsh light. "I'm glad he doesn't live in New York," I said. "I know we'd get involved, and he's just too unpredictable. How could I ever trust him?" Kim laughed, "Are you saying it's OK for you to kiss him, but not for him to kiss you?" I laughed back, letting that one go. I hoped I was being unfair, but I wasn't sure. After all, he was divorced and dating, just as I was. So he was entitled to look around, right? Or was he? I didn't really know what his deal was in Chicago.

If we were younger, I might've been more blunt, asked him what was going on between him and the woman he was seeing. But that kind of probing wasn't something I could do lightly or easily now. I was older and more wary. And if I ever forgot, I expected my girlfriends, who had been around the block a time or two themselves, to remind me or at least to help me stop and think. As for the dinner with Locke, I was grateful simply to reconnect in subtler ways now and with some safe distance, amazed that we'd had great conversation after all this time, glad to feel some friendship. At this point in my life, I was used to looking for reasons to hesitate with men. And when I did take risks, they tended to be with men I knew I wouldn't be getting serious with. Knowing that Locke was dating someone in Chicago was enough for me to hold my distance.

I reminded Kim of one of my favorite dating rules: "I don't trust men and I'm not about to change." Kim responded, parodying her own role of the helpful friend, "Oh yes, right, that's the spirit, stay tough, and whatever you do don't smile at anyone or pet any dogs or say hi to strangers on the street either." Easy for her to say. She didn't have to smile at anyone, strange or not. She was married.

After

In the weeks after our dinner I carried Locke around with me—certain days more than others. One early November morning, when I was slated to work in Scarsdale, I woke up to quiet. Looking at the pressed tin ceiling as always, I thought of how I loved this old Brooklyn house and sleeping up high in my apartment on the top floor. But five minutes later I was barely out of the bathroom when Jeanne, my landlady, called. She'd be by after work to look at the perpetual ceiling leak in the front. This was an old story. She'd come up two or three times a week, as if the leak were her garden to tend, rarely calling first, talking nonstop, nosing around. Sure, I said this time, but I'll be out. Out where? In Scarsdale, meeting with an art collector I'm working for, I felt obligated to answer for some reason. Looking around the apartment to see if I should hide anything from Jeanne, it hit me that this was no way to live at forty-two. Locke, I pictured in a house he owned, paying his mortgage on time. No renting, no landlady. Out of spite, I imagined it bland, like the midwestern tract housing down the street from my childhood home in Canton, Ohio. Squat, colonial style, flat and brick with new-looking white columns out front. Geraniums.

This kind of comparison only served to bring out the insecurities I had about my current life. Why wasn't I more settled, richer, thinner? Married. I had this idea of where I should be in middle age, an image that had been born in the 1950s when I'd been a child watching *Lassie* on TV. As outdated as it was, that blurred snapshot somewhere at the back of my mind actually *did* have a green lawn, a house, a picket fence, and two kids, a boy and a girl. In the corner, there was my husband in a suit coming home from work. And was that me at the front door in an apron? Did every woman my age have a similar snapshot in their mental scrapbook? In the decades since *Lassie*, maybe I'd managed to update the picture some. I'd erased the apron and added a home office instead. Still, there it was. And here I was, nowhere near it.

On the way to the subway, I stopped for tea and a chocolate chocolate-chip muffin to fortify myself on the long trip to Scarsdale and then immediately felt guilty about rewarding myself with food. Enjoyed the chocolate high, though. Once in Scarsdale, I was met by Stanton, the fifty-something financier who'd hired me to do a book on one part of his art collection, European prints from the 1920s. When Stanton started showing me all the gadgets in his car, I found myself telling him the story of seeing Locke just to shut him up. Stanton had gone to Harvard as we had, though some years before us, so he saw a distant connection to himself in the story. But when I described Locke's work against the death penalty with admiration, Stanton laughed dismissively. "Pretty specialized!" Subject shut. We spent the rest of the afternoon going through his print collection, while I secretly wondered what Locke's work was that day.

On the way back into the city, though, relieved the enforced politeness of the afternoon was over, I also was sick of thinking about Locke. I knew some things in early middle age. My life wasn't so bad, for one. For another, I'd made myself uncomfortable by comparing us and fantasizing that Locke's life was better than mine. I knew the contrast I'd imagined said more about my reality than his. Or what was missing from my reality. Security, for one. I was cobbling together too many part-time jobs—working for Stanton, teaching at N.Y.U., editing book manuscripts, writing for magazines, and none of them was secure or paid a lot either. I rented, didn't own my apartment. But there was a lot I liked about my life too. I loved to write, for instance, and preserved some time each week for my own writing. I had great friends like Kim. Thinking it over, I decided my life wasn't perfect, but then, I suspected, neither was Locke's. And I was grateful for much of mine. I left Locke on the Scarsdale train.

College

College girlfriend. It was a happy memory. Past. Distant. Yet part of
the deep texture of things gone by. If someone would have asked me
about whom I'd gone out with in college, I'd have given a wry smile.
Maud. Who even knew what had brought us together? I don't believe we ever asked ourselves that question. We were kids. We fused
together effortlessly—or at least that's how I chose to remember it.

And why hadn't I married Maud? Marry Maud? I'd have said,
well that was impossible. We were so young. And Maud and I,
we'd just fallen into place with each other. Happily, seamlessly.
But had I even chosen it? And then, of course, neither of us had a
clue of what we wanted to become. Somewhere near the end of
college, being with Maud and "growing up" started to seem like
opposing ideas. And I opted for growing up.

But I treasured the memory of our romance even now, years
later, when growing up had turned out so very differently than I
could have imagined.

I remembered. I first met Maud in 1972 in Harvard's Freshman
Union. It was always a decibel or two louder there than in any
other dining hall on campus. Freshman anxiety. Fourteen hundred
of us—barely not children—each one crying for attention, some
shrilly. Not an easy place.

By the middle of second semester, I had collected an assort-
ment of friends: P. K., my roommate, charismatic even then, a
lover of Broadway musicals and old cinema; M. B., only 16, a musi-
cal prodigy; J. K., socialist, theorist with laughing eyes. Allies, we
would sit together at a table off in one corner. Since I believed I
was a philosopher, I said little. I smoked filterless Camels, drank
coffee, and imagined the motivations of those who did speak.

One evening in May, Maud sat down at our table, directly
opposite me.

I had seen her before. Had probably talked to her, in fact. Her
musician-roommate knew M. B., so she knew him. And, lately, I
knew her, sort of. She was pretty, with an unwavering gaze. Men
greatly outnumbered women in our class. It was not a common
thing to be faced with one at the dinner table. She unnerved me.

I believe that she contrived to finish eating and stand up to leave just as I did. We walked out together (my friends tactfully melted away) into a heartbreaking early-spring night. It was perfect. I expected her to peel off, have some other plans. She didn't.

"You're not as smart as you think you are, you know."

"What?" I was too surprised to be angry.

"Michael says you're smart, though. And he's probably right. Except you never say anything, so who knows."

"Maybe I don't have anything to say." I had stopped to stare at her. Astonished.

"Maybe you should have something to say."

"Maybe you should stop trying to pick a fight with me. I don't even know you." I was trying to remember the last time I'd gotten in an argument with somebody about something personal.

Then she softened suddenly. "It's belligerence," she said, looking straight at me. "Natural belligerence. I have three brothers."

"Oh." I was an only child.

She said that her brothers were all great. If I wanted to be friends with her, I'd better not criticize her brothers.

No problem.

Which was not to say we would be friends.

Nobody's suggesting we're friends, I assured her. She seemed to talk in code. I couldn't figure her out. But her eyes continued to sparkle, and her skin looked very soft, almost translucent.

We walked down by the Charles River, over the Anderson Bridge, toward Storrow Drive.

"I want to go someplace. Like maybe to Walden Pond. I think this road maybe goes to Walden Pond."

I had no idea. But I did know how to hitchhike. Owing to her looks, it didn't take long to get a ride, which deposited us somewhere beyond the Boston suburbs shortly after nightfall. It was chilly wherever we were. And there was no traffic at all.

"Don't think we're going to have sex, because we're not."

"Maud, who said anything about sex?"

"I have a boyfriend. He goes to Yale and he's very smart."

"Well, I don't have a girlfriend, and I don't think we're going to have sex."

"You're probably wishing. I can tell."

I didn't say anything. I would have gladly consented to sex. There had been an aura of opportunity about the whole evening.

"To have sex with me, we would have to be friends first. And even then we might only be platonic. I'm not a promiscuous person."

We ended up spending the night at Andover, where she'd gone to high school. It had been far too late to start hitchhiking back, and we were completely stranded on that empty stretch of highway well out of Boston. Maud called one of her former teachers, who was not pleased but picked us up and loyally and firmly deposited us at her brother's dorm anyway. We slept, each on the floors of separate dorm rooms, which felt small and safe after all those months in college.

The next day we took the bus back to Boston. Side by side, I felt her shoulder touch mine. She was quiet for a time.

"We might be friends," she said. "But don't count on it."

I felt that I would like to be friends.

In the days that followed, Maud kept turning up. I'd see her at the Union. In the evening, I'd look up from my reading desk at Lamont Library, startled that she was standing at my shoulder waiting for me to notice her. I developed a sense for her travels through the week. And if she didn't appear where I expected her to, I'd feel a stab of loss, fear almost.

I didn't see this as falling in love. I did know that my feelings about Maud were complicated. I'd get so caught up in the figuring out of Maud—her peculiar way of talking, her brook-no-nonsense eyes—that I'd forget the part about wanting to sleep with her. And then (midway through some conversation) *that* would come up again, a hard shock.

Eventually, in the dark one night in front of her dormitory, I kissed her. Her mouth was surprisingly small and soft. And her tongue slipped between my lips for just an instant before she pushed away and ran upstairs.

Walking back to my own dorm, I felt giddy. When I got to my room, the phone was already ringing.

"I still have a boyfriend, you know." She said that without a "hello."

"OK, maybe I don't anymore. I'm a little confused right now," she added when I didn't say anything.

"Well, I guess I wish you didn't have a boyfriend."

"Really?"

"Yeah."

"I liked kissing you, Locke."

"Me too."

"But don't count on anything. You don't even really know me."

We didn't have sex together until after she'd announced that the boyfriend from Yale was gone. "He was only really interested in how smart we were. I told him just being smart wasn't enough. You have to have fun. Do things. Be ambitious."

When we did make love, it was hard and fast. We both came. We were breathless afterward. Staring at each other, almost in shock.

"You better not do this with anyone else, Locke."

"Don't worry, Maud, I won't," I said.

Breaking Up

Locke had this glint, this up-for-anything look. That's what I'd first noticed about him in the Freshman Union. That and a bounce in his walk. He was always carrying books, a serious student. But when he looked straight at me, his eyes gleamed. That's why I'd sat at his table that spring, to see what would happen.

By that summer, if we spent even one night apart, we missed each other. But we kept separate apartments. Locke and I were so young—nineteen and eighteen—that it hadn't even occurred to us to live together. Our parents would not have approved. For both of us, it was the first summer we hadn't lived at home. We'd found roommates and restaurant jobs.

I remember one night in particular, craving Locke. Like many nights late that July, it was too hot to sleep. I had the lights off and the window open. Dressed only in my cotton briefs and bra, I lay alone on my mattress listening to Bob Dylan on the stereo. I was buzzing in that sleepless, warm way you get on a summer night without air conditioning when you keep staying up later and later, feeling the hot breeze and hearing crickets. I was listening to "Lay, Lady, Lay"—even in 1973 it was already a classic. I would see Locke the next evening after his shift at Bailey's Ice Cream Shop. It seemed so far in the future.

I switched to Cole Porter's "I've Got You under My Skin." This was music that for us was so old-fashioned it was back in style. We knew that Cole Porter had been gay, and we imagined that all his romantic songs danced to at country clubs decades before by men in tuxes and women in full skirts were really coded ballads of then-forbidden yearnings. His songs were so sugary on the outside and so intense and indescribable at heart. *He* was a lover. I turned my stereo low so my roommates wouldn't hear and played the song over and over. Cole spoke in the clichéd language of acceptable love, but his was something wilder.

It was after 2:00 a.m. and I had the lunch shift at the Hungry Persian the next day. I thought I'd die if I couldn't touch Locke. I tried to find his smell in the pillows. I got up and put on my jeans, T-shirt, and sandals to walk over a mile down Mass Ave to Locke's apartment in Harvard Square. Then I stopped. It wasn't safe for a woman alone at that hour—the streets would be almost deserted. I picked up the phone and called Locke, waking him. His roommate too, probably. "Locke, listen." I played him the song. He listened. "I can't stand not touching you," I said.

"I'll be right there," Locke replied softly.

I wondered why those memories were more intense than some more recent ones. Were the romantic experiences they indexed deeper—like what all the songs say about the first love being the one you never forget—or was it that experiences felt more keen then because I was eighteen and with fewer buffers to my senses and emotions? Even simple memories seemed close to the surface decades later. I had a specific memory from our sophomore year, when we were both working as ushers to get into the plays at the Loeb Theater for free, of our sitting in the near-dark together. Locke's blondish-brown hair waved out around his ears, not long for the '70s, but untamed, as we thought of it then, and unshaped. He was wearing jeans and a white button-down shirt. Running shoes. I was wearing brown, thin-striped corduroys and a clinging purple and blue button-down shirt, an outfit that showed off my figure while also looking like I didn't care about clothes. A studied, sexy look of fashion nonchalance. My deep-brown hair was long, and I wasn't wearing makeup.

We both were well behaved as we showed the Harvard crowd to its seats—professors, students, Cambridge neighbors, also dressed down but some more expensively than we were. Then when the lights went out, we nabbed two empty seats toward the back, right on an aisle.

I watched the play and saw that Locke was getting engrossed in it. Then working my hands quickly beneath his belt and under his jeans, I reached down to touch him. "Maud!" He pretended to sound shocked, or maybe he *was* shocked. He moved my hands higher and held them tightly over his shirt and against his stomach. From time to time, I'd play at pushing them downward, he'd hold them above his lap at his waist, but pressed close, as close in as he could. I'd lean in, smelling him. We stayed like that, watching the drama. I had wonderful small memories like that one of being with Locke. Mental snapshots of us in college with rumpled hair and big crushes on each other.

I remembered images from the breakup too. In my bedroom with the sloping floor, I was alone in bed, crying, and unable to sleep. My bed was a queen-sized mattress and box spring with no frame, and either the mattress and box spring didn't quite fit or, more likely, the slant of the floor had them askew. It was something I'd hardly noticed on nights when Locke was there with me, and rarely before when I was on my own, but now it bothered me horribly. I had trouble sleeping for a while after that. I was wired, afraid to relax, to let down my guard, in case I'd be blindsided. But it had already happened.

Full and Rich

I preferred not to remember breaking up with Maud. We had broken up, that was the fact. And life went on. We grew up. That formulation had the advantage of not assigning blame. One undeniable aspect, though, of our split was that I had initiated it. It was my responsibility. I'd chosen for so long not to dwell on these things, that now I had a hard time trying to sort out why I'd pushed Maud away. Had we simply drifted apart? Certainly not. Maud and I were never casually together. We were always intense. I kept no secrets from her.

I'd met someone else. That was the easiest way to put it. Someone more like me, given to long silences, a believer in things spiritual. But why I'd been open to meeting another woman was the harder question. I was just over twenty, of course, still awash with hormones. That was part of it. If I really had to say, though, I ran away. Maud's vision was too acute where I was concerned. She saw exactly what I lacked. And she was blunt. She told me things I didn't want to hear. That I was smart, but fearful. That I was quick to judge and slow to participate. I wished she'd be kinder, warmer, more what later my therapist would call accepting. I thought even then that a more grown-up relationship would include more kindness. I had a lot to learn—on both subjects, kindness and relationships. Painfully. But I didn't know that then. I aspired simply to grow up. And the new woman was older, twenty-three.

I suppose there's some truth in this explanation. But it avoids the memory of the hurt in Maud's eyes as I told her goodbye. There is a simpler, more candid, and less pretty way to put it: Maud and I broke up because I'd been unpardonably careless with her heart.

I had not lived with regret over this history. I had more recent unhappiness, certainly. But more to the point, I improved. With time, and the hard lessons of two divorces, I became a more direct, more centered, more honest person. These were not vast, dramatic changes. I carried my scars. Instead, they were small, hard-won differences in how I talked and how I listened. Differences just large enough to open my heart to intimacy. I found that intimacy now, in middle age and a few years after my second divorce, most easily with my sons.

My youngest son, David, age nine, lived in Chicago and with me three nights a week. The days we spent together filled me with joy.

I'd rush from my law practice many evenings to catch basketball practice or a game at the park district program where he played. I'd sit on the top tier of the bleachers, amazed by my little son's skill. I'd see an open lane to the basket, and I'd sing out, "Drive, David! Drive!" And he'd lower his shoulder, shift hands with his dribble, and score. That's my kid, I'd think. Amazing.

In the summers we watched baseball together on TV. I'd see a player I liked, somebody with a quirky set of mannerisms. "Hey, David," I'd say. "See that guy? See how he steps out of the batter's box, rubs the bat with his hands, and takes two short practice swings? Just like that, see? Does it every time."

"Yeah," David would say.

"I like that guy. He's very smooth. I think he's a boy of mine," I'd say.

"No, he's not."

"Yeah. Sure he is. He's a boy."

"What do you mean? Like me?"

"Nah, not like you. You're really a boy of mine. Him, he's just smooth, he's slick."

"He's slick?"

"Yeah, slick. He's a boy."

"Yeah. He can be a boy of ours, yours and mine."

And David would lean his head on my shoulder, with his hand patting against my knee. A few minutes later, he'd say, "What about him, Dad? He's got a nice swing. Is he a boy?"

"Nah. Nice swing, but he's not a boy."

"Not a boy?"

"Not a boy."

"What if he gets a hit? Could he be a boy then?"

"You can't just become a boy by getting a hit," I'd say. "You have to be boy material."

"Boy material?"

"Um-hum. You gotta have a certain something. A boy is somebody you really like. A boy's got a spark."

"Am I a boy, Dad?"

"Yeah. You're the best boy of all," I'd tell him. "You and Kris."

Kris is my older son, seventeen. The child of my first marriage. Absent much of the time, in Alaska with his mother. And missed. Kris and I talked by phone. Planned for his college. I'd met his girlfriend on a winter visit to Alaska not long ago. He took me skiing cross-country. I'd glided along behind him, not quite able to keep up, loving every minute of it.

And I worked. I hadn't set out to become a lawyer. The 1970s, when I was in college, had an undertow of ennui. Mid-decade, with the end of the war in Vietnam, students on the left lost their rallying point. And, lacking that, it became so obvious suddenly (some of us, I among them, had seriously imagined otherwise) that the Aquarian Age would not usher in a revolutionary era of love, peace, freedom, and equality. We had a world of relativity to reckon with. We were bereft. And politics looked less like a mission and more like a gray sea of compromises. What were we to do now? I, for one, tended to turn inward. I majored in comparative religion. My subjects were the classics, medieval philosophy. I occupied myself with musings about the myriad ways in which humankind had sought out meaning over the centuries. I grew more hesitant to speak.

Not everyone seemed to be as confused as I'd become. I would listen in awed silence as the government majors around me held forth, voices loud and eyes alight with confidence, on topics that belonged to the hour—not the prior millennium. I coveted the *relevance* of their talk. Relevance was a weighty concept in those days, much to be prized. The study of law, I supposed, could be a way to get a seat at the table with the talking crowd. And it was within my grasp. The law school admissions offices, it turned out, did not see a background in religious studies as a barrier to entry. I applied on a whim in senior year and was promptly accepted.

Practicing law has been a blessing to me. I have always had a good sense of right and wrong. Law adds power to those concepts. Law makes it possible to say: you can't do that; justice won't allow it. There's both less and a great deal more to that than just knowing what's right and good. Law makes right stick. And, on a personal level, law has given me a voice in the public world—a remarkable gift to receive from one's work.

This did not come all at once. Early on, I spent several largely unhappy years in a corporate megafirm, where I was relegated to poring over box after box filled with financial reports and copies of executives' memoranda in order to prepare for tedious pretrial depositions in cases about breached warranties in multimillion-dollar transactions. I was overworked and uninspired. And I left for a position in the City of Chicago's law department, where the cases were about governance, the rights of citizens in interactions with the police, whom the city could hire and fire, the use of public space. I was in court almost every day. Harold Washington was mayor of Chicago at that time, and I felt a fierce loyalty and pride in his administration. It seemed as if we were reclaiming a place in the city's government for the people in the long-neglected black and brown neighborhoods on the south and west sides. Excitement was in the air.

I chanced into my present job nearly a decade ago. A small public-interest law firm hired me to be its legal director and to develop lawsuits that champion the rights of the poor in the criminal justice system. We fight against the death penalty, work for decent treatment of convicted prisoners, challenge and try to prevent police abuse and misconduct. I have a knack for this work. I can sense where a lawsuit might succeed in forcing the abandonment of an unfair practice. Or where a public relations initiative could move public opinion. I relish those battles.

Not long after I joined the firm we moved our office to the campus of a major law school. Students work with us on our cases, gaining practical experience and the chance to fight for justice. We teach them something that their professors by and large can't convey: that the greatest privilege of all in the practice of law is to stand before a court or a jury and to speak from the heart for what you believe to be right.

With all of this—my sons and my work—I counted my life as full, as rich. I had little thought of Maud in the aftermath of our dinner. I could have sent her more e-mails, written a letter, or called. But I just didn't have the time. My path was set and I had my eyes focused on the ground before me. I was not inclined toward adventures with far-off women whom I'd known in distant times. This was home.

The Proposition

In that time after remeeting Locke, one of my projects was writing for a cyberdrama called *The Couch*. *The Couch* was an ongoing tale for the Web, part serious, part goofy, about eight New Yorkers in group therapy together. We *Couch* writers met once a week in a Soho loft to write the group sessions, and then individually at home we wrote diary entries, all of which would be put on the site in January when we'd compiled enough material to launch. We each played fictionalized—sometimes wildly fictionalized—versions of ourselves. No one played the therapist. We didn't let the therapist speak in our scripts. We were sponsored by a hopeful San Francisco company that spliced its dreams of money with dreams of forming online communities.

This project was the most fun work I had. And my cowriters were more than colleagues—they were my writing group, my allies, my partners in eating Chinese takeout. We were all writers but unlikely collaborators—one worked at *Glamour*, another wrote for *New Age Journal*. It really was like group therapy without the therapist, but better. Adult playtime. Friendship, in other words.

My character, Celeste, I named after one of my nieces. I made her braver than I was. Bawdy. Unguarded. Otherwise the character I wrote was suspiciously like me. She was forty-something, a woman from the footloose '70s trying to follow the taut choreography of dating in the '90s. She complained about dating a lot, lustfully.

I had my Thanksgiving with a cowriter from *The Couch* and her family. And I think writing furiously in the soon-to-appear e-diary and sharing the entries with other Couchsters in the meantime helped me sail through the rest of the holiday season and past my loneliness. It wasn't a surprise that I didn't hear more from Locke: I hadn't really expected to. Perhaps we'd started a friendship, but it was one that would take its own long-distance pace.

A couple of weeks before *The Couch* would finally launch publicly, I e-mailed all my friends, Locke among them, and asked them to take a preview look.

Date: 18 Dec 1996
From: Maud Lavin
To: Locke Bowman
Subject: Maud in preview

It's a launch! I write and play a character in a cyberdrama, *The Couch*. My character, Celeste, is a fictionalized cross between me and Mae West. This week is our preview week. Please check us out at http://www.thecouch.com. Any constructive criticism and/or rave reviews welcome. Thanks for checking out our site.

Had I been spammed? I wasn't interested in hearing about *The Couch*. And, as a rule, I didn't appreciate unsolicited messages that asked something from me in return. If the e-mail had not been from Maud, I'd have deleted it in an instant.

Well, to be honest, the fact that it was from Maud—and that she had evidently relegated me to a mass mailing—added a spark of irritation. I hadn't seen or heard from her in weeks (nor written or called myself), and I supposed I had no claim to a personalized greeting. But I felt nonetheless a flash of unjustified disappointment. But I kept the e-mail, clicking it into a folder with a growing stack of messages that needed more in response than I was inclined to give them.

A couple of weeks later, just after the holidays, as I was going through old clutter, I encountered Maud's message again. I hesitated, half inclined to get rid of it. On second thought, though, I decided to look up *The Couch*. I saw this as a virtuous act. It would only take a few minutes of my time (I had them to spare on that particular day, I reasoned). I would admire Maud's work and type her a quick note to tell her so. With that I'd have done my part to stay in touch.

The home page of *The Couch* presented an array of options, including diary entries for each of the characters organized by categories—what each thought about love, work, pleasure, so forth. A swift couple of clicks brought me the introductory message from

Celeste, Maud's character, and another brought up Celeste's views on the subject of pleasure, next to a beaming photograph of Maud herself. Here is what I read:

Celeste, Introduction

Hi. I'm Celeste. I came of age in the seventies and I try never to forget it. I'm one of those slightly frazzled but still adventuresome baby boomers. . . .

Celeste, Diary entry: Pleasure

I can't get over that I'm 42 years old and I'm dating. I'm doing the personal ads, I'm meeting people in cafes and at parties. I tell myself I'm looking for love and yet what makes me happiest, if I'm really being honest about the whole thing, is just pure playtime—sex, joking around, chatting on the phone, kissing, the small intrigues. And what frustrates me the most is when someone doesn't realize that what it's supposed to be about is PLEASURE.

I don't think that everyone allows him or herself simply to have those daily doses of fun and hedonism and entertainment that make everything else, for me anyway, possible.

I want someone who thinks my company, even with its flaws, is a pleasure and will let me think of him, even with his flaws, as a giant box of chocolates.

I want to be a pleasure queen, a sand box, a whirring mind, a liquid tongue, a laughful, a handful, a mouthful.

Pleasure. In a nutshell, it was what my life had been missing. It was the second day in January, cold and dark in Chicago, and the rest of the world was in postholiday stupor. My boys were with their respective mothers. But that was insufficient reason to have driven myself into work. The phone had been deathly silent all morning. What was I doing there?

Divorce has a long aftermath. I had left a marriage—my second one—in which for years, there had been no fun, no emotional sustenance. Over time, my wife, a person of considerable professional accomplishment, whom I admired, had become a stranger. We looked at each other without affection. We had ceased to find amusement in each other's company. In the end, years of couples therapy had not succeeded in overcoming the central obstacle—that we no longer loved each other. And so, several days after I'd precipitously and uncharacteristically stormed out of a counseling session, I told her I was leaving.

She became businesslike. We fixed my departure date. She made a list of the items I'd be taking from our marital home. On the appointed day, I helped the movers load those meager possessions into a truck. And then, I drove off myself—in the aging, second car it had been agreed I would take—into something like an abyss.

No one who has experienced divorce has managed, I suspect, to avoid the sensation of having fallen off a cliff. In my case, I grew desperately anxious about money. I feared slipping out of the middle class. I rented a bare apartment in a multiunit building. My neighbors downstairs (kids in their twenties) blasted their stereo in the middle of the night. In my late thirties, it was as if I'd regressed to just starting out with nothing. The homes of my contemporaries (like my former home) were opulent, littered with possessions acquired over the years. Sound echoed off the walls of my near-empty rooms. Before, I'd slept easily. Now I started awake in the black of the night, heart racing, hands damp with fear.

But money, of course, is not the true measure of the loss that a divorce entails. Even in a loveless relationship, there is a miracle of interconnection that comes with the marriage, one you've built together as a couple. You share with your neighbors the life of the street where you live. The parents of the other kids at your son's school expect they'll encounter you and your wife at the back of the room on parent-teacher day. The folks at church smile at the two of you in recognition. And, of course, there are all those people you know because they were always friends with your spouse. Like possessions, these ties accumulate unnoticed over time. With divorce, all of them are threatened at least, and severed as often as not. The loss of them, like expanding ripples, magnifies the central emptiness of finding yourself going it alone.

I hadn't worked at forming close friendships. There were precious few souls with whom I could share my grief or to whom I could unburden myself. And how, in any event, does one explain the unraveling of a marriage? More than one of the friends I'd counted on made it clear they felt I'd done something unpardonable. My parents were ashamed and we stopped speaking. I saw in my sons' faces, as they watched me, a mixture of longing and sorrow.

I steeled myself. I went to work on the project of pulling together a life. Within days after the divorce became final, I bought a modest townhouse not far from my work—a place to call home. I shelled out for a new TV and a stereo. I wanted my boys to like coming there and spending time. I paid more attention to how I looked. I made a point of being polite to the strangers in my new neighborhood. I threw myself into my work. I helped coach my son's Little League team.

By the time Maud and I had dinner, three years had gone by and people were telling me I looked well. I felt well—happy even—well past the point of beaten-up despair. My head felt clear. I could smile easily.

I had found a girlfriend. It was a relationship entered into out of a pent-up need for physical intimacy. And one in which I stood to lose little. Typical of people in the aftermath of divorce, I was in no condition for emotional risk. I found a woman who expected little of me and with whom I could maintain a comfortable distance. Susan looked nice. She believed in good times. She liked my boys and they liked her. She encouraged me to cook, introduced me to her friends. And yet, this wasn't destined to last. The very safeness of the relationship—the easy-going, no-questions-asked approach that spared me pain and controversy—was bound to be our undoing. We ran out of things to say too often. We did not read the same books or laugh at the same stories. I began to imagine what it would be like to sleep with someone else.

And so I had an instant response to Celeste. Pleasure was the thing I'd been missing. And a liquid tongue. With a quirky, complicated mind. And large breasts. Full of ideas, and laughter. Sensuous. I began fantasizing about a naughty, sexual connection. I was ready for this.

I did not actually decide to send Maud a proposition. If I had *decided*, it would have been *not* to do anything so rash. Instead, I just did it. Why not? She claimed to be up for anything.

Date: 2 Jan 1997
From: Locke Bowman
To: Maud Lavin
Subject: Celeste

Dear Maud:

So I checked out your Web site. It was actually my very first (no, second) venture on the Internet. I don't know if you'll like me for saying this or not, but I think I want to be on your flirt list—in the sense of, uh, being interested, that is, sexually. It would be nice, I think. (But don't get pissed off or offended, please.) Write back.

Locke

With Maud, I knew, there was already more at stake than the question of sex and a simple answer. Either way, "yes" or "no," I'd have more to deal with than just the luck of the moment. Maud, though we barely knew each other now, still counted for a big chunk of my formative past. And so after my e-mail went irretrievably rocketing off, I had a sinking sensation. I'd been stupid to put myself out there so ineptly. I wondered what would happen now.

I didn't have to wait long. Maud's reply showed up on my computer exactly nineteen minutes later. The message title, "Hey," was thoroughly ambiguous: it could mean "Hey, go fuck yourself," and it could also signal a less deflating but equally alarming response, as in "Hey, let's fuck." But when I opened Maud's message, I found neither.

Date: 2 Jan 1997
From: Maud Lavin
To: Locke Bowman
Subject: Hey

I'm not at all offended, in fact, I'm flattered. But it's not possible to be on my list only sexually, I'm afraid. I'm a full meal,
bub, an overflowing, messy, delicious plate, as Celeste would say.
Maud would say much the same thing. I think your heart and
soul and mind are all interwoven with your sexiness too, no?

On New Year's Eve, the guy I've been seeing (also a Tau-
rus) who is very nice, but recently divorced (and Catholic!), he
and I decided to cool it for a while (maybe longer than awhile)
while he sorted out his divorce . . . and Catholic guilt.

All very confusing but it makes the warmth (heat?) of your
e-mail all the more welcome. Thanks, Locke. And plus you're
safely in Chicago. . . .

How will you respond to this e-mail, I wonder?

Yours for fun and for real, Maud

I took this as the offer of a genuine connection. And I was enormously grateful. Grateful, most of all, to have (apparently) sidestepped some deftly worded humiliation. But pleased, too, to hear
what seemed to be a friendly voice. I wrote back right away, thinking again that I'd tidy up the interchange and that I'd stay on safer
ground.

Date: 2 Jan 1997
From: Locke Bowman
To: Maud Lavin
Subject: Re: Hey

Dear Maud: What a very kind and arrestingly honest e-
mail. You're great. I'm really glad (actually) that I sent that (for
me) totally reckless message; on my end, it got us in touch in
a much more emotionally connected way.

I'm sorry about your relationship confusion. There was just a bit of melancholy (and I even think I detected just a wee scent of Jewish guilt) in what you wrote. Wear your best Celeste outfit—it becomes you totally!

Your friend and admirer, Locke

Date: 2 Jan 1997
From: Maud Lavin
To: Locke Bowman
Subject: Hi

I'm very glad too that you wrote, and you can definitely be on my list, even though I don't know exactly what that means.

I am blue today. I don't think it is going to work out with my friend. It's only recently that I really started to open my heart again and so this is painful for me.

Well, I could use an embrace, Locke. If you ever feel like hugging me, you're welcome. And if we never reach that utopia, I will definitely accept and enjoy your warmth via e-mail.

Thanks, Locke, and here's a hug for you, Maud

I hadn't expected her to write again. This one, I noted, was more softly titled: "hi," not "hey." Maud—I knew, because I remembered her—would not have changed the subject line lightly. And she would not lightly suggest an exchange of hugs—which I knew without a moment's hesitation I could use too. Suddenly feeling excited and shy, I offered up a delicate hint of my own longing.

Date: 3 Jan 1997
From: Locke Bowman
To: Maud Lavin
Subject: Timing

I'm sorry. These things hurt fearsomely don't they? I do believe in the cliché about timing being a big part of it. For me, it's turned out that I wasn't able to open myself to the right relationship (or wait for the right relationship) at the right time, which is so human, isn't it?

And I'm thrilled to be on your list, even though nobody knows what that means, Locke

— ✱ —

I had a shtick that I used with my girlfriends and other single women about dating. "Dating," I'd say straight-faced, "would be great if you were married." I'd pause, waiting for them to laugh or raise eyebrows or look politely puzzled. "Well," I'd continue with a half smile, "these dates are like adventures in anthropology, or like playing some kind of game; they'd be fun if only you could go home afterward, climb in bed with someone you loved, and tell the story." That would be met by knowing nods, bigger smiles. Dating could've been merely playful, lusty, fun, or just plain weird, if it weren't connected to real needs of the heart, to yearnings for family, to flights from loneliness, to the desire for a really good talk, to pining for a hug. I had achieved the mixed blessing at forty-two of being good at dating or at least competent. This meant that although I'd feel desire and attraction just as strongly as I had when I was a teenager, I could also as an adult do something I couldn't do as an adolescent. I could analyze, detach, and keep a distance no matter what I was feeling. Compartmentalize. This kind of distance once learned is hard to unlearn. Being playful was my dating style and my unconscious strategy to keep a safe distance. I could maintain a slightly brazen patter about food, sex, travel, work, and dating itself that I'd make humorous but I knew was titillating. It was like making up stories while being out on a date. This kind of talk kept interactions off center, and propelled them forward through the first date and into the second and whatever followed. Words were a kind of see-through veil that I never removed.

I knew other forty-something single women who were defiant about having fun dating. I *like* being single, they would say, telling about traveling to D.C. last week with one guy, going hiking in the Berkshires next weekend with someone else. It doesn't get much better than this, they would declare. Maybe I sounded like that too sometimes. But I was lonely.

At the same time, I felt proud—like I'd learned to keep in motion socially. Those of us who were baby boomers had never really dated when we were younger. We'd been more into serial love affairs. And in my case I'd been shy, to boot, even sometimes mortified at parties. On a one-to-one level, I could be brave, but the social whirl with all those rules had thrown me. Now I was meeting men at parties or gallery openings and then going out with them to dinners and movies. This was a kind of dating that had existed in the 1950s for my babysitters and now had been reborn in the '90s under the cloud of the AIDS epidemic, when dinners were safer than jumping into bed. Now I was moving, but it was stillness that was the problem—being still with someone, letting feelings open, cuddling without talking.

Of the women I knew, it wasn't the relentless daters I wanted to talk with about dating (although they had some good stories), and it certainly wasn't the ones who'd given up on dating (that men our age all wanted younger women was a line I was sick of hearing—and it wasn't true anyway). Ironically I liked talking about dating best with my married friend Kim. I didn't realize it then, but now I think it was partly because she and her husband had that kind of intimacy that my life lacked and that I was starting to crave.

By the time I started e-chatting with Locke, I'd had almost four years of date patter. I wanted a hug. And to talk! To really talk without playing all the time. Celeste wanted pleasure and so did I, but I was beginning to see that it had meant "playing" on a lot of different levels, some of which had gotten in the way of intimacy. Maybe it was e-mail or geographic distance that allowed me to start using words to go deeper, but I think I was simply ready. And when Locke and I had met for dinner in October we'd talked so much about our lives and about politics—including prison reform and the anti-death-penalty movement, which were his work. It reminded me how smart Locke was. And, I don't know, balanced: he seemed so balanced. I didn't want to waste that. As much as I'd expected some sex banter with Locke—we had imprinted each other when we were young with sex—Locke was also someone I really wanted to talk with.

Perversely and without thinking, I went first to the one subject most unspoken and sore for us: religion. I wondered at the time if religion and all it stood for is why we broke up in college. I wasn't sure, it was complicated. Probably we were destined to split not just because we were of different religions: how shocking, after all, was it in 1976 for a Jew and a Protestant to get romantic? But still, religion was the template by which we each modeled our bonds with our families, and we were too young then to form our own life together at odds with our families and their cultures.

Locke's father was Protestant clergy. At that time he was a Presbyterian minister. Of course Locke was not his father, of that we were sure. Locke seemed to be his own person, not particularly religious, not following in his father's footsteps. Locke studied philosophy and history of religion, an intellectual approach. But he'd felt a spiritual pull to his father's religion after all, I'd thought. Stunned as I was by our breakup at the end of college, it made a kind of bitter sense to me that he'd left me for someone who was adamantly Christian.

Date: 3 Jan 1997
From: Maud Lavin
To: Locke Bowman
Subject: Hey!!

What about you and religion? Do you think of yourself as Christian but not in terms of an organized religion? I wonder where you're at now with spiritual questions. I guess this is a tall order for an e-mail correspondence, but I would be interested to hear.

As for me, Judaism continues to be important as an ethical base, and a cultural and familial one, not in any literal sense though. I do believe in spirituality, which is only an incredibly vague concept in my mind, but I feel it really interweaves with so much, and matters more to me than when I was younger. I'd say that spirituality to me is love and kindness and ethics and caring when there are no strings attached, and that it's both entirely superfluous to and transcendental of (which is the point, to me, it's a kind of connectedness when connectedness has no "profit") and at the same time a basic thread of life.

Are you happy in the relationship you're in now? (Just a nosy question. You, of course, do not have to tell me.)

To be continued . . .

It was the second question that got me. Happy in the relationship? Well, "sure, pretty much" or "no, not really." The answer depended on whether you saw the glass as half full or half empty. It was, after all, just a question. But posed by a woman I'd just (sort of) propositioned and who'd in return suggested a warm embrace, there was more to it, of course. Maud hadn't really said no to anything. What did I intend here, anyway? I had no answer to that. So I left Maud's e-mail unanswered for a day. Until she superseded it with something lighter and provocative. And, to me, altogether irresistible.

Date: 4 Jan 1997
From: Maud Lavin
To: Locke Bowman
Subject: I'm glad

we started corresponding, and it can take whatever pace feels fun. I do feel lucky, though, that you wrote this week, which was a tough one.

As for you, well you're safely in Chicago and safely dating another woman. I am still intrigued to know what the grown-up Locke is like, and even willing (when I'm feeling a little more rambunctious) to play with abandon (isn't that what e-mail is for?). Sounds kind of nice to explore at a safe distance. I also asked myself what if? What if you were single and living in NY? What would I want? How would I want to connect? What would happen?

Disaster scenarios. Lush, sensual scenarios. Sexual scenarios. Sitting around and talking scenarios. Yes, this is where
the movie slows down and gets interesting for me. What I'd
really like is just to see you again, have another leisurely dinner—talk a lot, joke around, not jump into bed (sorry), have
a good time. (Well, I would like to jump into bed, and I'm
very sure it would be wonderful, but not out of the blue, not
quickly, not torn from what could be a luxurious and sensual
series. . . .)

So, I guess the good news is that we could do another
dinner next time you're in NY. Well, to put it as a question,
could we? Unlike Celeste, I feel pretty vulnerable (to use the
favorite therapy word, overused but accurate) in general, and
where you're concerned specifically. I'd like to do the wild
thing with you, Locke, but talking and dinnering seems like
where the weather vane is pointing.

And all that said, can we have some fun and play some
word games and write each other some wild stuff that'll make
us each laugh out loud when we open our e-mail in the middle
of a work day?

Here's a start: what I'm trying to remember is did we ever
have oral sex with each other? Or were we so young that it
was even before that time?

WB, Buckwheat. And thanks for listening (and playing)
this week.

At 30

What did I think about religion? And how about oral sex? Maud
had a knack for keeping me permanently off-balance. At nineteen
Maud had been a master at abrupt conversational transitions. It
was less a style statement than an all-out attack on my pretensions
of being almost adult. It had been fun. We had laughed. Since then
life had become altogether too serious. I sat in my law office with
the wintry light from the window and the fluorescent glow from

the ceiling reflected in my computer screen. As I absorbed Maud's message I thought back to when we'd intersected at all in our post-college lives before this year. We had only once—at a wedding reception when we were thirty.

It was P. K.'s summer wedding with a reception under a big tent in South Orange, New Jersey. P. K., a friend to us both, had grown up with all the privileges of that bedroom community of New York City. He had come to Harvard intensely verbal and charming. His ambitious heart yearned even then for the media world in Manhattan. By the time of the wedding, he was a young magazine editor who went out a lot at night and was seen with various members of the Kennedy clan.

Underneath that drive P. K. was a warm person, but the wedding reception was not a warm affair. More like a see-and-be-seen media party than anything else. I was wearing a wraparound blue-and-red print dress that showed a lot of my back and legs. It tied only at the waist, and I wished I'd worn something more conservative and less likely to fall off. I sat at a table with some of the other women from college. One was A., dark-haired and quick-tongued. I'd always been a little afraid of her. But at this reception she was my favorite person, her barbs aimed elsewhere. "Will P. stop by here, do you think? Or are our bank accounts not Kennedy-sized enough?" I laughed. "And did you *see* the woman B. married?" she said too loudly. "My God, she looks exactly like a Barbie doll." A. was definitely not behaving herself. I was, but at least I could listen to her. She continued, "So I had to go talk to her. And you know what? She not only looks like a Barbie doll, she sounds like one too." A. squeezed my forearm, "And how are you, dear?" she asked, always the sophisticate. I told her about my then boyfriend. "He sounds too good to be true," A. concluded. Announcing, "I've *got* to get that bartender to make me a martini," A. relinquished me, going on to other audiences. I saw Locke's back in the buffet line. I was surprised, I don't know why. Since he and P. K. had been so close in college, it made sense he'd be here. I hadn't noticed Locke before; he must've been sitting in the back at the wedding. He was wearing a dark suit. "Oh, yes," I remembered, "a lawyer." The suit looked uncomfortable.

I came up behind him, intending to surprise him, but he turned first and gave me a warm smile. "How are you?" he said courteously. He had dark lines under his eyes. "He's been working too hard," I thought. I searched his eyes for the old light, but I couldn't find it. He looked thin and serious. Was he having fun at this event? "Isn't this lovely," he said. I didn't know what to say back, he was so polite: "No?" We talked for a while. He seemed older than the rest of us. "What have you done with Locke?" I wanted to ask him. I wondered what I looked like to him in my arty Caribbean print dress, my braless back showing. I wished I'd brought some safety pins. I started to feel bored, and I made my retreat.

It was a decidedly undramatic reunion. I really didn't want to reconnect with Locke. I don't think that around thirty you're necessarily interested in honoring people who were pivotal in your life when you were younger. At least I wasn't. I was more interested in securing my own cool adult identity, and in that context Locke wasn't arty enough to attract me. Plus, I'm guessing, I'd killed him off in my heart. I'd diminished him, made him smaller in my memory because he'd hurt me. At thirty, I wasn't motivated to forgive him or discover whether he'd changed. That's another advantage of opening up in middle age. Then, I guess, you find the ability to forgive people who have wronged you or simply taken different paths—and even to be curious about them.

It was a khaki suit. How odd that I remember that suit as distinctly as Maud remembers her wraparound print dress. This suit was not the first I'd ever owned, but close to it. The business clothes I'd bought while still in law school were etched in my memory, freighted as they were with growing pain. "Here I am," they said. "A man in the big world. I've turned a corner; put away those childhood jeans." I was dressing up. With the tie and the fragrant leather shoes, I used to feel like I was putting on a costume.

By the time I wore that khaki suit to P. K.'s wedding, though, it had a few miles on it. I'd bought it several years before to wear at my law school graduation. It felt comfortable now, serviceable for an outdoor summer wedding. I'd felt ambivalent about going. I hadn't kept up with all those people from college. The South Orange country club was unfamiliar territory. I told myself I'd come mainly because the trip east meant a chance to see Kris in Rhode Island, where my first wife (who moved around a lot) was then in summer school at Brown.

I had, in fact, sat in front at the wedding, joined there by another old friend from college days.

Then I was at the reception, which was teeming with familiar faces. In spite of myself I began to feel a disconcerting sense of lightness. Cheerful, prosperous-looking people greeted me as if I were an old friend. I *was* an old friend. And they were my old friends. We were different now, of course. More solid. We were making money. Some of them were rich, probably. They must have had money when we were in college, though it hadn't been visible then. I noticed those distinctions now. But even though the khaki suit might appear shabby to some of them, it still didn't matter. There was something large that bound us to one another—a deep shared mystery of passing through time together.

In the reception line I turned and was startled to see Maud, right behind me. She was taller than I remembered, her hair very dark and her skin fair. Her dress was simple, not showy. In my memory, it was a blue-and-white print. She seemed serious. If she hadn't taken me by surprise, I might've shied away from saying hello.

"How are you?" I asked. I wanted to know. She said she was in graduate school. I told her I'd gone into law.

"I heard you got divorced," she said, not quite looking at me.

I felt ashamed suddenly. I half expected her to say, I told you so. Or to hit me.

"I'm sorry," she said, looking at me now. "I know it's very hard."

"It is. Surprisingly so." I was grateful. I hadn't expected her to care.

"Me too." Now I couldn't figure her out. I must have looked puzzled.

"I did. I got divorced too."

"Oh, I didn't know." Had I known she'd gotten married?

"It was horrible. The worst thing in my life. My family was all so mad at me."

I didn't know what to say. I felt a rush of sympathy, camaraderie even. But for some reason I couldn't get a fix on her. Each of us was wrapped separately, in our grown-up clothes, the cares of our newly adult lives now the measure of our own importance. Of course she wasn't angry that we'd broken up. Those times were behind us. It was, after all, so very long ago, and we'd been so young.

"Occasions like these are lovely, aren't they?" I said after an awkward pause. I was trying to convey the peculiar sense of weight-lessness I'd been feeling all afternoon. She looked at me oddly. And I realized I must have said the wrong thing. We talked for a few moments more. I remembered to ask about her brothers.

Then someone drew my attention away. A moment later I turned around again, and Maud was gone.

Seriously

There was a question pending, as they say in law. Actually, there were several: Religion? My relationship? And sex? And why had I started this e-mailing anyway? On one level, the correspondence seemed a little nuts. I'd mailed off a perfectly, predictably guy proposition—and done it for no particular reason (what had I been thinking anyway?)—and things had gotten instantly complex. I'd imagined Maud to be Celeste, which, of course, she was not. Celeste, was a nonexistent, fictional character. Inhabiting virtual reality, Celeste wasn't going to be responding to come-ons from flesh-and-blood humans. What was daunting though—serious, not nuts—was that the proposition had been received, in fact, by Maud, a formidable, fully dimensional person with a razor-sharp wit, a definite resemblance to Celeste (how deep that resemblance went, I wasn't quite sure), and no illusions whatsoever about me—though I'd seen her just twice in the past twenty years. This elec-tronic correspondence—instantaneous letters across an unimag-inably vast Internet and directly to each other's bedrooms—was making me want her. And that, more or less, is what I told her.

Date: 6 Jan 1997
From: Locke Bowman
To: Maud Lavin
Subject: Re: I'm glad

Dear Maud:

I'm glad we started corresponding too. It's turned out to be a whole lot warmer and deeper . . . and better . . . than I could have hoped for. It has far surpassed my fantasies, and my fantasies weren't at all bad.

I got stuck on the question of am I happy in my relationship (no, it's not a nosy question). I guess the answer is that I'm modestly happy. Susan is kind to me and good to my son. We like a lot of the same CDs (rock n roll, mostly; I never grew out of it). She likes my cooking (this is a big thing; grown-up Locke loves to cook). We almost never argue. But I never fell in love with her. This relationship happened almost without my noticing it—because of circumstances (her loss of a job, my loneliness and my worry about my kid) that made the relationship a great comfort for both of us. We tolerate each other's friends, but we really don't have friends in common.

Well, anyway, I'll tell you where I'm at with religion in another missive. This one already seems sort of weighted down. I'm very glad of the dinner invitation next time I'm in NYC. And, like you, I see no point in wrecking a great story line and rattling each other's fillings with sex in chapter two before the romance and warmth even get going. But I have had this image in the past few days: there's a long couch in your apartment; your legs are flopped over one arm and mine are flopped over the opposite one; your head is right next to mine, in the middle where we meet; we can talk all night that way, not quite looking at each other but with our cheeks touching. Oh well, dinner would be great and maybe holding hands.

Oral sex? Yes. The fact is we nibbled, just. I could do a whole lot better now. And am prepared to prove it.

Locke

Date: 6 Jan 1997
From: Maud Lavin
To: Locke Bowman
Subject: Prepared to prove it . . .

Hmmmm. Locke, you are so great. And I really did laugh out loud when I got your e-mail. Yeah, I'd like to stay up all night talking. I'd like it very much.

I'm wary of the fact that you are going out with someone. I know we're just at the getting-reacquainted e-mail stage so maybe it shouldn't matter, but I need to let you know that I keep relationships with men—what's the word? not simple, not uncluttered—how about with as firm boundaries as possible. Even G. being recently divorced was an exception for me and one that did create some stressful complications. Anyway, and this is self-serving and not very nice of me to say, but I think you deserve more. Lots and lots of women would enjoy your cooking, I'm betting. Love is important.

When are you coming to New York? Come soon, we'll have a wonderful time without flooding our engines, and we'll break rules but not hearts. I'm trying to think of another provocative question but my head is fuzzy with work. I think I'll just shamelessly fish for a compliment instead. OK, what is one thing about the way I look in my forties that you really like? Good night, dollface. Come visit soon. And maybe if you don't have a trip scheduled soon you could pretend. . . .

— ✳ —

There's a middle-age logic to this epistolary style of setting boundaries while also expressing deep availability and intuitive recognition. You've been through this before, in my case with the very same person, and you know how you feel—you know you want to go for it. At the same time, you've learned to speak up and set some self-protective rules. But in the middle of all that knowing, you wonder too: have I made this person up? The feeling is like when you dream you're so close, so intimate with a person whom in waking life you seem to know only casually and then you wake up and try to figure out if any of that dreamed intimacy really exists hidden between you or not. The dream is so present for you, but you question whether it's only the pull of your own imagination and needs that's the powerful force tugging on your heart. Or is there something there that your unconscious mind knows and your conscious mind never realized before? Maybe it's always that way with falling in love—you're responding to a mush of who the other person really is and the fantasy of whom you need. And it's that mix that helps you to leapfrog over hesitations as the romance develops. Falling again for your first love adds memory to the blend. And you never know and in some ways don't really need to parse what's what—emotional memory of your earlier fantasies, his earlier reality, your fantasy now, his reality now. For me, it's the eyes and the smile where they all meet. And it seemed to me that Locke had the same eyes and the same smile he always did. And that gave me the courage to leap in.

Sex and Religion

If we were more conventional, and if progress in a relationship were simply linear, Maud and I would have talked more at this point about "things that mattered"—religion, our values, and, bit by bit, our hopes and dreams. This is what our parents' generation would expect. They'd call it "getting reacquainted." It would involve long walks and then tentatively holding hands.

But our generation danced a different way. Our older brothers and sisters who came of age in the '60s robbed us of convention. We'd missed out, most of us, on prom night. We slept together before we went steady. Sex was never off limits to us. Unattainable often, but never forbidden. We had the pill.

And for that matter, no relationship progresses in a straight line. There is a flush of pleasure that comes with liking and being liked in return. But we catch ourselves and draw back. We try a more constructed, more artful pose—gathering ourselves and making sure before we venture further.

For Maud and me—odd though this may seem—sexual teasing was an easy way to step back and find a little distance. Not real sex, with flesh-and-blood intimacy. Just fooling around, and gauging the effect we were having on each other.

Date: 7 Jan 1997
From: Locke Bowman
To: Maud Lavin
Subject: One question

that's important to me is whether you think it's fun and exciting and useful to talk during sex. As children, I think, we used to just pant silently . . . a waste.

Best about you in your forties (so far actually, I've seen virtually nothing) is your face, which shows all your depth and maturity, but still glimmers the way it did when we were in our twenties—full of fun.

I'm coming in April, I think. Cheers, Locke

Date: 7 Jan 1997
From: Maud Lavin
To: Locke Bowman
Subject: Hard

as it may be to believe, I don't know if I talk during sex or not. Would I think it'd be fun and exciting and useful to try? Sure. I couldn't promise complete sentences though.

April?! Can't we pretend it's Feb. or even late Jan.? If I were a delayed-gratification person, I'd be thin. As it happens, I'm round, full of chocolate chip muffins, nicely sculpted by regular trips to the gym, and still with that very soft skin, and smooth.

Shamelessly and verbally yours,
but still eternally sappy,

Maud

p.s.—What I like about the way you look in your forties—your eyes. Well, OK, they are just the same, but they
say a lot and they see a lot and they've got laugh lines now,
and still that trace of Rasputin-like gleam.

Date: 7 Jan 1997
From: Locke Bowman
To: Maud Lavin
Subject: Re: Hard

Hard!? Well, yes, it is.

I'm thin. One of my ex-law-partners used to joke that
when I turned sideways, I would disappear. Actually, I think my
body looks a little better than it did when we were younger.
For one, I don't smoke anymore. Plus I run and lift weights
a few times a week (most weeks)—desperately seeking that
elusive third dimension. . . . All of which is not to say that I'm
big on delayed gratification. February?? How, I wonder??? You
certainly left me with a growing (full grown) curiosity about
the sculpted parts of you that I've not yet glimpsed.

You're the sappiest, Locke

— ✳ —

Sex with Locke back in college had been wonderful. It was embarrassing to admit it, since I'd had a lover at the end of high school,
but it was Locke who'd taught me what an orgasm was. That's not
something, once you learn, that you forget, or the person who
brought you there.

But I also remembered all too clearly the pain of our breakup,
and those were the images that made me afraid of connecting with
Locke in the present. I was e-mailing with him as if I were forward

and fearless, but then I often felt like pulling back even as I was playing Mae West. I argued with myself. Maybe I was so afraid of opening up to him in the present that I was forcing images of that long-ago breakup to the surface to ward off feelings before they took over. Maybe I was comfortable with the lusty yet essentially safe world of dating I'd built. Maybe I wasn't really looking or ready for more. The voice of scolding pragmatism temporarily won out: How stupid could a smart woman be, I asked myself. Did I really want to get re-involved only to go through a split with Locke, essentially the same split, twice? Time to start protecting myself. Time to put the brakes on. Or at least to give them a tap.

The thing is, I found out, those of us in our forties, we feel all the confusion and the mixed emotions hooked to the pull of attraction that we did at any age. We still have no power to stop any of it, it seems. But, I discovered too, we've also over the years acquired self-awareness, and with this now well-practiced insight we've gained some power. This combination makes us at the same time dazed, confused, *and* articulate. We can express the fear and pleasure of falling. The person who's listening, though, has to be roughly the same age, an adult, feeling both powerless and powerful himself, in order to hear all the frequencies.

Date: 7 Jan 1997
From: Maud Lavin
To: Locke Bowman
Subject: Talking the talk

Glad you're not into delayed gratification.

Locke, I have a girl caveat. You may be on such a guy tangent with this that you may not even want to hear this, but I would like to say it anyway, and hope that you're open to hearing it. Well, I do feel very drawn to you on many levels and it's a real pleasure. I even hope that the context will allow us to realize some of our fantasies, and am glad to continue to air them. BUT for me reconnecting with you is not mainly about sex. It may be fueled by sex, but it's much more about the joy of connecting or potentially connecting on so many levels (I really would like to stay up all night talking sometime, I really do want to hear what's going on with you and religion, etc.), and it's about a kind of gentleness I feel in each of us and that we (I hope) have between us too, or in any case I felt we did when we had dinner.

Having said that, here's what I'm thinking about us having sex again. I think the first time again with you I'd be really scared, and shy and awkward, and very excited. It would also be very emotional for me.

I would need to go slow and melt away all the nervousness with caressing and laughter and greediness and, yes, talking. And then, each time less shy and less scared, but feeling risk and feeling that it's real, and feeling that you feel at risk too. And I remember, Locke, some things in great detail, I remember the rhythms between us and you inside me and building and building towards coming—great sex. I don't know, now I'm just getting scared. Maybe I should just write you in the abstract, because when I think of you specifically it seems very real to me, very scary.

Yeah, Feb.?!? I don't know how. And I'd like to fly with you Locke but for me it can't feel like flying without a net, OK? It's uncanny how real you are for me.

WB obscene, fresh, thoughtful, funny—whatever you're in the mood for.

And thanks so much for reconnecting. It's giving me a lot of pleasure.

— ✳ —

Girl caveat to man on a guy tangent. I felt a little insulted. And unfairly criticized. Hadn't she been the one who had started the sex talk? Well, at least the dialogue about oral sex? Why was I now getting portrayed as a hulking hard-on and a one-track mind?

I did not have a one-track mind. But, more to the point, this was (already) not a one-track relationship. If it had been—if lust had been our only object—we might have derailed then and there. It's amazing how delicately the dance of pure physical desire has to be managed. Say the wrong thing, send the wrong signal at a key moment, and you risk turning everything off. Sexual heat can switch to hot anger in an instant. And, of course, sex is a sort of least common denominator. There are endless numbers of people to desire and be desired by. It's so easy to turn off, turn away, move on.

But between Maud and me there were other, higher frequencies. Our own personal memories were in the mix, after all. Memory, the thread of life, is of the spirit. So there was some reason in turning now to things more spiritual. I'd sidestepped Maud's question about religion because the topic was a painful one. Maud couldn't have known that of course. But she might have guessed. My father was a clergyman, and Maud must've remembered how, in college, I'd yearned for his approval and seen myself falling short.

I didn't want to risk a discussion of how my life had gone more recently without some assurance that I'd be listened to with compassion—or at least with sympathy. But Maud had given me reason to suspect I'd get what I needed. She'd coupled her girl caveat with an invitation to talk, to weave a safety net together. And I had no wish to stay on the defensive. I was ready to risk starting a conversation. I told Maud a story, one that revealed more of me than I'd have dared expose when we were college kids.

Date: 8 Jan 1997
From: Locke Bowman
To: Maud Lavin
Subject: On Religion

So let's change the subject for just a minute.

You remember that my father was a Presbyterian minister? In 1983, after converting to Episcopalianism, he became an Episcopalian deacon, then later a priest. I usually felt like I couldn't measure up to my father's expectations, and oftentimes this took the form of not being good enough, morally correct enough, to win my father's approval. I know that what I think and feel about religion today has a lot to do with this background.

Time was when I wanted very much to get back in the door of the Church, to feel like I was a good and regular person, as much entitled to be there as anyone else.

For the ten years I was married to my second wife, I was a more or less regular attendee at the Cathedral in downtown Chicago. What I liked about being part of that was mainly the timelessness of the Church calendar—seasons and feast days coming and passing with the perfect regularity of the year; expected colors; the majestic simplicity of the language in the Book of Common Prayer. I volunteered to be on committees—even taught Sunday School (totally not my thing), when there was no one else to do it.

In short, I can honestly say that I tried to be a good Church person. I really did. Thing is, I never really felt comfortable. And it turned out that when my ex and I separated, I got dropped like a lead balloon. I stopped attending, of course. The Church was one of the things that "belonged" to my ex-wife. Now, if I show up at church to drop my son off, folks look right through me like I don't even exist. Sort of an informal excommunication, I suppose.

What I believe is that we have a spiritual life, all of us. And that life is about more than what we see. I think that we have the capacity to a greater or lesser extent to be connected in a deep way to the rhythm of life in ourselves and in others and that to be better connected is to live a richer and fuller life. This is definitely an idea/belief that's still in process. But I'm pretty sure that the burdens of my past are such that I'll find the connectedness somewhere other than in the Christian church.

Locke

— ✳ —

So now Locke's father was an Episcopalian priest. When I first met him, when I was nineteen and he was (I think) forty-six, he'd been a minister, traveling often, teaching Presbyterian Sunday school teachers how to teach. Religious education was his specialty. He had written at least one book on it. I met Locke's parents when Locke had taken a semester off college, rebelling against the intellectual pressures of Harvard by taking a job as a stable hand back in Arizona where his parents were living then. Once the summer began, I went to visit. I got a ride with a friend to Topeka, Kansas, and took a bus from there to Phoenix.

I don't know what I expected of a minister's house, probably something wooden and decorative, with lace antimacassars draped on the backs of armchairs. Locke picked me up at the bus station. I was so glad to see him, and at the same time dizzy with lack of sleep and bloated by junk food. I'd been reading *Lolita* on the bus trip, and Nabokov's descriptions of Lolita's stickiness mixed in my mind with the smell of the bus cleaning fluid and my own stickiness. We drove up Camelback Mountain and lay outside on the ground kissing each other, breathing in the fresh air, and looking up at the clear, starry Arizona sky. By the time we got to Locke's parents' house, it was late. His father was away lecturing, and only his mother was there, graciously waiting up for us. She was a thin woman, with dark, intense eyes, and she spoke in a warm, slow, Missouri-born cadence.

Their home was a small apartment in Scottsdale, which Locke's mother kept impeccably clean and oddly sparse. The furniture was antique, much of it plain and wooden. There was no stuff, no clutter. Serious books, few magazines. There must have been a TV, but I can't remember one. And rugs, but they're not in my memory either. This was not a family with money.

Locke's mother was very nice to me, loaning me her car so I could visit Locke at the stable, talking books with me, taking me out to brunch.

It's funny that in the 1970s when so many of us courted variety and imagined we exercised independent choice in our beliefs, Locke and I were each fairly conformist in our unthinking attempts to follow our parents' values. We wore ponchos from Guatemala and read novels from around the world, we consulted the I Ching, but we still wanted to please our parents and that—although we never would've admitted it to ourselves then—meant finding mates from the cultures we'd been raised in. My parents are Jewish and my next serious relationship after my college breakup with Locke was with someone Jewish. Locke, too, found someone from his own faith. Hard to remember, though, how much we really thought about spirituality when we were nineteen—I guess Locke did, but I don't think I had much self-knowledge on this subject then.

By our forties, our adherence to our parents' worlds had faded even as our awareness of our familial bonds had sharpened. We now got that we were connected to their values, but we'd also become practiced at rewriting and adapting them and adding to them to fit our needs. And aging gave its own impetus to thinking about spirituality. When we remet, it didn't matter to either Locke or me that we were from different religious backgrounds. But that we'd forged similar values and politics, that we both valued spirituality in our lives, however unconventionally expressed—that was important. And a comfortable fit. We shared not so much our parents' pasts but our own. It was fascinating and perhaps predictable, too, that we'd each come to focus more on spirituality despite our different backgrounds. I was interested to hear that Locke had gone further into his father's church before pulling back, and I was curious about what his next step would be. I felt, from knowing him so well when we were younger, that religion would continue to be too important to him to simply let it go.

Date: 8 Jan 1997
From: Maud Lavin
To: Locke Bowman
Subject: Continuing

Locke, Thanks for the wonderful e-mail. I find it really fascinating, both the spiritual evolution (and your honesty about it) and how this intertwines with and eventually separates from trying for parental approval. I think it's great you're finding your own way outside the church or at least a traditional one, maybe there are others to connect with in the future, and other, more loyal communities.

What I think is so moving is this tension you describe between wanting to follow certain official church laws to please your father and then needing to break with that rigid structure and go with beliefs and questions you have that are in the end more deeply generous.

I don't mean to simplify what is in fact a hugely complex experience, but what I want to say is that what is/was very acute for you because your father is an Episcopal priest is also probably an issue in a less severe way for many people, and not even necessarily played out through a church. There are accepted moral codes that we try to adhere to in order to please. Then I think part of being authentically moral is to rewrite these traditional codes so that they actually function with warmth and principle and flexibility.

Warmly, Maud

— ✳ —

Maud had spoken of interconnection, of personal flexibility, of being in touch. I agreed with that. What I felt most deeply (though I hadn't said this) was the relationship, now as I grow older, between the spirit and my aging body. With the first faint whisper of decline, which most of us hear in our early forties, comes (paradoxically) a richer, fuller sense of the joy of simply living. Our bodies teach us that we're not meant to live forever. And knowing that (organically, not intellectually), we can connect more freely—more needfully—to our children, our lovers, to our past, and to our own magically still-beating hearts. Our relations—and relationships—become a treasure. Life resonates.

I sensed that these thoughts would not be foreign to Maud. That meant a lot. It really did. I did not take any pride in the story of how I'd become a fallen-away Episcopalian. It didn't show me in a good light—angry, hurt, resentful, pouty even. And yet Maud took it all in and seemed to put her arm around my shoulder. I felt like we were friends.

And then, after an hour or two, because it meant so much, I began to worry that she was just being nice. Being nice but not feeling connected. That was what I felt when I got her e-mail— connected. That seamless feeling between old friends, the sense not that your faults will be overlooked or forgiven, but that they'll be seen, rather, and tolerated.

Being nice, in contrast, doesn't last. It's cordial. But it's not friendship. And friendship was what I was looking for. I felt insecure, suddenly, uncertain I was reading Maud the right way. All I could do, I figured, was be clear about where I was coming from.

Date: 8 Jan 1997
From: Locke Bowman
To: Maud Lavin
Subject: Tonight's question:

Does this happen to you a lot? Getting into this kind of an e-mail relationship? I would not call this flirting. You're pointing out a big gap in my life that I didn't know existed. I love your e-mails, all of them . . . and want some more. I have this nagging fear about how do we break rules but not hearts. If you think I'm into a guy thing that doesn't want all of the connectedness, you're wrong. Please WB.

Date: 8 Jan 1997
From: Maud Lavin
To: Locke Bowman
Subject: And more

And a quick answer to your questions. No, this doesn't happen to me often. This is rare and precious. I think you've pointed to a hole in my life too.

I'm very glad that you feel the connections too, and enjoy them.

Sending you an electronic (electric?!) kiss, Maud

Pickled Sweeties

By the second week of January, work had begun to pick up. The law students had returned from Christmas break. They started showing up, hanging around my office, looking for work, wanting to talk politics and law. I was running on two tracks.

— ✳ —

Students may tolerate but they certainly don't anticipate and would probably prefer to remain ignorant of their teachers' affairs of the heart. I kept them in the dark. But more than once that required a guilty clicking out of my e-mail program when I heard a knock on my door. I'd put them off with a "Just a minute!" as if they were the parents and I were the child, hiding what I was doing in my room.

The e-mails were flowing now. I'm sure all our e-mailing made our courtship proceed faster than it would've otherwise—the way electronics speeds up so much in our lives. I try to think what the pace would've been like for us as guarded, postdivorce adults without that easy electronic touch. We'd have had that Halloween dinner. Then what? Exchanged thank-you notes back and forth. Next there'd have been a long pause due to being afraid and/or busy—like the one that had actually happened. Then, some excuse to communicate, like the cyberdrama (although not the cyberdrama), would've come up. (But *The Couch* was such a good excuse, because it involved some emotional unveiling on my part. OK, but there are other revealing moments and signs we could've shared that had nothing to do with digital technology.) Locke could've sent me a holiday-card photo of his sons. He would've shown his dad side. I could've responded to that glimpse of warmth by calling him. We could've opened up in that phone call too, but voice-to-voice communication most likely would have been too real for Locke to proposition me over the phone as he had via e-mail. On the phone, he never would've done that so early in our reconnecting. Then? Another safe pause, maybe until his spring visit to New York. Phone calls beforehand to arrange a dinner, more closeness. Maybe at the second dinner it would have dawned on us that here was the person who had all those qualities we'd been pining for. Compassion, honesty, humor, sensitivity, boldness, sexiness, affection, intelligence. And even more astonishingly, we might've started to see in each other a person who remembered and recognized those same qualities in ourselves, especially qualities like the skinless vulnerability we had learned over the years to hide. We each so wanted to be rediscovered and understood. From there, regardless of what mode of communication we used, things would have escalated. Fast. Because one of those qualities we'd liked in each other and ourselves when we were young and that remained only partly buried in middle age behind charm and fear was the desire and ability to dive in.

Date: 9 Jan 1997
From: Maud Lavin
To: Locke Bowman
Subject: Locke,

I am enjoying this correspondence so much it almost is like sex for me. But like with sex I wonder if I should delay gratification just slightly, or wait till tomorrow to answer this so I can draw out the pleasure of what I might reply? Then of course I want to answer right away.

I like being close to you, even on e-mail. I would be very flustered in person, I think, but that would be part of the pleasure. Really that kind of awkwardness is a compliment; it's like starting all over again. And I want that too—I want touching, not technique, and feeling slow and delighted and overwhelmed and totally blissed out. And not able to control things. And I want really corny music, like Marvin Gaye, music that would make us laugh, but at the same time make us feel excited and that we were living it.

Locke, I keep saying this, but this is such a pleasure for me, a pleasure on many levels.

Dreaming of you too, and listening to Marvin Gaye,

Maud

Date: 10 Jan 1997
From: Locke Bowman
To: Maud Lavin
Subject: Re: Locke,

Dear Maud: Thanks. Me too. Do you remember when we hitchhiked to Andover together when we were kids? I don't think I had any shoes on.

Hugs, L

— ✳ —

On that day my forty-plus-year-old feet were snugly wrapped (if not firmly grounded) in a pair of brown wingtips. With a group of my students, I'd sued the local juvenile detention facility for refusing to allow civil rights lawyers into the building to meet with young people who were locked up and might need a lawyer to help them present a grievance. I had returned from a settlement meeting with the chief judge of the Juvenile Court and the head of the detention facility and, after shooing the students out of my office, had found Maud's e-mail of the previous day.

My whole being softened when I read it. I can be a hard, unsmiling adversary. I had been as much that very morning. But in an instant Maud's words opened up an awkwardly tender spot at the center of my heart, and sent me dreaming of a barefoot time long ago. Who would have known this? Our exterior, public faces show almost nothing of our inner life. Maud and I shared a hidden place together. She wrote back almost instantly.

Date: 10 Jan 1997
From: Maud Lavin
To: Locke Bowman
Subject: Hitchhiking

Locke,

Yeah, I think you were barefoot. I think about my nephew Austin who's almost 13, and think we were not all that much older when we met—I was 18—and that gives me a thrill. But it's really the present that has the resonance for me now, the past is like icing.

Yours with excitement, Maud. And a longer, slightly more brazen and less scared, although still completely sappy kiss, or many kisses.

Date: 10 Jan 1997
From: Locke Bowman
To: Maud Lavin
Subject: Re: Hitchhiking

I wonder sometimes what my older son will think of me when he gets to be the age you and I were when we met (which isn't so long from now, after all). Will he have a girl-friend? What will the two of them say about me when they're snuggled up together and lost in each other's eyes? (Maybe they promise each other they'll never be divorcees; they'll find true love; and they'll stick with one love for always. If they do promise each other that, then I hope fortune smiles on them and all their dreams come true.)

It's very interesting about the past and the present and how they interrelate. I'm not saying I disagree—I mean, I don't feel the least bit of nostalgia. But this wouldn't be happening if it weren't for our shared sense of preserved sweetness, would it? A couple of pickled sweeties. And that sense arises out of our shared past. So, I'm just amazed. Snow's falling all around, but this has been two weeks of wonderful summer life.

These kisses are feeling deep and tingly.

Locke

Date: 10 Jan 1997
From: Maud Lavin
To: Locke Bowman
Subject: Pickled sweeties

I just got home to your e-mail, which just made me laugh out loud, especially the "pickled sweeties" line. Yes, we are that. Kisses, Maud

Questions

The next night I went out with my friend Kim. Since the birth of her son, Abe, Kim and I had developed a routine. We'd meet once a month for a New York Girl Dinner. In fact, our first one had been the first dinner Kim had experienced away from Abe when he was an infant. We'd chatted like we used to before Kim had become a mom, except every fifteen minutes or so Kim would go to the pay phone to call her husband, Jim, and check on Abe. But by now Abe was two and the number of phone calls during the evening were down to about one, usually at the after-meal-tea stage. Once this phone call was made and Kim was reassured, we could linger. This month we were trying out a new Thai restaurant in Brooklyn near Prospect Park.

Kim had beautiful posture, an expressive face, and humorous, questioning eyes. She was, like me, in her early forties. Kim and Jim had had Abe when she was employed as an editor, so she continued to work, and outside work she guarded her time with Jim and Abe wisely. But she liked girlfriend fun too. I respected Kim's adventuresomeness and smarts—she'd traveled in other years to Asia and Africa and written on environmental and political issues.

Kim and I had met at a friend's summer house on a lake in the Hudson Valley two months after my breakup with my New York partner. I was there desperately trying to relax, to stop thinking about the hole in my life. I wanted to lie on the dock and bake. Kim had gotten up that Saturday morning full of energy. While I was focusing on iced tea, she went running and biking. I was just venturing to the dock when she came back ready for a swim. I spread out my towel and lay down, and she jumped immediately into the water. She came up smiling.

"OK," Kim announced. "I've been running, I biked to the store and back, and now I'm swimming. For dinner I want steak and I want gin."

I propped myself up on my elbows and gave her a big smile. "And chocolate cake?"

"You bet."

I lay back down. Now this was a woman I could be friends with.

We were having our customary post-phone-call tea—spicy chai this time in honor of the Thai restaurant.

"So, remember my old boyfriend—the one I had dinner with this fall?"

"Yes?" Kim sat up even straighter and leaned in, turning her right ear toward me, parodying the pose of an intensely interested girlfriend.

"Well, we've been e-mailing each other fantasies."

"What kind of fantasies? About each other?" Kim affected a prim face.

"Oh, fantasy vacations we'd go on together. Trips to Hawaii. What we'd do there . . . to each other. That sort of thing."

"Didn't he have a girlfriend?"

"Yeah, he does."

"Still does? Well, I wouldn't take this too seriously. He could just be getting off on nostalgia. Or just . . . getting off."

"Um, my gut feeling is that there is something there. I am sort of serious, I guess," I said defensively. "At the very least I think he wants me as a friend."

"So, you're what—his jerk-off friend?" Now, she really did look prim and oddly angry. "What about what *you* want?" Therapy central.

"Kim, give me a break. It's not like I'm not out there dating. I'm not sitting at home complaining there aren't any men. But, come on, dating is a lot of work. So what if this is a little weird? It's fun." Why did I owe her any explanations?

"Are you dating anyone now?"

"No, but I don't have to be dating every second. What's your point?"

"He has a girlfriend and now he has you on the side. What are you getting out of it?"

"Look, I'm not married. And neither is he. There have to be some advantages to being single. This e-mailing is fun, it's easy. And, not that it's anyone's business but our own, but we don't just fantasize. We talk about real things too, friendship things."

Kim sat back. "All right, I just don't want to see you getting hurt."

I felt disgruntled. What about Kim's adventuring in her pre-married life? Here I'd wanted to make a light, bold-sounding anecdote, to update Kim on the college-boyfriend thing, and Kim—someone I could usually talk with about anything—had taken me seriously, too seriously. But I didn't have much room to complain. If I'd been completely honest with her, I'd have admitted how big reconnecting with Locke was for me. I was already afraid enough postdivorce. I didn't need her to scare me more. Now I felt painted into a corner. I went back to my tea.

I *had* wanted Kim to play the voice of reason. She usually went for substance. As an adult, I find I often turn to my friends for advice knowing in advance what they'll say. Kim wouldn't think this was just a game, and she'd want answers. I suppose that's how I was starting to feel too. If I'd wanted a lighter response I'd have gone to one of my relentlessly dating friends who might've suggested playing it for what it was worth or some other cynical tack. As much as I valued Kim's words, though, I wasn't necessarily braced to hear them, and I didn't feel compelled to follow her warning, no matter how sound. Kim's life was Kim's life, and mine was mine. I could listen but I could also pull back. This was not a sense I'd had with friends when I was younger, when I thought my girlfriends and I were joined at the hip and were set to go through life together step by step. That hadn't happened for baby boomers. We got married and divorced at different times, had kids at different times or not at all, stepped into and out of career fervor at different times, and moved around a lot. These differences in life rhythms were confusing and sometimes made me anxious. One advantage was that

I didn't expect even my closest friends, like Kim, to have the last word on my—inevitably different—life. The last word was mine.

Reality and the Big Picture

A couple of days later, Susan and I went on a real-life trip to Michigan, to cross-country ski and get away from the city's winter slush. I was miserable.

On Saturday night, in the lost middle of the night, I started awake from some unremembered dream of Maud and me. I couldn't stop hearing Maud's words to me. My world was full of her—and I didn't want to let her go. I had this recurring image of Maud and me, hitchhiking barefoot from Boston to Andover. I imagined our cheeks touching, talking into the wee hours of the night.

I slipped out of bed. Sat in an armchair. Propped my chin on cupped palms, elbows resting on my knees, feet on the seat of the chair. I figured it was about time for me to get a serious grip. I thought I was being a fool. My electronically accelerated correspondence with Maud had gotten way too far ahead of the reality of our situations. In our e-mails we were making love, sharing our hearts, falling asleep in each other's arms. In reality, I'd set eyes on Maud exactly twice in the past twenty-odd years. Despite the frenzy of our courtship these past couple of weeks, we'd never once even talked on the phone.

The moonlight reflecting on the snow outside the window made the winter night bright. I had always been a believer in the moon—yanking the tides, expanding our yearnings. But I doubted whether Maud and I would be spending any moonlit nights together soon. We were grown-ups, not portable people. We had lives, careers, lovers in our separate cities. I had children.

The reality was that we'd gotten swept away in an electronic word game. Let it get out of control. What had gone on between us was nothing more than an exchange of scores of e-mails. Nothing tangible. No deep kiss. No exchange of breath. Face it. This feeling I had of . . . well . . . of loving Maud was a pure wishful fantasy. Childlike. Crazy. I must be one sorry and vulnerable forty-something man, I thought. This could break my heart.

I got back into bed. And as sleep overtook me again I had the half comfort of reckoning that at least this whole e-mail fantasy had taught me one thing: how little contented I was with my life, how much more I needed than what I had.

Returning home the next day, I didn't—couldn't—rush to the computer to e-mail Maud. I had no idea what to say. I figured that to tell Maud I just plain longed for her, wanted to be with her, seriously, no fantasy—I figured that would end things. I wasn't ready for that. But I was in no mood for playful fantasy.

I held out from writing. Not being coy. Just not knowing what to do or say. Then Maud e-mailed. New mail; from Maud Lavin; entitled "Reality and the big picture." My heart sank. The reality would be: this made no sense. The big picture would be: we were adults and had lives to get back to and commitments to keep. So she had realized it too. Of course she had. Maud was no fool.

I let the e-mail sit, reading the title over and over. I let it be. Did other things. I'd read it when I felt up to it. And a few hours later, with an intake of breath, I clicked the e-mail open.

Date: 13 Jan 1997
From: Maud Lavin
To: Locke Bowman
Subject: Reality and the big picture

Locke, I had some time to think this weekend, and to feel, and I want to communicate some of it to you. It's frightening to say these things with e-mail; it would be so much easier, and more communicative, to say them in person, with some joking around and touching and body language and all that.

But, basically, most of this you already know, I think. Well, first I'll give you an image. I had been riding so high on our correspondence, and still am, but Saturday night, I really came down to earth. And I thought, well, this is great, but where is he? I want him here right now, in bed with me, and I had a powerful image of resting my head on your chest, just below your shoulder, and smelling you, and nuzzling into you, and staying that way for a long time.

I want to love and be loved, I want to be in a relationship, I want passion and I want cuddling and tenderness. I want eventually (although I don't think I'm ready for this right now) to remarry—I believe in the dignity, honor, commitment, and partnership of marriage.

Locke, I feel with you that I want a relationship with you. We can't predict or control the future, but I think people do know if they are at least going/desiring in the same direction. Maybe the question I want to ask you is not do you want a relationship—maybe it's way too early and e-mail-y for that—but would you want a relationship with me: are you thinking in that direction?

I know we're in different cities and there are logistical issues. But it's really the big emotional picture I'm thinking of. After finally starting to feel deeply again, I don't want to put myself on hold in a long-distance, yearning, can't-have-him mode. I decided to take the risk and tell you what I'm feeling.

I want to hear how you're feeling, at least in a general way—like is any of this even possible? We don't have to decide everything now. I just need to know if I can think of this in terms of forward movement.

Hope this e-mail isn't too alarming. I've just been stuck for so long, I don't want to get stuck again. Maybe I could've put this more delicately, but please, Locke, no matter what your response is, please be generous with me, as I know you are—I'm feeling a lot here, with you.

Date: 13 Jan 1997
From: Locke Bowman
To: Maud Lavin
Subject: Yes!!!

Dear Maud:

I'm rushing this out just to say that I have been feeling all the things you were describing in your e-mail and I lie awake at nights and think about you and I'm dying to talk to you only I didn't know if that was allowed or if this is just limited to e-mail fantasy. Please let me call you sometime, I'm absolutely dying to hear your voice.

L

Date: 13 Jan 1997
From: Locke Bowman
To: Maud Lavin
Subject: Re: reality and the big picture

I can't thank you enough for sending me this e-mail. All last week I felt just awash with you—full of sexual warmth and full of the treasure of your wit and your kindness and your perceptiveness and your just plain Maud-ness, which I have treasured in my heart for all these years. And, like you, I began to feel some—I don't know—fear/anxiety at the intensity of my feelings. Awash is probably as good a metaphor as any— soaked with my clothes on and out of breath and completely swept away from everything ordinary and predicted.

So the answer to your question is "Yes!!!" That is, no, you are not alone in desiring something to come of this and in thinking about forward progress. And, yes, I know in my heart that this is something very positive for both of us. I can't tell you the last time I had such positive feelings. And yes, too, there are some fairly major hurdles to a relationship between us:

1. I live in Chicago, work here, have a reputation here, feel a sense of career here, etc. I love my job and I feel I make a contribution through it.

2. My younger son lives here. With him here, I could never find it in my heart to move to another city. It would hurt him terribly. And me too.

3. I'm still involved with Susan. She has watched me become remote and less communicative . . . but I have not told her about you—yet.

I don't think e-mail is well suited to discussing these kinds of issues—not to be old-fashioned. So I have a couple of immediate and practical questions:

1. Would it be all right if I called you?

2. What would you think about a visit in February?

I think you were very smart to say we should not try to figure everything out at once. I don't know if love will find a way or not; but it definitely won't if we aren't patient and don't give it a chance.

You're great, Locke.

Date: 13 Jan 1997
From: Maud Lavin
To: Locke Bowman
Subject: Thank you!

Yes, please do call.

I was so relieved to get your e-mails, I can't tell you. I mean, literally, I can't tell you. I feel grateful and a little stunned that we might actually be in the same place (emotionally if not geographically) at the same time.

I do want to see you—February sounds good. And I want to protect a space for us where we can make lots of mistakes. It won't be perfect, Locke.

I feel like I can talk with you about almost anything except the relationship you're in now. First of all, I realized this weekend, I'm jealous. Second, I think I'd just say some really blunt things you wouldn't want to hear and you already know anyway—you've already said them to me. What I can say though is that I cannot play a mistress role, so that kind of holding pattern just wouldn't work. That's not an ultimatum—I'm talking about over time, not right this minute.

Patience. I agree. I need tons of it and am willing to give the same in return. Did my last e-mail sound impatient?

Maybe, but I think I was impatient to know if there were real possibilities and real feelings or not, not to resolve everything right away.

Chicago is an option I'd consider seriously. Huge subject. I have a career and a reputation here too. It is partly portable though. I respect the fact that you're close to your son. I like Chicago and the Midwest. All that said, it would be a complicated decision for me, and I do benefit a lot from being in NY. It's enough to say now that yes, I'd consider moving to Chicago, and that that's a realistic possibility for me.

Anyway, Locke, a giant, and at this point sleepy YES. Thanks—many thanks—for your e-mails today. (I was scared all day about what your response might be.)

A long hug, and a shoulder nuzzle, and patience, Maud

It never would've occurred to me when I was young that I could state what I wanted in a romance in detail, and that the guy could say yes and then be specific about what he wanted. Back then I probably thought that the point of romance was some old-movie kind of communion in silence. I guess I wasn't completely passive; I said yes or no at some key turns of the college relationship. Not often, though. I don't remember Locke saying much about what he wanted either. But now we were talking. I was forthright. Locke was listening. He was direct. This felt right. Age had its advantages. I was too old not to be demanding. I could hardly be someone in my work life who negotiated, who was frank, who insisted on clarity from the other party, and then be someone evasive with Locke. Or pretend I didn't know what I needed with him. The other side of that coin was that I no longer trusted everything to unfold dreamlike and perfect without my urging. That was lost. But so much else was gained.

That evening, while I was out, Maud called and left a message on my voice mail. It was short, rich with texture, so much fuller than words on a computer monitor. Simple, but it meant a lot to me, "Hey, Locke. It's Maud. Giving you the sound of my voice. So. You're not there. We'll talk soon, I know. I'm looking forward to that. Okay, bye."

Date: 14 Jan 1997
From: Locke Bowman
To: Maud Lavin
Subject: Not perfect

Hey Maud: Thanks for sharing your recorded voice and for your characteristically smart e-mail. I'll try and call you later in the day. I'm not looking for perfection or hoping for a perfect moment or perfect sex or anything perfect. You're wise of course to raise the caveat, but (for once) it's a thought I've thought too. Remember that song, "I'm happy just to dance with you." Beatles, I think. Not that I know how to dance (I don't), but I'm just looking to be with you and touch you and feel the happiness of it.

I've got to rush off into my day. Your sweet pickle, Locke

Date: 14 Jan 1997
From: Maud Lavin
To: Locke Bowman
Subject: I'm happy

just to dance with you too. And stumble, and kiss, and pickle.

I feel so tantalized now I can hardly focus. You drive me crazy, I wish you were here right now. Maybe I should just stick with boring NY guys who don't stir me up so much.

Please call me. Then I'll play hard to get and regain my whatever.

Tantalized by you and heated by e-mail, Maud

I'd like a kiss right now please.

There was the matter of Susan. Good friend. Kind to my sons. Kind to me. We had never been in love, though. And now, well, I'd gotten serious about someone else. It was time I'd better explain.

I told her.

"This is someone you've been sleeping with?" she wants to know, lips pressed together in a grim, straight line.

"Well, no, not recently." I start in on how the last two weeks of e-mails have rocked my life and made me realize that it isn't right for Susan and me to continue our relationship.

"E-mails? We're talking e-mails? For two *weeks*?"

"Mmm."

"Locke, you're crazy. Do you know that? You're really crazy." She walks out. Slams the door. She has a point.

Craziness held sway and, in the end, won out. In late February, after weekends together in Maud's apartment on Woodhull Street (to which I had been unhesitatingly invited) and my house in Chicago, I proposed marriage. Maud said yes. On April 16, 1997, Maud and I were married in Chicago's City Hall. Later that spring we carted Maud's possessions to Chicago in a rented U-Haul and deposited them (and Maud) in my townhouse.

At that time Kris was seventeen and David nine. Together, Maud and I have watched the boys grow up, and have loved them at every stage. Surprisingly, that ended up being the part of our relationship that was most continuously satisfying—maybe because we didn't have any past of parenting together to live up to or in comparison with. In other areas, dreams of the future seemed to conflict more and more with those youthful memories and with appreciating each other in the present. Still, we honor our pasts—two of them now, one from our late adolescence and one from our forties—and, in middle age, the desires and goals we helped each other crystallize, the professional work we encouraged each other to contribute, the feelings about our different approaches to aging we shed light on, our attempts to connect and love, and the parts of our midlife we celebrated, even if in the end in a bittersweet way, together.

Acknowledgments

For generous contributions to *The Oldest We've Ever Been*, of different but all invaluable sorts, Maud Lavin would like to express gratitude to Richard Babcock, Alyson Beaton, John Day, Shay DeGrandis, Gioia Diliberto, Jane Doyle, Kristen Hagenbuckle, Patti Hartmann, Terri Kapsalis, Katrina Kuntz, Kathy Livingston, Teena McClelland, Ann Pandjiris, Isabel Swift, Chris Tomasino, and Lori Waxman. She is indebted, as always, to the Visual and Critical Studies program of the School of the Art Institute of Chicago. She, and also Locke Bowman, deeply thanks Kris and David Bowman, Amanda Steen, Audrey and Carl Lavin, and Locke Bowman, Jr.

Calvin Forbes would like to thank his family. Dave King is grateful to Kim Larsen, Maud Lavin, and Wendy Lukomski for their invaluable help in editing his piece; also to the late Marianne Danner, who gave him his first collection when he was a boy and set a powerful example of how to go through life with vigor and humor. Kim Larsen would like to thank Anya and Abe and Josh and Jim. And she wants to thank Laurel for teaching her what courage means. Ellen McMahon would like to express her appreciation to Alice and Della for their inspiration and to Moyra Davey, Holly Hickler, Miwon Kwon, and Maud Lavin for their careful eyes, sharp minds, and warm encouragement. Peggy Shinner wants to thank her father, the late Nate Shinner, for taking her to the ballpark. Allan deSouza would like to thank family and friends who have made birthdays something to cherish and celebrate (and especially Yong Soon Min, who has been at the center of celebrations in more ways than can be listed). Thank you to fellow writer Ellen McMahon for proposing him for this book, and also to Rebecca McGrew, curator at Pomona Museum California; Deepak Talwar, at Talwar Gallery, New York; and Gerry Craig, at Cranbrook Academy of Art, for publishing previous versions of this essay.

Contributors

Since 1992, *Locke Bowman* has been Legal Director of the Mac-Arthur Justice Center, a public interest law firm now located at Northwestern University's School of Law that litigates significant cases involving the criminal justice system. He writes occasionally in a variety of venues on criminal justice issues.

Allan deSouza is a Los Angeles and San Francisco–based artist and writer. His photographs, sculptures, installations, and performances have been exhibited extensively in the United States and internationally. His writing has appeared in various artist catalogs, journals, and anthologies, including *Battle of Visions*, *Critical Art of Korea* (Kunsthalle Darmstadt, Germany); *Shades of Black* (Duke University Press); and *Looking Both Ways* (Museum for African Art, New York). He is a contributing editor and regular columnist for *X-TRA*, an L.A.-based contemporary arts quarterly, and is an Assistant Professor in New Genres at the San Francisco Art Institute.

Calvin Forbes is a poet and writer, author of two books of poems, *Blue Monday* and *The Shine Poems*, and Chair of the Writing Program at the School of the Art Institute of Chicago. He is currently working on a book on the social history of jazz.

William Davies King (known as Dave) is Professor of Dramatic Art at the University of California, Santa Barbara. He is the author of *Henry Irving's "Waterloo": Theatrical Engagements with Arthur Conan Doyle, George Bernard Shaw, Ellen Terry, Edward Gordon Craig, Late-Victorian Culture, Assorted Ghosts, Old Men, War, and History* (winner of the 1993 Joe A. Calloway Prize), *Writing Wrongs: The Work of Wallace Shawn*, and *"A Wind Is Rising": The Correspondence of Agnes Boulton and Eugene O'Neill*. Since the writing of "Nothing Gained," he has married Wendy Lukomski, a writer and teacher of writing and an eminently sweet woman, and they reside in Santa Barbara. A book about his collecting, *Collections of Nothing*, is due to be published by the University of Chicago Press.

Kim Larsen has published essays and articles from Burma, Congo, Japan, Nepal, and Zimbabwe—all pieces, in one way or another, that look at the intersection of culture, conservation, and national identity. Her work has appeared in *Discover*, the *Village Voice*, and *OnEarth*, among other publications. She is a recipient of a grant from the New York Foundation for the Arts in the category of literary nonfiction. She lives in Brooklyn with her husband and son.

Maud Lavin is Professor of Visual and Critical Studies and Art History, Theory and Criticism at the School of the Art Institute of Chicago. She is the author of *Clean New World: Culture, Politics, and Graphic Design* and *Cut with the Kitchen Knife: The Weimar Photomontages of Hannah Höch* (named a *New York Times Book Review* Notable Book) and the editor of *The Business of Holidays*. She has received a National Endowment for the Arts grant and a John Simon Guggenheim Memorial Foundation Fellowship.

Ellen McMahon is Associate Professor in the School of Art at the University of Arizona. For the last twenty years her work has explored the psychological and social forces that determine the politics of intimacy within the family. Her handmade artist books are in the collections of UCLA, Scripps, Occidental, Texas Tech, the Center for Creative Photography, and the New York and Boston Public Libraries. Her essay "A Little Bit of Loss" can be found in *Mother Reader: Essential Writings on Motherhood*, edited by Moyra Davey. Now that her daughters are older, she is returning to her earlier interest in the world outside the family. She is the recent recipient of a Fulbright Scholars Grant to contribute as a writer and visual artist to an interdisciplinary conservation project in Puerto Peñasco, Mexico.

Peggy Shinner's fiction and essays have appeared *in Alaska Quarterly Review*, *Another Chicago Magazine*, *Bloom*, *Daedalus*, *Fourth Genre*, *The Gettysburg Review*, *TriQuarterly*, *Western Humanities Review*, and other publications. She has been awarded several Illinois Arts Council Fellowships, an Ausable Press Fellowship, residencies at the Ucross and Ragdale Foundations, and a Pushcart Prize Special Mention. Currently, she teaches at Roosevelt University and Thousand Waves Martial Arts and Self-Defense Center, and is at work on a book of essays about the body. She lives in Chicago with her partner.

Library of Congress Cataloging-in-Publication Data

The oldest we've ever been : seven true stories of
midlife transitions / edited by Maud Lavin.
    p. cm.
  ISBN 978-0-8165-2616-1 (pbk. : alk. paper)
  1. Middle-aged persons—United States—
Psychology. 2. Middle age—United States.
I. Lavin, Maud.
HQ1059.5.U5O53 2008
305.2440973—dc22   2007029698